Song of the Sparrow

Song of the Sparrow

A MEMOIR

Tara MacLean

HARPERAVENUE

Published by Harper Avenue, an imprint of HarperCollins Publishers Ltd

First edition

Pages 335–37 constitute a continuation of this copyright page.

HarperCollins books may be purchased for educational, business or
sales promotional use through our Special Markets Department.

HarperCollins Publishers Ltd
Bay Adelaide Centre, East Tower
22 Adelaide Street West, 41st Floor
Toronto, Ontario, Canada
M5H 4E3

www.harpercollins.ca

Library and Archives Canada Cataloguing in Publication

Title: Song of the sparrow : a memoir / Tara MacLean
Names: MacLean, Tara, author.
Identifiers: Canadiana (print) 20220426147 | Canadiana (ebook) 20220426155
ISBN 9781443465120 (softcover) | ISBN 9781443465137 (ebook)
Subjects: LCSH: MacLean, Tara. | LCSH: Musicians—Canada—Biography.
LCSH: Singers—Canada—Biography. | LCSH: Composers—Canada—Biography.
Classification: LCC ML420.M164 A3 2023 | DDC 782.42164092—dc23

Printed and bound in the United States of America
23 24 25 26 27 LBC 5 4 3 2 1

FOR MY DAUGHTERS

The sole purpose of human existence
is to kindle a light in the darkness of mere being.
—CARL JUNG

This book contains detailed accounts of child abuse,
self-harm, addiction and domestic violence.
Please read with caution and care.

Contents

The Key

I still had sand between my toes when I stepped barefoot onto the plywood stage at the country fair.

Like most mornings the summer I was nine, when we were living in the tent by the beach, the best way to get clean was to jump into the ocean. The waters of the Gulf Stream that flow around Prince Edward Island were as warm as a bath some days. The mornings could be a little brisk, and the soft, cool breeze made us shiver as we emerged from the ocean and walked onto the shore. It was like being born every day.

Our bathing suits were hung on the tent lines to dry, and inside, the constellations of mosquitoes on the nylon ceiling were fat and full from a night of feasting on the children. So many children. At the time, my mother had three of her own. Her new boyfriend, Izzy, had four boys from previous relationships. They were often around, our little scavenger wildling brothers. We were all free-range kids, raised by the earth. We had no money, but we had each other and we had the Atlantic Ocean.

To be honest, I wasn't a huge fan of my mother's boyfriend. I was old enough to be able to compare my relatively unstable life to the lives of most of my friends at school, who lived the coveted "normal" existence. In the 1980s, Charlottetown was a small, conservative, churchgoing city with a wild fringe of hippies. Many who had resisted the US draft nestled themselves into that scene, and Izzy was one of them. He was an alcoholic, an eccentric, and didn't seem to take much fatherly responsibility. He came and went as he liked and couldn't be counted on, except to fulfill his own ever-changing, inexplicable needs. He was a wanderer.

We lived in what we could afford at the time: a cabin, a bus, tents, shabby country homes, other people's houses. Food was often scarce. If we didn't have money for gas, we would hitchhike. But the biggest thing for me was that I didn't think he deserved my beautiful mother, and before we knew it she would be pregnant, I was certain.

Mum was the most exquisite, talented and brilliant human being that had ever existed, and she was a queen in my eyes, as so many mothers are to their daughters at that age. What was she doing with this clown? And he was literally a clown. He had a rainbow wig, a red nose, face paint, a penny-farthing bicycle with one giant wheel on the front and a tiny one on the back. He was the master of juggling and balloon animals. Most kids loved him, but I was on to him and he knew it. Even though he was smarter than everyone on *Jeopardy!*, even though he was a brilliant Shakespearean actor, I took eye-rolling to Olympic levels with him. He was always wary of me and felt my searing judgment, but when I would sing, he would close his eyes and smile softly to himself.

My mother used to tell me I was a bird, because I sang before I spoke. Her little sparrow. People would tell me I had a beautiful voice, and I did love to sing, but I was determined to become anything but a musician. I was going to be "normal" if it was the last thing I did.

The country fair in Kings County was filled with the scent of fresh-baked pies and burgers on the grill. In a giant field under the sapphire Island sky, children ran happily and freely from picnic blankets to farm stands, gleefully bringing back treasures and treats. My little sister Shaye loved catching crickets and squealed as they tickled the cave of her clasped hands with their sticky legs.

Fishermen, farmers, families and even folks from other counties came to feast and dance to the music coming from the little makeshift stage at the centre of it all. Maritime fiddlers and step dancers were backed up by the Rubber Boot Band with their long beards and sweet smiles.

I was wearing my one sundress that tied at the shoulders and had combed the salty tangles from my long, chestnut hair. I was excited to hear the fiddles and hopefully run into my best friend, Jenny, who lived around there.

I noticed Izzy approaching me. I tried to look busy retying my dress, peeling some skin from my sunburned shoulder, hoping he'd take the hint and go away. Instead, he sat down beside me on my blanket and told me he had an idea.

He convinced me to come with him to the stage and ask the band to back me up on a song. I was mortified at the idea of approaching strangers to ask if I could sing, but I was more fascinated than I was afraid. I had a few songs in my repertoire that most people would have known, but Izzy wanted me to sing his favourite, "You Light Up My Life."

As I moved toward the stage, heart pounding, I noticed Izzy's hand on my shoulder as he steered me through the crowd of people. What normally would have irritated me suddenly felt cool and comforting. Izzy, for all his faults, had a fearlessness about him that was contagious. He was unapologetically always himself and there was no box he could be put into, even on an island made of boxes. That's what made him so embarrassing and, at the same time, so deeply intriguing.

The band welcomed us with a smile, and Izzy nudged me forward. I looked back at him, and he gave an encouraging nod. He wasn't going to ask for me. If I wanted to do this, I had to be brave. I heard myself asking the band if they knew the song I wanted to sing. They laughed kindly and said of course they did. It had been a huge hit in the 1970s. They asked what key I sang it in.

Well, I sure didn't know the answer to that. I didn't know what that even meant. I felt my cheeks burning. The guitar player, seeing my hesitation, grabbed his instrument, sat at the edge of the stage and asked me to sing it softly to him. In about ten seconds, he had figured out this mysterious "key" and told the other musicians. They all nodded and asked me to come back in five minutes, once their break was over.

I couldn't believe it. I turned around and hugged Izzy tight, something that never happened. We walked slowly over to the lemonade stand and he took a few coins out of the pocket of his bell-bottom jeans. He bought me a cold drink and walked me quietly back to the stage. There was nothing to say. He knew my mind was racing and he was just present with me, letting me prepare.

My father came into my mind. He had taught me almost all of the songs I knew. When I was small, he would sing at the foot of my bed every night with his guitar, and I would sing harmony, and everything was right in the world. But he was gone now, somewhere "down south," on a boat where there was no winter. There was no way to contact him; we just had to hope the southern winds would blow his ship toward the harbour of our family.

As I moved toward the stage, I realized that I'd forgotten my sandals on the blanket. I looked down at my bare feet, at the pink sand from this morning's rebirth. The stage looked splintery. I didn't have time to get my shoes because my name was being spoken into the microphone and the crowd turned their attention to the stage. A hand reached down and pulled me up. My little sandy feet walked me to the microphone, and it was lowered in front of me to the exact height of my lips.

I looked out and saw my mother smiling. Jenny had appeared and was beaming at me, surrounded by the other kids. Shaye sat on the grass right in front of the stage, looking up at me with giant blue eyes and thick, uncombed hair, all crickets released into the grass. Most of the faces in the crowd were kind and expectant. Parents hushed their children. The music began to play.

Where are the words? I thought. *I know this song. What are the first words?* My heart jumped into my throat. What if no sounds came out? The words flooded my brain just in time: "*So many nights, I'd sit by my window, waiting for someone to sing me his song . . .*"

I thought of my father and how often I would wait for his headlights to come down the driveway and light up my wall, throwing dancing shadows that promised the sound of his voice. I closed my eyes and poured all my pain, all my longing and all the love I had onto the people in the field. My voice carried over the land, through the trees and into the sky. My arms raised up beside me and it was like I was conducting the clouds. I pulled the sun into my hands and through my body, and my voice was amplified a million times, resonating in every cell the sound could reach.

"*Rollin' at sea, adrift on the water . . .*"

I saw myself begging my father to take me with him, to not leave us again. So many things I couldn't say. I couldn't tell him that it seemed like every house had hands that wanted to touch my little body, that I was so hungry sometimes, that the world wasn't safe. All I could do was sing it that day. Sing everything I couldn't say. Sing what I couldn't scream. My heart felt like it was on the outside of my body, and I was all inside out. And then something happened. Something I can't describe, really. Something lifted out of me, and I was . . . I was the sun. And the clouds. And the field. And the people. And the song. I was everything.

I was free.

My mother always said that faith is simply knowing a little bit of light can illuminate the darkest room.

When I finished, there was silence. It felt like it took a long moment for the applause to begin. But it did. I smiled shyly, bowed and turned to thank the musicians. They had tears in their eyes. I got offstage and Izzy was there. He pulled me into his arms for a hug, shaking with emotion.

"Look around," he said. As I lifted my eyes to the crowd, there were grown men sobbing into their overalls, wiping their faces with dirty cloths, looking at me. Izzy, with his arm around my shoulder, walked me over so I could meet them. I shook rough hands and looked into tender eyes. Even though I was determined to be "normal," I had to admit I loved making people cry.

It was different from a cry of pain. It was a cry *out* of pain. There was often a smile with the tears. A sun shower. Something mystical. Something healing. Something light in the ever-expanding darkness, guiding us home.

What I didn't know at that moment was that I had just found the key. The key to my survival.

I.

The Wilderness

Wild eyes in the wilderness
Where're you going with the devil in hand?
—DANIEL LANOIS

My father bought the land in 1973 from a man named Erskine Smith, who had bought it from a man named Ishmael Moon. Twenty-six acres of soggy marshland in the backwoods of Prince Edward Island. DeGros Marsh, Cardigan. Mr. Moon was an American, and he didn't own the land; his ex-wife did. He was a bit of a hustler, and it was the dawning of the Age of Aquarius, when anyone with long hair was considered trustworthy. Sweet Erskine, unaware that he didn't own this beautiful, mosquito-infested piece of red earth, sold it, in turn, to my trusting (some would say naive) father. There was no paperwork, no deed. That's how it was done. He shook Dad's hand and took the five thousand dollars. It wasn't even my parents' money. Marty (that was my father's name) had borrowed it from a family friend without telling my mother and "bought" the land before she had seen it. Men used to do that, because they thought they owned the world.

Cardigan was originally named Samkook by the Mi'kmaq, the First People of the land. It means "sandy shore." Of course, the fourth Earl of Cardigan, George Brudenell, named it after himself in 1765. British men used to do that, because they also thought they owned the world.

I made my entrance on October 25, 1973. Our dog, a giant, black Newfoundlander named Contessa (Tessa for short), began circling my pregnant mother, which was their first clue that something was happening. They had just smoked some homegrown pot and decided that they should go to the hospital to check things out. It was a long drive to Charlottetown. On Prince Edward Island in 1973, it was still illegal to give birth at home with a midwife. There were no contractions, just a slight leak of water. When they arrived at the hospital, the nurse checked my mother and informed her that she was ten centimetres dilated.

For those unfamiliar with this medical term, let's just say the journey from water to air seems short if measured with a ruler. The transformation from girl to mother is a multi-dimensional crossover. Space-time bends and we balance on the folded seam of existence.

As birthing mothers, we learn that we can make a deep, primordial sound. It is an underground river that opens the portal. It is the sound of infinity and it is low. Cello and bass. Timpani drum. Drone. Om. Those few inches are a burning threshold that, when opened completely, initiates the woman into the realm of goddess. Creatrix. It is a door she cannot go back through. Only forward.

There is no fullness like being with child, and there is no emptiness like the void that follows. There is no joy like having your child in your arms, and no agony like losing one, as my mother would later learn. Birthing teeters on the precipice of life and death. The girl is gone and the mother is born. This is a time of celebration and a time of mourning.

Mothers used to die all the time in childbirth, especially once it was decided that the wise women attending births were evil witches. The men took charge of "delivering" babies. This still happens in many places today, where men still think they own the world and our bodies and keep robbing us of this rite of passage. So much of our knowledge was burned, but our bodies remember, and they rejoice, they grieve, they dance, and they open on their own, gifting the world with life. We are fierce.

I was born minutes after they arrived at the hospital, at ten thirty p.m. My wide-eyed father in his pale green scrubs and muddy rubber boots fell in love with me at first sight. My mother took one look at me and said, "Far out," which in modern-day English would be translated to "Amazing!" The nurses tried to take me to feed me the requisite sugar water from a bottle. My mother adamantly refused and insisted that she breast-feed, which was seen then as a filthy and barbaric practice. I nursed right away because I was born with the munchies.

I was the only breastfed baby in the Charlottetown hospital at the time.

My father, who couldn't contain his joy, ran outside to a pay phone but didn't know who to call. He picked up the phone and told the operator that he was the father of a baby girl. After hearing her warm congratulations, he hung up and stood alone in the crisp, fall night air, looking up at the stars. Stars. Tara.

Introducing Tara Margaret Charity Martirano. Ta-da!

They had to stay in the hospital for a week because I was jaundiced. On Halloween (Samhain), they took me home and cast a magic circle on the floor. Incense and candles burning, they placed me inside it and introduced me to the ancestors.

The log cabin we lived in had no running water or electricity and was insulated with mud and moss. Water had to be brought in from the hand pump in the yard and heated on the crackling wood stove. If the pump was broken or frozen, my parents would go down to the stream deep in the forest with buckets and haul it back to the cabin. It had a bright kitchen with a wood-burning stove, and a living room with an airtight wood-burner that could go for eighteen hours unattended. We slept in a loft at the top of a ladder. My memories of my parents' faces are illuminated by the soft light of a kerosene lamp and my father's guitar shining like a golden sun in the darkness, his hands casting shadows over the strings. He sang me to sleep every night, except on those rare evenings when he was away playing music.

My mother loved to garden and much of our food came from her dance with the seeds, the ground, the rain, sun and seasons. She knew when to plant with the cycles of the moon, what to plant with what, when and how to harvest. She was a master. The pot plants were taller than my dad.

They didn't have much money, and Lord knows songwriters can't feed a family. Mum had put aside her aspirations of acting professionally for the time being, in order to play the role of Mother Earth, a hippie witch, vegetarian, back-to-the-lander. She embodied this so beautifully. At sundown, Mum would often stand at the top of the hill and look down at her garden as the moon rose. She wondered if this was how life was supposed to feel and what it had felt like for the ancestors before her in the continuum of living with the land, in harmony and unity. Interdependence.

My mother, Sharlene MacLean, was then only twenty-three years old, but she had been on an accelerated evolutionary path. Having grown up an army brat in the small community of Charlottetown, Prince Edward Island, entangled in a highly dysfunctional, military home life, she rose above it all to become a scholar and a beauty queen, an actress and a seeker of something beyond the shape of her small town. As a wave of feminism rose up in the late 1960s, the rhinestone tiara came off. She had a boyfriend she loved but left him behind to travel Europe, and settled in London, England, where she was drawn to study the occult.

There, she met Alex Sanders, who was the "King of the Witches," joined his coven and began her Wiccan training. She wanted to be a mage. Sharlene had a sharp, academic mind, and the first part of her training required constant reading. It was important, magically speaking, that she begin with the teachings of the religion she was born into, so she read the Bible. Though her disdain for organized religion was strong, she found that she resonated deeply with the teachings of Jesus. Then she went through stacks of books, including the Quran, the Bhagavad-Gita, the Upanishads, *The Key of Solomon* and the writings of Aleister Crowley. She noted that his last words were "What a fool I have been." She was beginning to realize that she herself was a bit foolish, having spooked herself a few times practising magic alone. Her training was powerful, and by the end of the year, if everything went well, she would meet her "Guardian," a good spirit who would stand by her always. She just had to be careful to call the right one.

She worked in the dusty, Dickensian basement of Watkins bookshop on the cobblestoned Cecil Court, right behind the old Wyndham's Theatre in Leicester Square. Surrounded by all the old magic books, she had access to one of the most treasured libraries in the world, including the original volumes of Aleister Crowley's *The Equinox* in his own handwriting. Sharlene still aspired to be an actress, and Mary, who managed the astrology section, had worked with Noël Coward. Anything could happen in London. It was in full swing.

Before she'd left Prince Edward Island, she had met and fallen for a handsome singer-songwriter named Marty. Her heart was torn between her boyfriend, Danny, and the charming troubadour, both waiting for her back home. When she asked Alex what to do, he answered her in his Liverpudlian accent, "All that glitters is not gold, Sharlene. You must learn that. Hardship is coming."

But a woman in love is stronger than any magic. She soon discovered she was pregnant, and so Marty, thrilled with this development, joined her in London.

Marty was a devout Christian and, unbeknownst to Sharlene, had come to London on a rescue mission, to pry her from the clutches of the witches. But the ancient wisdom of The Craft and the coven's dedication to the deep study of all the sacred texts fascinated him. They delved deeply into their studies together, as I grew in her belly. A Wiccan wedding was held for them, and the coven bestowed three gifts upon the unborn child: beauty, music and a pure heart.

The doctor who was to attend my birth was the famous Arch Druid Dr. Thomas Maughan. He became like a grandfather to my mother and invited her to join the ancient rites at Stonehenge for the summer solstice of 1973. As the sun rose over the stones, I dreamed in her belly, each chant wrapping us in blessings.

Shortly after the wedding, Marty got a panicked call from his mother back in Canada. He had been married before and already had two daughters. He was told that his first wife was in crisis and that he had to go home immediately. Sharlene quickly packed her bags alongside him, promising their coven and her doctor that they would return before the birth. Alarms were going off inside her, telling her not to go, but all she could do was follow her love, no matter the cost. She looked back over her shoulder at her sweet, bright flat with the stained-glass window over the bathtub and the beautiful life she had created there. It was a moment she would ponder for the rest of her life, wondering where life would have brought us had she stayed. She chose the man over the moon.

They flew to Canada so Marty could tend to his family, and by the time things were sorted, they needed to find the money for their flight back. Marty got some gigs around the Atlantic provinces and took a willing and increasingly pregnant Sharlene along with him. (I was on tour even before I was born.) However, the money could not be earned in time before Sharlene was considered too pregnant to be allowed to fly back to England.

She would never see her beloved Dr. Maughan nor Alex Sanders again. They would be dead by the time she was finally able to return to London with me fourteen years later. And the King of the Witches had been right. Hardship was coming.

So I took my first steps on the beautiful island paradise surrounded by the Atlantic Ocean. There was almost no income. There was a monthly federal family allowance cheque for twenty-five dollars that should have been coming to them, but for the longest time Dad refused it, saying he didn't want anything from the government. The rest of our food came from generous neighbours, the occasional visiting relative and the local store, which had a running tab for us that I'm pretty certain is still unpaid. Sometimes the food would get down to almost nothing: oats, flour, yeast and water. My mother would make bread, and the cabin would fill with the smell of it and they'd feel rich and abundant. Dad loved to follow her around the cabin singing sad country songs, trying to make her cry. They laughed all the time—I suppose because they were happy and very, very stoned.

The cabin also had an outhouse, which to this day is my least favourite thing in the world. It was across the front lawn, past the firepit and in the woods. I would have nightmares about falling in. The smell was revolting and there were flies in the summer. I would try not to gag while doing my business super fast. If there was a gateway to the underworld, it was that outhouse. If I just had to pee, I would go into the woods as far away from that frightful structure as I could get, squat down and feel like a happy little wildling. I admit I pooped outside a few times to avoid the hell bog.

One day, my dad went down to get water and found a naked woman hanging out by the stream in a teepee, which wasn't even surprising during those days. Being naked in the forest on PEI was just the thing to do in the 1970s, at least for our sort.

Mum bathed me in a galvanized metal tub with water that had been heated on the stove. I loved nothing more than being in the water. I would splash and sing, and Mum would laugh. These were the sounds of pure, exultant joy.

On icy mornings, they'd cuddle me between them, and eventually Dad would get up and start the fire. He'd make coffee and toast right on the top of the stove, and again the house would fill with the delicious scent of warm bread. They were dirt poor, but they were in love. We had everything.

In the winter, there was often no way to go anywhere because of the snow. No way in, no way out for days unless the plow came. When the plow men would show up to clear the three kilometres of logging road to get to the cabin, they would come bearing moonshine. They would all sit together by the fire, and Dad would sing for them in exchange for the plow work and the shine.

Those were sweet days when Dad wrote songs by the fire and sometimes carved things out of wood or chopped down trees to keep the fire going. He would talk to the tree and thank it. Once, he argued with a tree and the tree won, so he moved on to another, less defensive tree. Mum painted, cleaned or played with me, and they practised magic together, made incense and performed rituals. Their mage training was still in process, and their Guardians hadn't yet shown themselves. They were constantly studying holy texts.

The sunrise would paint the whole world pink, and Mum would go back outside, stand on the porch and look out over her little slice of Eden, holding me, her little elfin-like baby, in her arms. To get me to nap in the afternoon, she found that if she bundled me up and put me in a bassinet outside, I would sleep for hours. The fresh air and the forest sounds would lull me to sleep, and I was cozy and warm. She would come to check on me, and my cheeks would be rosy from the cold. I wouldn't cry when I woke up. She'd find me looking around with my big blue eyes, content and calm. I didn't need soothing. The breeze would kiss my face, the birds sang me lullabies, and the birch trees said "hush" in the wind.

I didn't have many toys, but I had a Raggedy Andy doll and the magical Fisher-Price castle with a tower, a drawbridge and a trap door that led to a dungeon that housed a pink dragon. It had a queen, a king, a knight and a little baby that I fed to the dragon daily.

Dad wrote me a song and sang it to me all the time. Its melody flowed through me like my blood.

Baby, tiny though you seem
You fulfill a dream, a dream I never even dreamed of dreaming.

Baby, you don't know who you are.
You must be the lucky star to shine your light on me.

One snowy Christmas Eve, there was almost nothing left in our cupboards to eat. In the distance, Mum and Dad heard sleigh bells. It was a hippie friend from the woods of Cardigan making a delivery. Rice, dried milk, flour, soap and other basic necessities as well as treats filled his horse-drawn sleigh. It always seemed that just when things were dire, a miracle would happen, and an angel would appear with life-saving sustenance. To them, their little haven in the woods was an exercise in trust and surrender, and an experiment in what could be conjured through devotion to higher powers.

In the spring, also known as "mud season" on PEI, it was harder to get down the driveway, and we were often stuck. Prince Edward Island is a sandbar in the ocean. Just add rain and you have a giant mud pie.

Though our cabin was small, we didn't need much space because we lived outside. My world had no real walls. There were no locked doors. From the moment I could walk, I spent much of my day wandering barefoot. Sometimes a hand would be holding mine, but often I was alone, naked, wild, exploring. I knew the land in all her seasons. I knew the secret apple orchard and was intimate with the bees and blossoms that changed to apples. I could find all the wild strawberries and pick a meadow clean, coming home with red fingers and a satisfied smile. I was a forager and berries were treasure.

The only rule was not to pick the lady's slippers. I could come home with fists full of wildflowers, bulrushes, lupins, pussy willows and feathers, but the lady's slippers were to stay in the ground. These were the sacred wild orchids of the island, the holy grail, glowing in the forest. When I would happen upon one, I would sit beside her and observe with wonder her fluffy, feminine petals.

Before I could talk, I would sing. I was told I was a bird because I would imitate their calls and hum the melodies of my father's songs. When I saw winged creatures flying overhead, I'd sometimes project myself into them to see myself from their perspective. I would circle my little self in the air. Bird's-eye view.

So there I was, curious, free, surrounded by the song of the island. Each sound, in connection with another, created a symphony. This was my home, my sonic landscape, the biosphere of my little auditory universe.

I remember, though, that there was a song missing. A song just out of reach. Sometimes I would hear it in the distance and follow it, but it would disappear before I got there. It was like trying to find the end of a rainbow. The song would come from the forest, and the clay ground became cooler under my feet where the canopy above grew thicker. I found my way along the worn path to the stream. The elusive song had a heartbeat.

One time, it led me deeper into the woods than I'd ever gone. I was off-trail. Once I realized I was lost, I cried for a moment. Then I stopped and listened to the forest. It was darker and colder than I knew a forest could be. I did the only magic I knew how to do. I sat on the ground and started to sing. I don't know what the song was, or if it had a form, if it was my father's or my own, or the earth's. Maybe songs don't belong to anyone. Maybe every song is one song. It came through the ground. Perhaps it had been woven into the roots of the trees, carried there on the backs of ants through deep tunnels, kept warm under the moss, guarded by the flowers and fungus. My fear left me, and I noticed tiny fingers of sunlight reaching down through the leaves. Had they been there the whole time? I reached my arms toward the light.

Two hands scooped me up. It was my father. Tessa had led him to me, as she always did. They never had to worry about me because she was there and would always find me. She knew my song.

I made friends with all the creatures. I loved watching frogs grow their legs, and I'd let them jump all over me. I tried to keep snakes in my sandbox. They weren't into walls either and would always leave before I was finished telling them my story. Snakes aren't great listeners. Spiders, however, are little vaults for all your secrets. I could tell them anything and they'd just hold space knowingly, spinning their mystical webs. There is nothing in the world more beautiful than morning dew on a web sparkling in the sun, especially if you know the spider that made it. It's like hearing a perfect song when you know the writer.

Soon, two more creatures were added to the collection. A little girl named Shaye and a boy named David. We had three swings hanging from the giant tree, one each. We didn't dare touch each other's swing, but everything else we shared. We loved each other and played all day in the fresh air. Hide-and-seek, tag and my least favourite game, smell-my-finger.

Every sparrow, butterfly, bee, chickadee, tiger lily, firefly, bunny rabbit, fox, bug, kitten and snowy owl was our family. Immersed in the natural world, we had a whole group of people who would come and sing by the fire, bringing oysters, corn and lobster (poor people food). I would huddle close to someone and sing along, and watch the sparks go up to heaven and become stars.

Every night, my little bare feet climbed the ladder to the loft, Mum and Dad close behind. Shaye would be tucked in beside me. The baby would already be asleep. Dad would play any song we wanted. It was like a concert every night. Sometimes we would sing harmony, but his soothing voice would put us in a trance, and we would get sleepy. Any fears I had disintegrated in the melodies, and every cell in my body resonated with his vibrato and the strings on the wood of his guitar. I imagined every animal, bird and insect surrounding our cabin at night to hear him sing.

One song that made my heart swoon was the song he wrote for my mother. It was called "M'Lady." He would look at her as he played it, and she was a queen being worshipped in the forest by her lover. He masterfully painted a portrait of her with words. To my young, romantic heart, this was what it was for a woman to be truly seen.

M'lady's a dancer, the whole universe is her stage
Her cup of tea leaves will tell of the places she's played
Her mystic manner will plant in your mind like a seed
When her story is written, it might make a mention of me
She flies in the sky when she's sleeping
A flickering candle will call
Part of my soul she is keeping
Until she returns in the fall
She's a friend to the rain and a silhouette seen in the mist
Cleansing her body and soul with each drop to her lips
A statuesque figure in black and a Raggedy Ann
She turns to the Mother of Nature when she holds my hand.

As Dad went deeper into his mage training, he realized that he wasn't spending as much time with the Bible as he wanted to. Mum happened to have her grandmother Margaret's Old Testament in a suitcase upstairs, tucked away. Dad began to read it again from the first page and was hooked. It sank into him in a way the other texts didn't, possibly because of his childhood indoctrination in the Christian church. Those messages had been pushed deep into his mind in his most formative years, and his study was excavating familiar narratives. When he reached the end of Ecclesiastes, he fell to his knees.

This book of the Bible was written almost three thousand years ago by a mysterious author who identified himself as "the Preacher," though many believe it to be the story of King Solomon, who was a great seeker of wisdom. His father was King David, which was a lot to live up to, I suspect. King David was the same guy who slew the giant Goliath with a sling. He was also a musician and a poet and may have been the first king with his own logo, the six-pointed star. In the story, there is an existential crisis. What is the point of life? It's all vanity, this meaningless accumulation of material things, a foolish desire for fame. It was all empty, the root cause of suffering and misery. The only duty of man, says this book, is to follow the commandments of God. That's it.

It seemed so simple to Dad. This understanding spread through his body like a golden light, and he felt in that moment that he was being called to serve. On his knees, he begged for forgiveness, and he felt the weight of the world fall from his shoulders. He went out and bought a New Testament, and from that moment on, he wanted to be like Jesus, to be without sin. If he could just figure out how Jesus did it. Tricky.

He shared his "awakening" with my mother, and then took all the Wiccan books and tarot cards and burned them. For the "spiritual safety of the family," he broke her sword and threw her crystal ball into the river. He didn't ask her permission, but he did consult with his closest friend, who agreed it was the right thing to do.

Dad's best friend was a man named Gene MacLellan. They were more like brothers. Dad asked him to be the best man at their Christian wedding on PEI. Gene, his wife, Judy, and their children would come to the cabin, and he and Dad would sing together long into the night. Gene was already a famous, brilliant songwriter and a devout Christian. He had written a song called "Snowbird," which made Canadian singer Anne

Murray a household name. Elvis Presley had recorded the song as well, and then he recorded "Put Your Hand in the Hand," a work of Gene's that was to become the most recorded gospel song of all time. But Gene wanted nothing to do with fame or fortune. He just wanted to spread "the Word."

Gene and Dad read the Bible together, prayed and created new music right in front of us. Two poets sat by the fire with guitars, drinking coffee. Sunbeams would pour through the windows. There was no high hum of electricity to take up the top of the sonic sphere, no droning fridge in the low end, no traffic filling out the middle. There was just space. Space for music. One moment there would be nothing, and the next, a song would be born. The melody was the ocean, and the words were the waves. We were all standing at the gates of creation. Now, this was magic. We all knew not to make a sound when this was happening—it could break the spell.

At the time, money was particularly scarce, and Gene wanted Dad to drive to Toronto with him, to play some music in churches and prisons. One night, Gene left the cabin after a long night of fellowship and music. When we woke in the morning, Dad opened his Bible to read, and inside it, nestled into the delicate, translucent pages, lay a cheque from Gene for seven hundred dollars so our family could eat. The amount could feed us for a year.

Dad ended up going on that trip. He and Gene had stacks of Bibles to give away everywhere they went, and the music they made captivated congregations of every denomination, prisoners and anyone else who was lucky enough to hear their voices together. They worked so well with each other onstage. Dad's natural humour put Gene at ease, and they had all kinds of hilarious bits worked out. They were an incredible duo on a mission. As the crowds cheered, they had an agreement of understanding between them that the applause wasn't for them. There was to be no taking the glory away from God. The worship was for the spirit in the music. They would stay humble and not be trapped by adulation or by fame, as the Bible had taught them.

One winter's night when my father was away on that trip, Mum had to go down to the river to get water. The moon was full and her babies were sound asleep in the cabin. As she hauled the buckets in each hand, she suddenly felt something behind her. She was still secretly working on her mage training, even though Dad had given that up. She had scared herself again by practising alone. Had she conjured something accidentally? Something unwelcome? The fear inside her chilled her blood. She began to walk faster, certain that if she turned around, she would see it. Whatever was behind her, it was not her Guardian.

The water in the buckets splashed as she started to run, but she knew she couldn't outrun it. Just before she felt it was about to reach out and touch her shoulder, she dropped the buckets and fell to her knees. The incantation that came to her was the Lord's Prayer. Uttered incalculable times by the human tongue, in countless languages, over millennia, it had the cumulative protective power of every time it had been spoken aloud.

Whatever she felt behind her evaporated. The chase was over. She was safe. But she wasn't alone.

The forest filled with light.

She spoke to him out loud, "Oh, it's you. You've been here the whole time."

Her Guardian had appeared.

2.

The River

So deep, so wide, will you take me on your back for a ride
If I should fall, would you swallow me deep inside
River, show me how to float
—PETER GABRIEL

When I was four, my mother took me down to the river.

We were spending the summer of 1978 at an evangelical Christian ashram in Nova Scotia, and they were doing baptisms down the stream. Her long, shimmering black hair was kept off her face with a scarf. She wore a long denim skirt to cover her ankles. My goddess of a mother. I had been to this river many times alone, having snuck out of the tented church when no one was looking.

My father was getting work as a gospel singer and my mother was teaching Sunday school. Since the night in the forest, Mum had completely relinquished her Wiccan studies. More and more hippies in the woods were coming around to talk about Jesus. Soon, a revival swept Canada's East Coast, and the fields were littered with paper temples. Instant altars.

It was hot and boring in that tent. The only time I paid attention was when we were singing.

> *God sees the little sparrow fall,*
> *It meets his tender view;*
> *If God so loves the little birds*
> *I know he loves me too.*

The grown-ups were always praying or singing, or singing prayers, doing things that made them feel "closer to God." I'd heard someone say that God was inside us. I didn't know how much closer you could get than that, so what were they looking so hard for?

If children were silent and still in church, we could be given the Quiet Seat Prize at the end of the service. I never got it, which I felt was deeply unfair. I admit I was squirmy, but who wouldn't be when they were sweating and bored out of their minds? So I'd leave while everyone was in the throes of rapture, when they wouldn't notice me sneaking out.

Once liberated from the sauna of sermons, I would head down to the river to throw stones into the water. I loved the swallowing sound when they connected with the surface. Near the shore, it was so clear I could watch them sink and listened for the little click as they touched bottom. I imagined they were joining their friends. If no one was there, I would strip off all my clothes and watch my reflection rippling on the face of the water. Sometimes, I would pee standing up and laugh hysterically at how funny I was.

The spiders laughed with me. We were friends. They got me.

The river was so close to our cottage at the ashram that I could hear the water rushing at night. It was much wider and louder than our little stream at home. I discovered that it had a pathway that went all the way across, just beneath the surface. If I balanced just right, I could make it to the other side and back. I couldn't wait to show my mother.

One sunny day, I brought her down to the shore, and she watched attentively as I made my way across. What I didn't know was that rivers aren't like streams. They have moods and ever-changing levels. I can still see the sparkle of the sun on the surface of the river, smell the green water, feel the slippery stones beneath my feet.

"Look, Mama! I'm like Jesus! I can walk on . . ."

I saw her jump, with the lightning speed of any mother animal, as I slipped. She must have realized she was too far away to get me because as I surfaced, fighting for air, I heard her scream, "Get her!"

Rivers carry you. They lift and pull and have their own direction. As I went under, the voices muffled, but the sound of moving water was loud. I couldn't tell up from down. The air bubbles weren't even able to tell me where the surface was, so tumbled were we by the turbulence. A pair of hands reached down and pulled me out. I remember that breath. I still wake up sometimes inhaling that deeply, that fast.

Those hands belonged to a young woman with a kind, sweet smile. One of the group from the baptism, or maybe an angel hovering nearby. Chest-deep, she was in exactly the right place to catch me, and she was steady. She brought me to my mother and placed me, shaking, in her arms. My mother's skirt was dark and wet from coming in as far as she could. I wept as she held me.

That night, my mother insisted that we go back down to the river's edge. I didn't want to go. Resistant but knowing better than to argue (the Fifth Commandment: Honour thy father and thy mother), I found myself standing in the moonlight at a calm part of the river, an estuary where its mood was still. There was a slight hint of salt, night bugs singing, fireflies silently dancing. My mother picked me up and walked into the water until it was up to her waist. I clung to her. I could feel the warmth of her neck as I buried my face, and the cool water on my feet. She lowered me into the dark pool and told me to float on my back. I squeezed her tighter. "Trust me," she said. Slowly, I loosened my grip and unclenched my body. With her hands underneath my back, I stretched out and lay on top of the water. She whispered, "I am going to let go, but there is a trick. If you think you are going to sink, you will sink. If you trust that you will float, you will float."

As her hands moved away, I felt the water pull me down, my body heavy, a stone girl. I began to panic and went under. She pulled me up and held me as I clung to her, eyes shut. "Now," she said softly, "again. Tilt your head up so you can see the moon, forehead touching the water. Chin up, relax, breathe and trust." She whispered a prayer, an incantation to life, asking that I be taken care of when her hands couldn't hold me. A protection spell. Mother calling on the Mother to keep me safe.

Her hands left my back, and something else rose from the depths to take her place. Something held me, kept me from sinking. I became moonlight. I trusted the river. I trusted the water, my mother and the moon. I trusted myself. That is what held me, and always has.

That was my baptism.

Shaye and I were only eighteen months apart. I don't have a clear memory of ever not being her know-it-all big sister. I had come first to earth, so I knew the lay of the land. I introduced her to the flora and fauna and introduced them to her. I pulled her through the forest, pointing out the essentials, but she developed a different relationship with them. Instead of talking to the spiders, she would sit quietly with them. Instead of singing with the birds, she would listen. Instead of sharing her thoughts, she kept them in her own little web. I could see the awe and wonder in her eyes as we wandered barefoot through the world, but she rarely said a thing. She'd almost died in childbirth. Born breech in the Summerside hospital linen closet because all the rooms were full, she almost took my mother's life as well. The result was that she always seemed a little darker and enigmatic, more in touch with the things we couldn't see, comfortable in silence, followed more closely by the shadow of death.

Her inner world hadn't yet developed a release valve like mine through song and story. Instead, she created a profound and mysterious dimension inside herself that only a privileged few would ever glimpse. Shaye was deeply loving, curious, poetic, observant and funny. We would laugh and laugh until we cried, rolling on the forest floor, covered in dirt and pine needles, leaves in our hair. When we would sing together, we harmonized flawlessly, even as young children. Shaye also loved my songs and knew every note and every word I had ever written. She was my first fan.

The thing about the quiet ones is they make better prey.

Back then, people didn't explain things to children the way they tend to now. Suddenly, we were leaving everything we knew. Mum's grandfather Lou MacLean had passed away. He had been playing Santa at the Holman's Mall and was on his cigarette break when he went into his dressing room and fell over dead, still in his red and white suit and beard. Lou had been more of a father figure to my mother, and left her with a small inheritance and a place to live in town. Mum and Dad wanted to be closer to the Calvary Temple Church, so this worked out for them.

One night, we were packed up into our van with the "Holy Roller" bumper sticker and driven away from the cabin through the snow, past the sleeping secret orchard and the puddles of frogs frozen beneath the ice. We could see the full moon through the back window of the van. Shaye and I watched it as it followed us down the road.

The next thing we knew, the trees were replaced by telephone poles, and the blue moonlight was exchanged for the unnatural yellow light of street lamps. Instead of birdsong, we heard sirens, and there were no fires to start, no bare feet allowed, no mud puddles to be naked in. In fact, we had to wear clothes all the time.

We were able to live in Lou's place in Charlottetown while Mum packed and sorted through his things. His wife, Margaret, had died a few years before. (Mum called her "Mummy," which confused me, because Margaret was her grandmother.) The apartment was on the corner of Fitzroy Street, above The Flower Cart, and right across the street from us was Garden City Dairy Ice Cream. There were so many flavours, and I was just tall enough to look into the freezer at the huge tubs of swirling colours. Chocolate and Grapenut were the best. I can smell the cool, sweet air and see my breath fogging up the glass, the thin, transparent barrier that separated me from the greatest thing ever created by humanity. The smiling, jovial man behind the counter was the answer to my ice-cream prayers. I can imagine he must have loved his job. He made so many people happy, and I'm certain my joy level was among the top of all his loyal customers.

My great-grandparent's place even had a flushing toilet, which we thought was hysterical. I don't know how many times we'd flush it just to watch the magical, spiralling whirlpool of water.

When that lease was up, we moved on to a little town called Murray River, which had a small Pentecostal church, where the preacher's name was Pastor Cross. For real. Our rundown house was white with green trim and stood bravely in the wind at the top of a hill. I could see the fishing boats in the ocean from my window. I had a white and black tricycle and would race around on it. There was a new litter of kittens born in the house, and there was nothing I loved more than their soft fur and little mewing sounds.

One evening, in this new house on the hill, my parents had another family over for dinner. There was no fireside singalong, no potluck-style meal to graze on, no falling asleep to the sound of laughter and song. We sat at the table with the quiet children, a frail-looking woman who was their mother, and their father, a large man across from her. There was a palpable tension and I could hardly eat. Suddenly, their father leapt up and threw his chair back. He reached across the table and grabbed his wife by the wrist. She screamed feebly as he pulled her across the table toward him, over the food and onto the floor. Their children looked at their laps like nothing was happening. Dad talked the raging man into letting her go and took him into another room to pray, while my mother tended to the broken dishes and broken woman.

I ran out the back door into a field, sat alone and watched the sun go down, trying to erase the sound of the whimpering mother, the shattering glass and the deafening silence of the helpless children. I looked down beside me, and on the ground was a dead, dried frog. I picked it up and turned it over. Its belly was full of maggots. I went home when I was sure the family was gone.

Why were those people in our house?

With my parents' newfound devotion to Christianity, they started to believe that they had an expertise to offer in the spiritual realm. They wanted to save people. Though they deeply understood the power of the teachings of Jesus, they didn't understand that they were not qualified to determine who was safe to absorb into our home life. They had no idea how to secure the perimeter.

Dad never had a father who protected him. Anthony Martirano left when my father was two years old, never to be seen again. Without explanation, without a hug goodbye, he had slipped into the emptiness that swallows people when they don't want to be found. Dad never had an example of a father who stayed. And Mum, well, she never had a chance to know what it meant to be safe. When both parents have no idea how to form a protective shield, the children are left to the elements.

From somewhere deep in my little psyche, a pattern began to emerge that gave me tremendous comfort. As I looked into the eyes of Mary in my Bible, a mother who also couldn't keep her child safe in this world, a connection began to form, an understanding of the sacrifice and power of women. I knew enough to know you can't be a virgin *and* have a baby. What was Mary up to? What were her secrets? Who was she really? Why was she looking at me like that?

One day in a library, I laid eyes on an image of Aphrodite in a book. Time stood still. She reminded me of Mary. Not of the innocent images in the stained-glass windows of the churches, but the Mary who remained when those windows were smashed to pieces. Mary broken open.

Aphrodite is the enchanting, insatiable Greek goddess of love, beauty, fertility, passion and pleasure. Known also as the goddess of the sea, she rises from the ocean, shells in her hands, encircled by sparrows. She has many lovers, both mortal and immortal. Pomegranate. Swan. Rose. Venus. Her beauty unparalleled, her thirst unquenchable, she is a fierce and violent warrior for love.

I realized when I saw her that she had somehow always been with me. I don't know when she first appeared, but it may have been in the river that night with my mother. She appeared again when I was about five years old in the form of a kindergarten teacher. I adored her. This teacher taught me the magic of painting over crayon wax: how to draw a white moon on white paper, a wolf howling, and then paint a black sky over it. The invisible became visible by adding darkness. I couldn't wait to see her every morning. She was pure love. There was no man in this classroom who was going to pull her over a table by her delicate wrist. We were safe in this room. I was safe with her.

I wish I could identify the woman in whom the goddess appeared to me next. She was beautiful, with black hair. She had a large body that even my young self found heartbreakingly exquisite. I was six. I think her name was Marilyn.

One winter's night, when our parents left us sleeping in the car while they were visiting with friends, I awoke shivering. I don't know how long we were left there, and it wasn't illegal to do this in the 1970s, but it was long enough that it got really cold. Shaye and David were asleep beside me on the back seat. We were wearing winter coats, but there was no blanket that I could find. I looked out the window. It was entirely frosted. The spectacular patterns of ice on glass with the light coming from the other side soothed and distracted me from the cold. I could see my breath. I went up close to the window and used my breath to melt the spiralling fractals, and I saw an old farm-house. The porch light illuminated the falling snow. It was an unfamiliar place, and I was afraid to go inside. My body began to shake and I huddled back with my siblings, trying hard to stay warm.

I remembered how, a few months before, Daddy was furious that another litter of kittens had been born and put them out on the porch overnight. In the morning, they were all huddled together in a pile of multicoloured fur, frozen solid.

Would we be frozen solid by morning? I searched my imag-ination for warmth, and Marilyn appeared in my mind's eye. She smiled and opened her arms to me. I climbed on her lap and laid my cheek against her breast. No man could pick her up and throw her—she would crush him. I fell asleep wrapped in the imagined heat of her body and a blanket of stars. She sang softly to me as we floated in the cosmos. Perhaps this is who my mother summoned on the night of my baptism. Maybe she was my Guardian.

It was around this time in my life when I began to experi-ence a sensuality in my body that was ignited by the presence of certain women. I couldn't explain it then—it just felt like the most natural thing in the world, though some part of me knew better than to mention it to anyone at church. It felt pri-vate, sacred, holy. They could paint all the black over it they wanted, but the moon and the wolf were emerging.

We moved back to Charlottetown, to 9 Park Street, to be closer to Calvary Temple Church again. The house was a duplex, and my bedroom window looked out over the Char-lottetown Driving Park, the horse-racing track. We could hear the hooves hitting the dirt, the announcers and the crowds roaring at night. For a week in the summer, known as Old

Home Week, it turned into the fairground, and the smell of cotton candy and popcorn wafted through my bedroom window, the lights making spinning patterns on my wall.

Nana, my mum's mother, would take us to the fair and eat all the candy and go on all the rides with us. She was laughing so hard on the Scrambler that she swallowed a moth. Was there anything in the world more glorious than the fair?

The yard in May was covered in forget-me-nots. I had not lost my talent for presenting my mother with flowers, and on her twenty-ninth birthday, by the swing set, my fist bursting with purple, I gave her a bouquet. She knelt down to my height and looked into my eyes. Some part of my psyche grabbed that moment in time and has held it like a steel trap. I felt so loved, so seen, so appreciated. To this day, eye contact is my favourite thing. And flowers, of course.

One day, a man was brought to the Park Street house by an old friend from the woods. He was asleep on the floor of the back seat of the car. A drug addict and a pimp, he had to be peeled from the car and carried into the house. They laid him on our couch to sleep it off. He ended up "finding the Lord" and living with us for years. For some reason that I will never understand, my parents thought that in exchange for a place to stay, he could help take care of the kids. Dad and Mum thought it was the Christian thing to do to help a guy out. His name was Gilles. He was a monster.

I began to understand that the church could be used as a sanctuary, and it could also be used as a cover. People could be seen washing their sins away in the river, but it was just a show, a bit of theatre, a hollow ritual. Some hearts are stones that go right to the bottom.

3.

Monsters

*Whoever fights monsters should see to it that in the process
he does not become a monster. And if you gaze long enough
into an abyss, the abyss will gaze back into you.*
—FRIEDRICH NIETZSCHE

My grandmother Madrien (née MacLean) and grandfather Albert "Smiley" Ferris lived in a very nice house in Charlottetown. It was a testament to mid-century, middle-class opulence, with wall-to-wall carpeting and velvet furnishings—a far cry from our log hut.

There was always plenty of food, and every can in their cupboard faced the same way, in neat little rows. My grandparents were meticulous. Though they had a cleaner, Ruby, Nana would go around picking lint off the carpet and straightening the beds and the towels on the rack. Nana was a large woman, thanks to a hysterectomy at twenty-seven that messed with her hormones, and she was always on a diet (except at the fair, and in bed late at night, and at the Dairy Queen drive-through, and . . .). But still she was elegant and immaculate, and always smelled faintly of flowers, like lily of the valley, my favourite. She taught us to care for our hair and teeth, to make our beds with hospital corners, and to have table manners so that we could eat with the Queen in case such an opportunity arose. She trained me so well that when I was five, I got a special pin with a tooth on it from my dentist, to mark excellence in dental hygiene awareness. I wore it on my coat like a sheriff's badge, and to this day, I have not had any cavities in my adult teeth.

I tended to slouch, my toes turned in a little when I walked, and my two front teeth were crossed in the front and stuck out, like a happy little donkey's. Nana was constantly pulling my shoulders back, bought me corrective shoes that looked like the ones you wear bowling, and slapped a retainer on me the moment I was old enough. She would make me sing for her all the time. In the car, before bed, and anytime "the relatives" were over from Ireland, I was the entertainment. I made it my secret mission to find songs that would make her cry. That's when I knew I had been successful. Dad had taught me well. She especially loved it when Shaye and I sang together in the car, and from the back seat we would watch the rear-view mirror as the tears flowed from behind her sunglasses.

She favoured me, but it wasn't obvious to the child I was. This is the thing about privilege: we don't know it's happening because it's just how it is. Now that I know why, I shudder.

My grandfather Smiley had been a regimental sergeant-major in the army. He had swum the English Channel, was a Golden Gloves boxing champion and a true war hero. He was a tall, dashing Irishman from Tandragee, Northern Ireland, with the quintessential sparkling eyes and a smile that never stopped—hence his nickname. He was greatly respected in the community, and all eyes would turn when he walked into the theatre or down the street. He looked the part of aristocracy, and his sister, Winnifred, was every bit as glamorous. She lived in Ottawa but visited PEI for long stretches. When she and her brother were together, you'd think the King and Queen had entered the room.

How I loved Auntie Win. She was everything I wanted to be when I grew up. She had a refined quality that we didn't see in many other people. She sat upright, her long swan-like neck holding her beautiful head and perfectly coiffed hair like a sculpture. And she was funny. I may have spent more time staring at Auntie Win than at any other human in my childhood. I kept my adoration to myself, but she knew. She would let me sit beside her, and she would give me little gifts and sweet compliments that made me feel grown-up. She made me feel that one day, I—little pigeon-toed, slouching, donkey-toothed me—could be a movie star, an Aphrodite-level beauty like she was. I see now that by having me sit with her, she was purposely keeping an eye on me.

Legend has it that they were the descendants of a duke, an English lord in Ireland, who had an affair with his maid Julia, thus resulting in the birth of a girl, my great-grandmother Mary Addy. She was never acknowledged as an heir. Mary's husband, my great-grandfather Isaiah, sick from tar poisoning from roofing, passed away in the arms of my nine-year-old grandfather.

Smiley actually had three younger siblings. Winnifred was next in line, then a brother, Walter, then baby Clara, who was seven when she got sick from diphtheria. Smiley was outside that night, bringing the cows home, when he heard the banshee cry. In Ireland, a banshee is a spirit that screeches a warning to signal a death in the family. He ran home at full speed. Clara was gone by morning.

At fourteen, he came to Canada by boat to work on a farm in order to send money home to his family. The other farmhands beat him pretty badly, and he ran away a few times. I imagine his bare feet on the dirt roads, his face bloody and bruised as he looked frantically behind him to see if he was being followed. They always found him.

We don't know what the farm owner did to him, but we have our suspicions. He became a powerful, high-ranking sergeant in the military and a champion fighter so no one would beat him again. Now *he* handed out the punishment. *He* was the hunter. *He* had control. He was a killer with a killer smile.

When my grandmother first laid eyes on Smiley, that was it. He was thirty-five and married with a son, and my nana was just fifteen. She was already curvy and big-breasted with giant blue eyes that could disarm any soldier. He was a friend of her father's from the army. They had served in the Korean War together. Lou MacLean was not happy about his daughter's obsession with someone his age. When Madrien was seventeen, Smiley got her pregnant. Shortly after their baby girl was born, with no father listed on the birth certificate, Madrien went to nursing school while her own mother, Margaret (née Diamond), raised the child as her own. Madrien had no say in the matter. Baby Sharlene was sickly and in hospital for most of the first three years of her life. Seventy years later, she still dreams of the bars on her hospital crib, a tiny prison she couldn't escape from.

In order to do "the right thing," Smiley left his wife and wed his child bride. Though she had gained more weight than he approved of, she was able to reach a "respectable size sixteen" before the nuptials, as per his instructions. They married at the army base in Petawawa, Ontario. She was resplendent in a robin's-egg-blue suit and pillbox hat with a veil, and he was elegant in his flawless uniform, medals gleaming in the sun. They burst from the chapel as the wedding bells rang and passed through the sabre arch of the Canadian Guards. Sharlene was there, in a little dress covered in forget-me-nots. The irony was not lost on Margaret.

Madrien gave birth to a son, who was a sweet, gentle and cherubic little boy, deeply adored by his mother. She lost her womb after the birth due to cystitis, but the baby weight stayed. Smiley told her that she was no longer a woman, and he never touched her affectionately again. Madrien lavished on her son all the love she couldn't give to her little girl. She saw Sharlene often, but the family insisted that Sharlene always believe Madrien to be her big sister. When Margaret had a heart attack, Sharlene, only nine years old, went to live with her "sister," her "brother-in-law" and her "nephew," having no idea that they were actually her mother, her father and her little brother.

We will never know if it was Smiley's father dying in his arms, his sister's death, the abuse at the farm or the horrors he saw in the war. We will never know what compelled him to hunt my mother. Her earliest memories of him touching her were when she was five years old, when he would visit. He had regular access to her then, but once she lived with him, from nine to sixteen years of age, she was his prisoner of war.

We often wonder how my grandmother didn't know. I suppose some things are too horrible to see, but it's clear that somewhere in the depths of her, she knew there was a monster in the house. She protected her son fiercely and left Sharlene to be eaten alive, night after night. Like a sacrificial lamb led to the slaughter, my beautiful, bright, blue-eyed mother, in her little nightgown, endured horrors no child should ever experience, as my grandmother turned up the volume on the TV, ate the candy she hid under her bed and held her son close.

When we were born, my mother went to her father and made him promise he would never touch us. He assured her that he never would, that what they had was different.

This is what they do. Predators groom their victims to think they are the only ones, that everyone else is safe, that they are "special" to them. She told him she would rip his heart out if he ever touched us.

He did, and she didn't.

So, when the moment was right many years later, I took it upon myself to make sure that he paid.

4.

Saved

If nothing will free us from death, at least love will save us from life.
—JAVIER VELAZA

"You've been left behind. You've been left behind."
The film they showed us at church repeated this mantra. I looked around the dark room, my little bum hurting from the hard pew. Everyone was transfixed, staring at the screen, watching the little girl come home from school only to find her parents gone, a lawn mower idling on the half-cut yard, food burning on the stove. They had disappeared. The Rapture had come and she hadn't accepted Jesus as her "personal Lord and Saviour," so she was left behind on earth. Soon, our beautiful world would be on fire, decimated by demons, and she'd burn for eternity.

The film ended and everyone applauded. Shaye reached for my hand. I gave her a look that was meant to let her know this wasn't real, but her fear was the most real thing of all. Her eyes were wide and her hand was trembling. I am thankful that for whatever reason—and *reason* is the operative word here—my mind didn't allow this message to penetrate.

The pastor brought up the lights with a wave of his hand, the music started, and he began to speak. He sure wasn't speaking to me. Something about fire and brimstone and blood and lambs. We'd heard it a million times. He was inviting people to come and find Jesus in their hearts. Streams of weeping believers flooded the aisles and made their way to the altar at the front, where Pastor Power (I could not make this up) brought the religious fervour to fever pitch.

People were speaking in tongues, making sounds that were coming from some subconscious place. Fast, unintelligible words, often in monotone. Many people had tears running down their faces, their arms in the air reaching for the hand of God. The pastor came up to each of them and laid his hand on their forehead. "Catchers" stood behind each member of the hypnotized congregation in turn, and as the pastor prayed, he pushed them backward. They fell trustingly and were placed gently on the floor, where they were left to stay as long as they needed to be there, until their voices were still and their beings filled with peace.

Shaye and I called this "bowling for Jesus" and we found it quite funny, as two-year-old David sat on the floor in front of us, chewing on a hymn book. However, there were times when our family would be at the front of the church, singing gospel songs while this parade of parishioners moved toward us. The view from the front was different. The "words" that flew from their lips had an effortless quality to them, like their mother tongue was releasing from deep in their minds, from an ancient time, a primordial communication. Words beneath words.

There is so much we don't understand about the nature of healing. We do know that making vocal sounds, or "toning," can be helpful in releasing trauma from the body. We use it in birth to help open the birthing canal and bring life into the world. The meditative centring practice of chanting and prayer can focus the mind. And, of course, there is the power of song. I have no doubt that those people were having beautiful and transcendent experiences. I just couldn't get on board. Clearly, I was going to be left behind, and that was okay with me. I wasn't afraid of demons. I hadn't met one yet that I couldn't kill, and I had an army of birds and spiders behind me.

To me, the church was an elegant spire that pierced the sky, though not my heart. But as an echo chamber for the music, that made sense and opened me up into an exultant, praying, communing little being. That touched me. God was in the songs. How sweet the sound.

Mum could see I wasn't buying what they were selling. She saw me light up only when it was time for the music. One night as she was tucking Shaye and me in, she brought in a Bible and sat on the edge of our bed. She gave it to us and told us that the only thing that really mattered was the words of Jesus, and that they were in red ink in this version. She told us that he was a great teacher of love and that all God really was was love. She told us about how the church at the time rejected him and how he was a rebel. She told us about forgiveness and about the way he died. He said, "Forgive them, for they know not what they do." Then she told us he was just one of many great sages whose teachings we would study. From what she said that night, I understood something new: Jesus was just the beginning of an opening into the understanding of how to be a revolutionary, a freedom fighter for love.

After Mum said prayers with us and left, Shaye cuddled up to me as usual. Even though she was my little sister, she was taller, so it made sense that she was the big spoon. We would talk about life until we couldn't keep our eyes open. We were always told that there were angels guarding us as we slept. Shaye was my angel. Her love for me kept me safe. Her body was a protective shield. Sometimes, we would quietly sing our favourite hymn in harmony.

> *Come to the water*
> *Stand by my side*
> *I know you are thirsty*
> *You won't be denied*
> *I felt every teardrop*
> *When in darkness you cried*
> *And I strove to remind you*
> *That for those tears I died.*

Luckily for me, my best friend, Jenny, had parents who were Jesus Freaks too. She was almost my age, the eldest of five kids, and she was having none of it, either. Our families met through the church when we were small, and though they lived in a different town, we were often at each other's (dilapidated, borderline condemned) houses. The parental units would be downstairs praising the Lord, and we'd be in a closet playing with a homemade Ouija board.

Jenny was smart, bilingual, beautiful and mischievous in the very best way. We had our own secret world of stories and adventures that lifted us up and out of our poverty-stricken, fundamentalist reality and into a realm of original creativity and reason.

We loved our parents, but we agreed that they were out of their minds. (Not because they loved Jesus, but because of the degree to which the church permeated our lives.) We saw ourselves, sometimes resentfully, as the caretakers of the younger children and the adults. I don't know what I would have done without Jenny. We adored each other, and she encouraged me to sing, to write and, always, to rise. She never judged me, and we lived in constant curiosity and awe of nature. We would wander through the forests and along the shoreline, weaving ourselves into the mystical landscape, developing an even more profound intimacy with the world. We were elementals, dancing ourselves and each other into being, unfolding like ferns in the sunlight.

Most importantly, she thought I was funny. In a world where everything is crumbling around you, humour is essential and life-affirming. Her laugh is one of my favourite sounds of all time. No matter what was happening, together we were able to find joy amid the suffering and comedy in the tragedy. We had a dark sense of humour. *Noir.* This ability to reach for and remember the beauty and wonder of the mystery of life became the guiding principle in our own version of faith. She knew me better than I knew myself. Chosen sisters. My rock on this island made of sand.

Often at church services, I would listen as my mother testified about her night in the forest and how Jesus appeared. Then Daddy would sing. What a voice he had. He played his guitar with the nylon strings—more soothing than steel—masterfully. The people, rapt by the magnificent storytelling and beauty of my mother, would be lifted. They were stars in the temple. I was surprised there weren't stained-glass depictions of them in the windows, with halos and lutes. The pastor would pass around the collection plate, and we would receive a "love offering" at the end of the service. This money would cover gas and food.

Sometimes, we would stop at a store and get black licorice on the way home. Everyone but me loved it. I'm still traumatized from an incident when I thought I was biting into chocolate in the dark and discovered it was licorice. Some things you can never recover from, no matter how much therapy you get.

When I sang in harmony with Dad, it was a transcendent experience. Now, this felt like communion. We would not only do hymns, but also songs by the Everly Brothers and Bette Midler, and my favourite, "Somewhere Over the Rainbow." The songs "Tomorrow" from the musical *Annie* and Kermit's classic "Rainbow Connection" also changed my life and certainly affected the songwriter I was to become. All of these songs were about dreams, faith, love and longing, about waking up and answering your calling, following your heart.

Then I got my hands on *Bella Donna* by Stevie Nicks on vinyl. Her songwriting and voice awoke the young priestess in me and called on some underground river to spill out. She changed everything for me with her confident bohemian glamour, her seductive, serious demeanour and her fearless poetry.

The voice of Sam Cooke permeated my heart. His version of "Peace in the Valley" had soul like I had never experienced in our predominantly white church. *Slow Train Coming* by Bob Dylan was huge in our house. I later learned that the album is a master class in production and instrumentation. At the time, I could just *feel* its brilliance. It has to be the greatest example of non-secular music mixed with the most renowned funk musicians of the time. Jesus had appeared to Bob in a hotel room. He was baptized shortly after, born again.

Nana had a record player, and I listened to ABBA's *Super Trouper* and danced around in front of the mirror. She had many albums of old Irish folk songs, and she'd always weep when we put on Mahalia Jackson. There was something about "Row, Row, Row Your Boat" that always gave me peace and clear direction. Do what now? Row your boat. How? Gently. Where? Down the stream.

But the gem of all gems, the song above all songs, was "I Will Always Love You" by Dolly Parton. I listened to it over and over and sang along until the tape wore out. I still think it is the most perfect song ever written. It taught me that you can love something more than life itself and let it go with grace. I still think it was the song that taught me that the greatest pain can be transformed into beauty, into music. It also taught me that you can love someone forever, that you *must* love forever, that our hearts are infinite, and that true love sometimes—no, *always*—means saying goodbye. That song is a hymn to love, and if I had had a religion as a child, well, Dolly would have been the preacher.

The songs of Gene MacLellan sank deeply into my psyche differently than the other gospel songs because I got to hear them live from the writer himself. One lyric always stood out: "Take a look at yourself and you can look at others differently." I didn't know what it meant at the time, but I had a feeling it was important.

Dad shared with me what he and Gene discovered about not taking the applause for yourself at the end of a song, staying humble, taking their thanks as proof that they have done God's work, and then sending all their love back up to the Spirit.

"You are just an instrument of God," he would say. "When you think you are the god they are praising, that's when you get in trouble. That's when you get lost." This was probably the most important advice I've ever been given. Since the word *God* didn't resonate for me, I would always change it to *love* in my mind, like Mum suggested. I was an instrument of love. This made sense to my little self. Even though I had a naughty streak, I was sure I was a loving being.

We packed up the van and went to Waterdown, Ontario, for a while, to live with Gene and his family. Gene and Dad would write in the kitchen, and I would sit at their feet and close my eyes, letting the flawless harmony move through my body, trying to understand what the words meant.

They made an amazing album together, which was released by the now extinct Pilgrim Records. I got to sing on a song called "Mommy." I'll never forget the first time I heard my voice coming through headphones!

Dad's other daughters had come to live with us. Donna and Kimmy. They were older and beautiful, and they could sing. At first, they were resistant to the church, but then they made it work for them. It gave them a stage, a way to connect with Dad. It felt like they didn't like me so much when we were young. Some part of them understandably blamed me for their father not coming home to them. One day, feeling dejected, I ran away and took Shaye with me. The police found us a few blocks away and brought us back before anyone had even noticed we were gone.

Here was my mum with three kids of her own, two stepchildren and no creative outlet except teaching Sunday school. She wanted to act again, but of course that was out of the question. Only whores acted, said the church. Yet according to the Bible, Jesus hung out with them all the time.

Fun fact: In some ancient Sumerian languages, the word *whore* originally meant "womb." Once upon a time, the priestesses were called "holy whores" to represent the sacred birth of creation. A *hag* was a wise woman. The conical hat of the witch represented the connection to great and otherworldly knowledge, not wickedness. Female power was spun to represent evil, the downfall of man, the snake in the garden, the weakness of women, and pain in childbirth was said to be a curse. So little did they know.

My dad had shown signs of having a temper—the frozen kittens should have been a clue—but the church's general policy on the man being the master of the house didn't help the growing tension in our house. "Your desire will be for your husband, and he will rule over you" (Genesis 3:16). Welcome to Patriarchy 101.

However, my mother had a mind of her own and she was very, very hard to oppress.

One night after we moved back to PEI, I woke to the sounds of screaming. Both my mother and father were in a rage. Shaye and I sat on the stairs to listen, knees to chins, huddling close to each other. Two quiet little sparrows on a branch.

They were fighting about money. The coffers were empty, and Marty had refused a record deal because it was "of the world." He was also feeling guilty for taking money from the church for singing.

SMASH!

We ran downstairs and saw our father holding his forehead. Blood was starting to gush through his fingers from a wound in his head. He had thrown a Coke bottle in my mother's direction and caught a shard as it bounced back. We didn't know what to do; there was glass everywhere. Suddenly, they both started to laugh. I suppose the tension had broken with the bottle. Dad told us to go upstairs and get dressed because we had to go to the hospital. This sent them into hysterics. I took Shaye's hand and led her upstairs. I don't know where

Donna and Kimmy were that night, but the baby started crying.

Other incidents followed. Our home was frighteningly tense. People came over to try to counsel my parents.

I have no doubt that my dad loved my mother, and I understand the pressures of poverty and that strict religious dogma can bring out the worst in people. But we had nothing. Not a crumb. And it felt like the love was dissolving. Though my mother could fix up any rundown house with a roll of wallpaper, it was beginning to peel away, and the writing on the wall beneath it was showing through. Black ink hypocrisy.

I wanted to go back to the cabin, where the walls were made of trees in their original form. The Genesis before the Genesis. The garden before The Fall.

The final fight was bad. On the way to the hospital, bleeding and bruised from a broken nose and cheekbone, my mother stopped at the church to see the pastor, to show him. He asked, "What did you do to anger your husband? What did you do to him?"

She walked out and never went back.

Dad swears it was an accident that she was hurt so badly. I only know that afterward and for the rest of his life, he never raised a hand to her or to anyone else again. I think something finally broke in him. They were like caged wild animals, and only one would get out alive. So he left, and when he did, my exquisite actress of a mother once again took to the stage.

He took my baby brother and his guitar and caught the wind on a schooner headed south to the Caribbean. *The Avenger*, she was called. The southern seas were filled to the brim with wayward musicians escaping the confines of society, breaking free of the prisons of their own making. I think the ocean calmed my father. Perhaps it held a mirror to him, forcing him to face his own tumultuous nature, to make seaworthy the wreckage of his life. He took a look at himself.

He had permission to take David for a few weeks, but they were gone for what seemed like forever. Even though Mum was terrified, waking at night from nightmares of storms, her baby lost at sea, she never said a bad word about my dad, which in hindsight was one of the great lessons of my life. No matter how much pain we are in, or how betrayed, lonely or broken we are, there is never any reason to disparage a parent to their young child. The kids see enough; let them also witness compassion and kindness. It's not that she turned the other cheek or hid things from us. She was strong. It's just that she loved the part of him that lived in us and never wanted us to be ashamed of that, or to be more deeply wounded by his inability to be a "traditional" father to his girls or a husband to her. She forgave him. The result was that we never felt we had to take sides, we could be open about our love and longing for him, and we could one day forgive him too.

I imagined him on the deck of the boat in the sun, strumming his guitar with his tanned, calloused hand. He was made of music, and songs swam around him, deep underwater songs that glowed in the dark. A bioluminescent bard.

I'd heard somewhere that all oceans are connected and that water is a conductor, so I would go down to the shore and listen for my father's song, and cry until the sea levels rose.

I don't know what sounds I made to release the pain. I recall a silent, open-mouthed scream one night in bed. Absence has a shape, a shadow and a spear. It is hollow. Empty. Eventually, I would sing myself to sleep, and for a moment when I woke up, I would forget he was gone. Then it would hit me, the blinding pain. Morning sun is the spotlight of grief.

I'd been left behind.

Gilles, the man who had stumbled into our house and was "reformed" by the church, stayed on after Dad left, to help Mum with Shaye and me. She needed household support, and we needed help with our homework. Since he spoke French, he was valuable for our schooling in the language. *Être*: "to be." *Avoir*: "to have." *Aller*: "to go." Over and over, he conjugated verbs with us, had us write them down, helped us with *les devoirs* every night.

He had a pay scale for us. Since Mum was working so much, trying to pay bills and raise us on local theatre wages, getting money from him here and there was helpful, sometimes for basics, sometimes for treats. Only we couldn't tell our mum where the money came from, or, he said, she would send him away, and then who would help us with school and cook dinner? We could starve, he told us. We knew what it felt like to be hungry.

What we had to do for him in return for the money was as wide-ranging as the dollars. It went from five dollars for touching him to fifty dollars for fellatio. That's where he drew the line, though. Anything more would have been inappropriate, because he was in his thirties and we were seven and five.

This went on for years as we moved from house to house. He would follow like a long, thin, toothless shadow. He was the kind of man who would have picked a lady's slipper. Shallow river believer.

One house on Fitzroy Street had an attic, where he stayed, with a window that looked out over the avenue. The Gold Cup and Saucer Parade went by one summer day as I stood watching the families below cheering, the floats sparkling, the marching bands playing and the legion looking so proud in their uniforms, preceded by a piper. The drone of bagpipes always moved me, transported me through time to another place, a land I was indigenous to. The pipes let me know I was lost in the world and called me home.

Gilles pulled me away from the window, back into the dark musty room as the pipes dissolved into the distance. He took his glasses off, lay back naked on the bed, smelling of cigarettes and unwashed sheets, and waited for me to choose what I "wanted" to do. The cash was always given to me directly after, and I would immediately go and hide it in my closet. I guess he got his money from dealing drugs, but I can't be sure. I would lock myself in the bathroom, climb into the tub shaking and try to scrub him off me, try to wash him from my mouth, scour him from my tongue.

There were other men lurking in other houses who had access to us and who were the handsy, flower-crushing sort. One would film us naked in the bathtub, show us pornography or slide his hand under our nighties while we pretended to sleep. One would pull us onto his lap and grind himself against us. One put his fingers inside my little sister as she sat on the couch, his own children playing obliviously in the room. Always someone we knew. Always someone trusted. Always someone no one would expect. But if we are grading on a curve, Gilles was the worst, at least for me.

One day, he disappeared. No one explained it to us. It turns out someone had ratted him out, but no one came to us to see if we were all right. We stored the secrets inside our bones. I thought only Shaye and I knew what it was like inside the mouth of that monster, but we weren't the first, and we weren't the last.

Later, in my teens, I saw an old home video with him in it. I took it into the police station and reported him. They made a still shot from the tape, they put out an alert, and he was found sleeping on a park bench in Quebec. He pled guilty and went to a warm jail cell with three meals a day for only eighteen months, even though it took decades for me to not see his face between my legs.

5.

Connection

Nothing happens until something moves.
When something vibrates, the electrons of the entire
universe resonate with it. Everything is connected.
—ALBERT EINSTEIN

There is no feeling like walking onto a stage.
A blank canvas, an empty page.
It is the darkness waiting.
For the mystery to be revealed.
Creation. The field.
Exhilarating. Terrifying.
Everything echoing, birthing and dying.
The entrance: the sound of footsteps on the deck, the heartbeat all through the body, the lights, the sudden hushed silence

and attention of the crowd. The heights. A performer can feel the audience immediately. Are they holding back at first, opening slowly, or are they with you from the start, cheering you on, laughing and applauding easily? Is the audience hungry or cynical? Do you need to win them over or have you already won? Songs are spells of the most powerful kind with the intention to open and connect.

This is an ancient arrangement. The storyteller and the listener. The witch and the bewitched. The spotlight is the sacred fire. New stories are thrilling, but the ones heard over and over are the ones that keep drilling down. The hits. The favourites. The requests. The classics. The mythological songs that become part of the fabric of society. The old folk tales that tell deep, unchanging truths about the human condition. The melodies that unlock something within us. Songs make you laugh or weep or dance or bond, or they can change the course of civilization, just as long as they make you feel something, move something, touch something. A song might be heard by one person or by every person. It doesn't matter, as long as it's heard. It isn't complete until then.

All I knew as a child was that music just happened. Like the sun coming up or a snowstorm on St. Patrick's Day, it was certain.

Prince Edward Island's first known name is Epekwitk, loosely translated as "Cradled on the Waves." It has four distinct seasons: summer, or pothole season; fall, when the colours explode on the deciduous trees; winter, which is filled with snow that can cover a house; and spring, mud season, the time of the lilacs.

The island has always been a place of deep music, from birdsong, wind song and waves to the magical sands that sing when a foot falls upon them, like the earth rejoicing at our touch. The calls of the coyotes ring through the night in concert with the crickets and cicadas. The three notes of the chicka-dee, descending into a minor third, is a song on an icy winter morning or a balmy summer night. Songbirds abound.

Then came the lullabies of the First Peoples to the babies in that cradle, and the drums, the honour songs, and the chants of the warriors. Stories were told in song and passed down, generation to generation, for thousands of years. These people, or *L'nu*, are the Mi'kmaq. All of what is now called Atlantic Canada (Newfoundland and Labrador, New Brunswick, Nova Scotia, Prince Edward Island and parts of Quebec) is Mi'kma'ki. About ten thousand years ago, as the ice age was ending and the glaciers receded, these places were attached by a plain and were easily travelled by *L'nu*. But five thousand years ago, as more ice melted and the ocean rose, Epekwitk took its form as an island.

Many of the old songs were lost in the near-decimation of the Mi'kmaq and their language, but so many have resurfaced, found their way back to the rising voices of their descendants like sap from the root moving into body and branch. Songs of hunting, feasting, dreams and tides. Some songs never die, no matter how hard we try to kill them. They live and hide underground until they are unearthed, breathing, dancing fossils come to life.

Then the Vikings came, and they sang too. Great and epic sailing songs of leaving behind their loves and of steeling their hearts to face the sea.

When the settlers came from Europe, they brought their songs, instruments and customs across the ocean. What it must have been like to cross the Atlantic, fleeing famine, persecution or war, or holding the dream of a new world. Music would have accompanied them from one shore to the next as the ships rocked on the waves. Prince Edward Island has a strong Scottish and Irish population that loves to dance and play the fiddle.

Many French Acadians who live on PEI are the descendants of settlers deported from the Maritimes during the barbaric British rule of the 1750s. Those Acadians who returned from Louisiana brought back the mystical alchemy of Cajun music, which was infused with the German accordion, Spanish guitar, African rhythm and Acadian fiddle. The influence this music has had on the world—from Hank Williams to bluegrass to Elvis to modern pop music—is impossible to measure.

When enslaved people in the United States escaped, becoming fugitives on the run, they moved in quiet waves northward to Canada, doing whatever they could to avoid detection. They often found their way through songs that were passed on to give hints on how to find the path northward. To name a flower in a song was code for the time of year it blossomed, perhaps a time when it would be safest to follow the stars and secret trails. "Follow the Drinking Gourd" is a song that survived the journey, a song about the Big Dipper pointing toward Polaris, the North Star. Many of the survivors settled in Atlantic Canada, bringing their traditional spirituals and deeply enriching the culture of music on the East Coast.

New songs were being born in the home, in the logging camps, on the fishing boats and in the mines of Atlantic Canada. To be a musician was not to be "an artist"; it was to be human, to be alive, to be an expression of our ancestors. Music is to life as breathing is to the body.

Music healed people, and as it happened, I was supposed to be one of those medicine carriers. I was told that I had a responsibility to sing because I had a gift.

Pffft. There was no way I was going to do that.

I was nine now, and all I saw around me were people who had no plan. People who lived day to day, trying to stretch every dollar. People with mismatched furniture, broken-down cars and crumbs in their cupboards. No matter how magnificent an actress Mum was, I rolled my eyes and crossed my arms at her, her actor friends and her clown boyfriend. The whole lot of them were ridiculous to me. If one of them tried to make me laugh with their puppets, I would look at them with my "you're dead to me" stare and imagine taking scissors to their stupid socks with googly eyes.

They would play games. They'd play board games all night long, while I cleaned up the ashtrays and washed the dishes. At least I learned the map of the world from the Risk board. They'd often pass me the joint by mistake if I was nearby watching. I would politely decline, which would send them into fits of giggles as I stomped away, causing them to laugh harder. Songs would eventually start up and take them into the wee hours. They were like children, thinking they could just roll along in life being whatever and whoever they wanted to be at any time, with no sense of responsibility, while I'd had to sell my body in the attic.

But they had no idea what had happened to me. They were just trying to enjoy life, to have fun, to play. I was sour. If I didn't get to be a child, then neither should they. But that summer, after Izzy encouraged me to sing at that country fair, everything changed. I caught a glimpse of something magical, something truly rapturous. I heard a call from deep inside myself.

I auditioned for a "triple-threat" school—one that taught singing, dancing and acting—and was accepted and given a partial scholarship. Mum said we couldn't afford the leftover tuition. She said it like I should know it already. I was livid.

I ran away again but didn't get very far. I turned around after a few hours, realizing I didn't have anywhere to go. Mum didn't say anything when I got home, but I knew she knew some part of me was trying to break away. And she knew I knew she knew. She noticed how I would look at her judgmentally, oozing dissatisfaction. I'd meet her loving looks with my death stare.

I had friends who had parents with "real" jobs that made money. They got the same cheques every week. They had dishwashers, and microwaves, and food, and sandwich bags. They didn't have to reuse everything all the time. They didn't have to wonder if they were safe.

At our new little apartment, my mother pasted up pretty wallpaper in a valiant attempt to beautify the slightly rundown dwelling. Shaye did all the cooking, which consisted of a lot of potatoes and pasta. We weren't vegetarian anymore, so meatballs were an exciting addition. Shaye had sworn on the Bible that she would never wash a dish, which was super sneaky since that still somehow held weight with our mother. I did all the cleaning. It made me seethe. No matter how hard I scrubbed, I couldn't get the black off the end of the butter knives that Mum and her friends used for smoking hash. Ashtrays made me want to throw up.

Since Mum grew up in a military family, her standard of clean was off the charts. If the house was messy, Mum would be more stressed. She'd say, "We may not have money, dear, but we have breeding. We must set the house in order and wait on the will of heaven. Now, bring your poor, dear mother a coffee." I tried to protest having to always be the one to clean up after the parties and the other kids, but she made it clear that this was my job as the eldest, and there would be no swearing on anything to get me out of it. To this day, I prefer not to cook, but my house is spotless, and I am so thankful to Mum for training me well.

Single mothers, who raise their kids and work at the same time, require co-operation from the children. One day, Shaye said, "I want to be a single mother, like Mum."

"Why?" I asked her.

"Because she doesn't need a man to be happy."

That made me look at Mum differently. Shaye saw all the things she did and all the joy she exuded. Perhaps because I was older, I was privy to the tears and the challenges. Money was so tight, and yet, somehow, Mum managed to get the rent paid from working in the theatre. There were triumphs every day that I didn't see.

My best friend at school, Johanna, came from a huge Mormon family. Every day, she would subtly slide extra coins to the lunch lady so I could get cold milk in a little Styrofoam cup. Some days when I'd have a meagre lunch, I would see my teacher sneak two quarters to that lady, and a hot dog would magically appear before me, soft and warm and salty. I cried about that when I was older and it hit me: the deep and private kindness of those gestures.

I planned to be that kind of parent one day, the one who made sure their children and their friends had enough. That meant I could never be a musician or an actor, and I would never call myself an "artist"—ugh, so pretentious. It also occurred to me then that being an artist meant walking the tightrope of sanity. In my young observation, to be a truly great artist, you had to lose your grip on reality and responsibility. I would not, under any circumstances, allow that to happen. I vowed to hold on to my mental health as everything crumbled around me. No one could take that from me. They couldn't take my mind or my voice. Those were mine.

Also, I could write. I won a French poetry contest and was encouraged to keep writing stories. One essay didn't make it into the hands of my teacher because I asked my mother if she would proofread it, thank goodness. It was all about autumn and why it was my favourite time of year because it's my birthday and Halloween and magic mushroom season. I wrote about how I loved that our family picked them together and how I could tell which mushrooms were edible and which ones weren't. My mother laughed so hard she had tears streaming down her cheeks. That was the day she explained the difference between legal and illegal drugs, how ridiculous the laws were and how some things needed to be kept secret. I recognized then that we were a family of outlaws. I rewrote the essay.

Mum loved to blast the Eagles on the way to school. We'd pull up to the building, often late, and when I'd try to get out of the car, she'd say, "No! The song isn't over." Over and over the lyric *"Take it to the limit"* would repeat—the song never seemed to end. Mum would sing it at the top of her lungs and make me sing it too. The song was sacred and had to be heard from intro to outro. Finally, when it was over, she'd let me go, laughing at me because I was such a little priss sometimes, and she was like the cool kid. And she really was.

At a school concert, all the other parents were seated together as the music began. My mother slipped in (late) and situated herself against a window ledge at the side. I noticed some other parents observing her. She wore a beige figure-fitting sweater dress and high brown boots with a classy heel. Her hair was cut in a stylish bob. She was tall, slim but curvy, and walked confidently. I smiled with pride as her beauty and presence eclipsed everyone in the room. When I sang my solo during the concert, a song in French called "Evangeline," she moved to the aisle to take a photo. All eyes followed her, but I didn't care. I loved this fascination everyone suddenly had with my mystical mother.

She crouched down to take the photo, I saw the flash, and then she smiled at me. We locked eyes. I understood in that moment that she had powers beyond my understanding. Even though we struggled at home, she taught me there and then how to show up in public like a boss, chin up, shoulders back, proud. This was also known as the Glamour Spell. We could be fascinating, mysterious, wild, beautiful, even if we were the subject of so many whispers. Small towns love a fallen beauty queen. But my mother hadn't completely fallen apart. Not yet.

Often after a late-night performance, Mum would come home exhausted. I would pull her brown leather boots off her and rub her feet, and she would tell me about the show, sipping Southern Comfort, a sickly sweet excuse for whiskey. She would usually sleep in and we'd be late for school. Since Gilles the monster had disappeared, I'd get Shaye ready, combing her long, thick, knotted head of hair. I'd try to scrape some breakfast together from the cupboard and make Mum a coffee to help her wake up, all the while experiencing a feeling of exasperation with her. So often, I would sit on the cement steps after school, waiting to be picked up. Her car would pull into the empty parking lot, music blaring. She was actually incredibly cool, working hard, and her friends were operating at the height of original creativity, but I was as disapproving and judgmental of her lifestyle as a nine-year-old first-born female could be.

To this day, if I'm running late, I get an anxious feeling in the pit of my stomach and feel panic rising. To me, it's so disrespectful to waste someone's precious time. I've always been the first one to arrive in the hotel lobby for "bus call"—ask any of my bandmates. Parents can be excellent examples of how *not* to be.

Sometimes, Nana would bring over bags of groceries and unpack them, looking with disdain at the empty fridge. Well, not exactly empty. There would be Carnation evaporated milk for the instant Maxwell House coffee. Usually, there was beer. If Mum was having a rough day mentally, which was happening more and more frequently, Nana would take me and Shaye to her place, where we could have a luxurious scented bath, wrap ourselves in clean, fluffy towels and, with little pink

curlers in our hair, climb into a cozy bed with an electric blanket and snacks. The only price we had to pay for this visit was
the "Go say good night to your grandfather" toll.

With trepidation, we would walk to the huge wooden door.
There was always a pause before we knocked and a knowing
look shared. He would say, "Come in." Holding hands, holding our breath, we'd enter.

His room was like one belonging to the captain of a ship.
There were giant windows, dark wood furniture and nautical
bedding. It had a large bathroom and a walk-in closet that
held his uniforms, and all along the walls were pictures of him
wearing them with his medals and his swords, looking like
Lawrence of Arabia. Even in the photo of him with his boxing
gloves up to his face, he was smiling. The message was clear:
He was the king of the castle. He was the hero. He was Smiley.

I would step forward first to kiss him on the cheek. He
would pull me toward him and run his hands all over my body,
between my legs. Sometimes, he'd put me on his lap, so I could
feel his erection. This is what men did. It was normal. Then he
would dismiss me and tell me to close the door, leaving Shaye
there for him. There was nothing to be done except to abandon her. It was how it was. I was sure that all he would do was
feel her up, like he had with me. If only I had known that he
would lock the door, bind her little wrists, and point his sword
at her chest, smiling all the while. How could I have known?
She was so quiet, and to survive, she created a deeper, separate
world, dissociated from me, from anyone, even herself. Perhaps I should have noticed how many times I had to fix Shaye's
curlers when she came back from his room, but I didn't make
the connection. Or maybe I just couldn't bear to. I was like
Mum and Nana, compartmentalizing the horror.

I would head back to Nana's room and cuddle up with her.
Sometimes, she'd ask me to sing her a song. *"This little light of*

mine, I'm gonna let it shine. Let it shine, let it shine, let it shine." I could sing and I could shine no matter how disgusted I felt. She would let me watch whatever I wanted, which was either *The Nature of Things, Star Trek, Three's Company* or my favourite, *The Muppet Show.* I dreamed that I would one day be a musical guest on that show and meet Kermit in person. *The Golden Girls* was Nana's favourite.

She never asked where Shaye was. There was always candy.

One night, I stayed at their house because Nana had entered me in a talent contest and the performance was the next day. She told me to go in and say good night to him. I left her and stood outside his door. The large, wooden gateway loomed before me, and I waited quietly, more afraid to knock because Shaye wasn't with me. I had no sacrifice to offer the ravenous beast. Trembling, I turned back toward Nana's room, composed a smile and pretended like I had done her bidding. Rebellion.

Nana was very clear that music wasn't a valid career, and I agreed. I would use my mind and be an academic. However, since I was good at it, she felt I should be onstage. The arts were important to cultivate if I were to be a "well-rounded woman."

For a time, she had me enrolled in a choir called Sing for Joy. We sang in Italian, German, English and French. I loved singing in other languages. It tapped into a different, universal place inside me. I couldn't read the music, but I memorized the melodies easily and then referenced the page for the lyrics. The problem with reading music for me was that music didn't look like that in my mind—treble clefs and straight lines and dots. I did try to let it in, but something inside me refused to allow myself to become literate. To me, each note was more like a snowflake, a seashell, a flower, a fern, a galaxy. Songs were always a circle, never linear—a round, *around.* I've seen other things in my life that look like music, but the notes on the page looked nothing like what I was experiencing, and so I rejected those symbols. In my mind's eye, music would remain the psychedelic, spiralling mystery it was. There are now microscopic pictures of how different notes affect water. Mystical mandalas appear as the water reacts to the sound vibrations. We are mostly water, so of course different frequencies of sound will affect us. It's science.

Not being able to read music, I did miss out on a shared language that has been handed down for thousands of years. The first example of music notation was discovered on a Sumerian tablet that was four thousand years old. Without written music, countless masterpieces would have been lost, and musicians wouldn't be able to communicate across space and time the way they do. Had I looked more deeply into those little black dots, maybe I could have seen what I was envisioning, seen the entire cosmos, but I didn't. Whatever was inside of me that rejected being able to read chose to experience music in a different way. My conscious mind never entered the arena when it came to music. It was all feeling. It limited me in some ways and freed me in others, the way someone who can't see develops and sharpens other senses.

Whatever course music was taking through me, it felt like an ancient, oral tradition requiring memorization. When a song came, it would be burned inside me, never to be forgotten. Future me would be asked by a musician in a recording session, "How did you decide to go from that note to this note?" I didn't know how to answer because I was unaware that I was making decisions. But, of course, I was. However, my choices were completely subconscious. Some part of me was trying to create a series of notes that unlocked something inside myself, and it had one purpose: to release the pain. The only way I could tell if I had the combination right was if I felt relief, if I felt open, if I felt free. The key.

I got let go from the Sing for Joy choir because you only got three strikes and Mum kept forgetting to bring me to practice on time.

For the talent contest, Nana wanted to make sure I was rested, bathed and dressed in a clean outfit. She took off the residual polish on my fingernails and reminded me that the worst thing I could do was look tacky. That would be embarrassing to her. I stood in front of her mirror curling my hair, looking at my little round face and tiny nose, wishing it would grow and look more like Shaye's and David's. They looked like Italian twins and were so much taller than me. I was this short little thing with no profile to speak of. So unfair.

Nana came up behind me in the mirror.

"You're perfect," she said with loving admiration, pulling back my shoulders as she often did. Then she added, "You're the perfect weight. I'd say you're about a hundred pounds. Don't gain any more than this. Men don't like that, and you don't want to end up alone."

I nodded in understanding. To be tacky, fat and alone was clearly the worst of fates. That would never happen to me. She taught me the calorie count of every food. I would repeat them like a mantra to myself. Instead of seeing the nourishment, I would see the number.

Diet and weight loss back then was already one of the fastest-growing industries in the world. Women were judged on their weight, and a low-fat diet was heavily promoted, which we all now know is a terrible idea. To be slim, women were depriving themselves of what they wanted and needed, and still we were gaining weight. It seemed that the more "liberation" women achieved, the tighter we had to make our belts. The backlash for the headway we were making in terms of power was that we seemed to be rendered powerless when it came to our bodies. It was a control mechanism of the most sinister kind and created epidemic-level cases of eating disorders and took countless lives. You would have been hard-pressed to find a woman without an eating disorder or a dangerously low level of self-esteem. If we didn't measure up (or measure down, as it were), then we were worthless. As Gloria Steinem said, we could be financially independent now, but we "couldn't afford" to eat that muffin. The more we rose, the more we were expected to diminish ourselves. Heaven forbid that we take up too much space.

My grandmother, in her voluptuous body, was a sitting duck for this brainwashing. Her pedophile husband, who preferred "his" women to be childlike, was constantly broadcasting his disgust with her, putting pressure on her to lose weight. From the time he told her he would only marry her if she got smaller, until the day he died, she measured and saw herself through his eyes. Being thin equaled being of value. To be skinny was to be worthy of love. She only wanted love for me.

I began to see myself through my grandmother's lens. No matter where I went, the echo of her voice and the shape of her shadow standing behind me in the mirror were with me. I was haunted by a hungry ghost.

The afternoon of the contest, confident that my hair looked pretty, my outfit was perfect and the song was deep inside me, I stepped onto the stage at the exhibition grounds for the Island Talent Show. All the other kids were on the rides at the fair, but not me. I was working.

What a rush it was to be introduced by CFCY's famous radio DJ Loman MacAulay to the cheering audience, to be handed a microphone, to be bathed in light.

"Tara Reno, everybody!" Martirano was too long for a stage name. "She's going to come on up here and sing us a song that would make Kermit jealous," Loman said in his iconic voice. To make matters even better, my uncle was playing the piano in the band. He was brilliant and I felt so calm knowing he was there. I didn't have to know my key; he just knew where my voice sat and what tempo would bring out the emotions of the song. It was a definite advantage having him there. (On PEI, you're always related to someone, so it wasn't frowned upon.)

The moment the music started, I disappeared. I heard myself, amplified and reverberating, but I was gone. I was lost in the words, flying on the music. Defying gravity. When the key change came, I felt like I caught air. It's called "modulation," and I'm pretty sure that's because you're suddenly in a space module blasting through the atmosphere. When the song ended, I came back into my body. The sound of the applause got louder and louder. My uncle smiled at me. I won second place singing "Rainbow Connection."

After I got my prize, people came up to Nana and me and said they just wanted to tell me how much I touched them. *Touched them.* With my voice. I did that. I remember one older gentleman shook my hand and said he would never forget this moment, as Nana looked on with pride. That pride reminded me not to take the compliment for myself, like Dad had taught me. I thanked him and silently gave the praise to Kermit, the earthly incarnation of the god of all amphibians.

On the way home in the car, Nana was unusually quiet. I looked out the window, still high from the experience, going over and over it in my mind. When she finally spoke, she said, "You could do this. This could be your ticket out of here."

At the time, I didn't register that it was an exit strategy she was laying out. All I knew was that I had experienced an ecstatic state, a kind of liftoff, and everyone felt it, the lovers, the dreamers and me.

6.

Goodness

Surely goodness and mercy shall follow me all the days of my life.
—PSALM 23:6

loved my teacher in Grade 5: Mrs. Mary Lou Morrison at West Kent Elementary School. She had a gentleness and a sparkle in her eye. She would read to us and then have us write our own stories. Anything we could imagine could be projected onto the blank page. I couldn't wait to get to school. It was my first year of having full-length days of English learning and I loved it. Though singing and writing poetry in French were wonderful, English was so much easier, and I felt like I could be funnier in that language. She encouraged me to write and illustrate my own books. Under her gaze, I felt seen, not just for who I was in the moment, but for the oak tree that could come from the little acorn of my heart and mind. In her garden, I bloomed.

This was also the year of the first school dance I attended. "Every Breath You Take" by The Police played as Peter, the cutest boy in my class, danced with me, and I felt the tingle of having a boy I liked touch my waist. It was thrilling.

One day, another teacher came into the class. He was there to teach us sex ed. He sat sideways on a desk in a friendly, casual pose. The kids in the class were awkward and giggly about it, and he smiled kindly and patiently, expecting this reaction as he shared about the mysteries of life. I didn't laugh at all. I knew all of this already. He became serious as he spoke about inappropriate touching. He said, "This is your body. No one can touch any of your private places. If they do, tell someone you trust, a parent or a teacher."

I stopped breathing.

What? This is my *body? Tell someone. Tell someone. Tell someone.* My thoughts came crashing all around me. What had been going on all this time was *wrong.* I knew this was the truth. I had to tell Shaye.

When the bell rang, I quickly gathered my books and flew out of the classroom, knowing exactly what I had to do.

We had just moved to an apartment on North River Road, which was within walking distance of my school. Shaye attended Spring Park, and to "help" Mum, our grandfather volunteered to pick up Shaye after school and take her to the motel he owned for a few hours. He would drop her off around suppertime.

I knew if I followed North River far enough, I would get to an intersection, and I'd be able to see the motel from there. *Follow the river. Listen to the river. Trust the river.* I ran as much as I could, my lungs screaming, my heart pounding in my ears. Finally, I got to the crosswalk that led to the huge front lawn of the Zenith Park Motel. His car was parked in front of the office.

I looked in the front seat. Shaye's backpack was in the car. I opened the office door. My grandfather came out of the back room looking surprised to see me. He was wearing pants and an undershirt. His blue wartime tattoo of a dancing girl on his forearm was on full display. He was limping slightly—he had been to the hospital recently because of some surgery on his inner thigh. We had to visit him in the hospital, where he showed us his scar.

"Tara, what are you doing here?" He spoke in his lilting Irish accent, trying to conceal his irritation.

I stared at him severely, my heart racing, feeling like I might throw up. "I came to get Shaye."

He looked at me curiously, almost amused. "Why?"

I summoned all my courage. "Because . . . if you don't give me Shaye, I'm gonna tell." Dead. Silence.

His eyes betrayed a hint of fear before they turned to ice. But I saw.

"Tell what?" He moved toward me, looking at me closely and coldly. His voice changed, got low, ferocious. "You think anyone would believe you? You're bad. You're the worst kind of bad."

There are moments in life when being small is to your advantage. Somehow, I managed to get past him into the back room. There was a TV, a single bed, a chair, a table with an ashtray. Shaye sat perched on the edge of the bed. No shirt. Her long, thick hair fell across her back, her little shoulder blades cutting through like the wings of a baby bird. Her shirt was folded neatly across the back of the chair, which he must have done, because she never folded anything. I threw it at her and told her to put it on. I knew he was right behind me. Shaye grabbed the shirt.

"Shaye," he said in a frighteningly calm voice. "Don't listen to your sister. She is a bad girl, and you . . . you are my good girl." I turned and looked at him. He was right there, huge, towering over me. In memory, I see a shadow, not a man. Goliath. His words didn't land. I knew I was right and that was my weapon, my sling, and the information that I had been given at school was my stone. This was war and I had the advantage.

"Get out of our way," I yelled. He didn't move. With all the strength I had, I kicked him in the leg, right where he'd been cut open. He went down in a cry of pain. I grabbed Shaye's hand and we ran past him, out the door, and followed the river home.

The next day, I asked to speak with Mrs. Morrison after class. I told her all about Gilles and about our grandfather. She was quiet, listening intently. I will never, as long as I live, forget the love in her voice when she finally spoke. She reached for my hand and looked in my eyes.

"Thank you for telling me. I will take care of this, okay? Leave this with me. It was good that you came to me."

Good.

I was good. I believed her.

Mum was called into the school. After being informed of what I had said, she thanked them calmly, then peeled out of the parking lot and went straight to the motel to lose her mind on her father. She threatened him legally and physically. When Mum's temper was released, she was nuclear, an instrument of decimation.

When she got home, she said, "It's done. He won't touch you again, I promise. But listen to me: This is just what happens to little girls. He did this to me too. Please don't tell Nana. It would crush her. Don't tell anyone. And Gilles will not be coming back." We were shackled again with the secret and the responsibility of protecting my grandmother and the rest of the family. But we never did have to say good night to him again. Nana didn't seem concerned with his change of heart when it came to his grandchildren. Maybe he was just getting grumpy in his old age after his surgery and his "fall" at the motel.

Soon enough, my uncle and his wife would have two beautiful baby girls. If the secret remained, they would be fresh sacrifices.

The only way to kill a monster is to expose it for what it really is.

The only way to kill a monster is with the truth.

The truth will set you free. I learned that in Sunday school.

When Dad and David would come home, we rarely had advance notice. At Christmas, we would leave notes if we went anywhere, in case they magically showed up and didn't know where we were. Little faces pressed against windows, watching the driveway for headlights. Breath fogged the panes as little hearts ached with longing.

I wonder how many women throughout time have waited for their fathers and brothers to come home, be it from hunting, from war, from the sea or just from having a wandering spirit. Loving my father taught me to wait and wait and wait. My tenacity was born of this waiting.

When he did make an appearance, he would only stay a few days. Sometimes, he would leave David for a while. Sometimes, he would take him. He would make a game of having us comb the house for change so he could buy cigarettes. He always had his guitar, and we would sing together and work on harmonies, and he would do his bedtime concert. He regaled us with stories of hurricanes, of swimming with fish of every colour, of eating cheeseburgers in paradise.

One night, he sang us a new song called "Out Where the Buses Don't Run," which was about being on the sailboat. He said, "When you write a song, you always have to write somethin' true."

"How do you know when something's true, Daddy?" I asked.

"You'll just know." He gave me his rum-sad, hound-dog smile.

In the morning, he packed the car.

I hid on the floor of the back seat, thinking he would drive away with me, and when we got "down south" I would pop out and surprise him, and we would live happily on the boat and just play music all day. I made myself as small as I could, curling up tight like a fiddlehead. If I held my breath when the door opened, maybe he wouldn't detect me. When I was found, they had to tear me from the car as I screamed. Shaye just sat quietly on the doorstep, staring at our father as he drove away. The look on her face would haunt him in the rear-view mirror of his life forever.

From then on, he would always leave in the middle of the night to avoid a scene, leaving notes for us. Once, he left a calendar, and at the bottom of each month he'd written, "I love you, Daddy." As if that was enough love to fill the heart of a little girl. I wanted to tear the calendar to pieces.

Mum's clown boyfriend, Izzy, was a problem, but not in a monster way. Kids adored him, and though I thought he represented the height of irresponsibility, you couldn't help but love him. He had many children with many women, and he thought he was so fucking smart. He came and went from our house at his convenience, dragging new configurations of kids along with him like a Pied Piper who made balloon animals instead of music.

He decided one day it would be a good idea to buy a sheep. So he piled some kids, myself among them, the sheep and a couple of chickens in the back seat of his blue Buick Skylark to bring us to the cabin where we were staying that summer. The animals kept defecating all over the seat and my lap. Ugh, the smell! He caught my eye in the rear-view mirror and started laughing at my look of fury and disgust. I had an iron will of disapproval of him and he was not going to break me. A chicken jumped on me and I screamed, which sent him and the other kids into delirious laughter. I couldn't help but burst out laughing. We laughed all the way home. That was the moment I let myself love him.

Legend has it that sheep still roams the forests of eastern PEI.

Sometimes, when we didn't have money for rent, we would live in a tent or a bus in the summer. This was wonderful at the time, because we were wild, all of us. Though I tried to separate myself from the pack as a more sophisticated creature, I was really just another animal, swimming all day in the Atlantic Ocean, with my little nose constantly sun-kissed, salt in my hair, wood-fire smoke in the air, sand between my toes and a heart full of wonder at the natural world. We spent glorious Prince Edward Island summers dining on shellfish, which us kids would gather from the shoreline, and freshly picked strawberries. Wild roses lined the sand dunes, where the marram grass would bow in the wind, a million tiny monks in prayer.

The earth raised us. Nothing calms my heart more to this day than the offering of sparkling diamonds on the sea from the sun and moon. The human eye has witnessed this marvel ever since we crawled out of the ocean onto land and looked back over our shoulders, secretly longing to return to the womb of the Mother, the shimmering light beckoning us home.

Then Mum and Izzy announced to a seated crew of children that they were going to have a baby. *A baby?* He didn't even take care of his other kids—how was he going to care for this one? He was drinking more and more and passing out in public. Once, I found him rolled up in a blanket in a ditch. Kids weren't allowed to come to my house to play because he was so eccentric. How would I ever live this down at school? I had to get out of there. I stomped out of the room, furious.

The next time Dad and David made an appearance, I pleaded my case like a criminal on death row. He finally agreed to take Shaye and me with them to the Caribbean. I was elated. David was less thrilled because it meant he wouldn't have the front seat all to himself—he'd have to take turns with his sisters.

I informed Mum that we were leaving, and she cried but agreed to let us go. She knew there was no stopping us from packing our bags and heading south, a direction that always held deep mystery and adventure. I imagined warmth, palm trees and turquoise water. Eternal summer with no dark places for monsters to hide. I'd take a hurricane over a pedophile any day. That would be paradise.

I awoke on my tenth birthday on our little boat, the *St. Moloris*. She was thirty-two feet long and anchored in St. Maarten, a little half-French, half-Dutch island in the Caribbean. Dad preferred the French beaches because the women were topless. As we did every morning, Shaye, David and I jumped off the boat with our snorkelling gear. We would make a flour paste and bring it into the ocean with us to feed the tropical fish. We lived in a dazzling underwater world. David could dive the deepest, but he'd been living on the boat since he was two, so he had an advantage. The number one rule was to not swim after six in the evening—that's when the sharks fed.

After a swim, Dad would row our wooden dinghy onto the shore, tie it up and go into the hotel restaurant for fresh orange juice and pancakes or scrambled eggs. There was a parrot that lived in the restaurant that liked to snack on the salt in our hair.

She'd sit on our shoulders and tickle our necks as she sucked the sea from our locks. We never wore shoes. As a birthday gift, I was given a yellow sarong with a flower fastener. I felt like a princess. I never wanted to leave.

None of the children's bathing suits were sold with tops. Even the little girls wore bottoms only. As I walked through the hallway of the hotel in my suit, a maid stopped me. She was a Black woman and was with two other maids. She reached out and put her hand under my little sprouting breast. She jiggled it up and down and turned to her friends and laughed. Then she looked at me, smiling, and said in a thick Caribbean accent, "It's time for you to cover these, girl." I made my dad buy me a top that day. I still laugh when I think of her grabbing me like that. There are so many kinds of touch. So many kinds of love.

Dad would sing in the open cafés and bars, making a little extra money to keep the boat afloat. He sang songs I'd never heard him sing, while we sipped grenadine and water and watched the iguanas scurry.

One day, I woke up and decided I was ready to row by myself. We were anchored in the harbour in St. Barts. There were boats everywhere. I woke Shaye and David, and we quietly piled into the little rowboat. They trusted that their big sister could handle it. We'd all taken turns rowing and everything had gone fine before, so what could go wrong? David untied us and we began to drift. I tried my best to steer us, but the current was strong that morning. We were drifting out to sea as the sun was coming up. A huge ship was anchored farther out, and between the three of us with two oars, we managed to aim ourselves at it. I grabbed onto the huge chain, and we stopped. We could see our little boat in the distance.

David yelled, "Look, Dad sees us!" Dad, the size of a lentil, was standing on the deck. Suddenly, he dove into the water.

He swam all the way to us and grabbed the line. Rather than get in the boat, he towed us back. He was a very strong swimmer, his lithe, tanned body cutting through the tropical water in the morning sun. To my astonishment, he didn't get mad at me when we got back to the boat, though I was braced for his fury. All he said was, "We'll have to get you rowing more so you get stronger." Row, row, row your boat.

One day, David had a temper tantrum of epic proportions. He drew a knife on me and forced me backwards onto the bowsprit. Did he think he was a pirate or something? Dad, smiling, came up behind him, picked him up and threw him overboard. That cooled his little Mediterranean temper right down. We all laughed about that for weeks. Well, David didn't.

Dad had friends from all over the world with boats and kids. There is a culture of people who raise their children on sailboats, living at different ports, spending months out on the open ocean, home-schooling. These kids are a different kind of wildling than Canadians. They get to be naked all year round! Dad tried to home-school us for a minute, but then he let that go. We would sail between St. Barts and St. Maarten, and Dad would pull out his guitar, light a cigarette or a spliff (tobacco and hash) and let each of us take a turn at the helm. Open sea and song.

There was a beautiful girl I met who was ten as well. She had an English accent and long, thick hair. I was mesmerized by her. In the evenings when her parents would hang out with my dad, she and I would go up on deck and lay there looking at the stars. One night, she surprised me and climbed on top of me, straddling me. We smiled at each other. She began to move her hips in circles, and I realized something was happening that I had never felt, a tingling fire all through my body. Everything about that moment felt right—the sky, the sound of the water against the boat, the warm breeze.

She climbed off me and we lay on our sides looking into each other's eyes.

"Doesn't that feel so nice?" she asked. I nodded. I had no words. In only a few moments, she had activated my body to want sensual pleasure. Until then, my body had been for others, but now I belonged to myself, though a little bit of me would always belong to her too. What beautiful medicine she gave me. It was pure goodness.

That winter, we travelled back to Canada. I was fiercely missing Mum. Missing a mother is a different ache. It's more primal, more disorienting. She is your compass and the stars you steer by.

Dad dropped Shaye, David and me off at Nana's on a freezing cold night. She welcomed us with hugs and tears, and said, "Have I got a surprise for you! It's a good one."

7.

Metamorphosis

Everything is in a state of metamorphosis.
Thou thyself are in everlasting change and in corruption
to correspond; so is the whole universe.
—MARCUS AURELIUS

We walked into the tiny hospital room. Izzy, sitting by the window, acknowledged Shaye, David and me with a quiet nod. Mum was lying in the hospital bed, and we surrounded her with love and kisses. It was so good to smell her. In came a smiling nurse pushing a cart with something inside. As I looked over the side of the bassinet, my life was changed forever.

Nothing could have prepared me for the beauty of that baby. Even as a newborn, she had huge, wise, calm eyes, wispy curls, a perfect nose and little lips like a rosebud. I vowed then and there that I would be her protector for life and that no man would hurt her. I didn't do it consciously. In the blink of an eye, she became my heart.

I had to guard her from all the madness. The force of my love for her hit me like nothing I had ever felt until that moment. Though I loved Shaye and David, this felt different. This baby, she was mine. Her name was Bryde. Bryde is Irish for Brigid, Mother Saint of Ireland, poets, babies and sailors. Legend has it that she could turn water into beer.

We all lived together, with this new little bundle always in our arms. Shaye and David kept growing taller, while I remained small. They teased me about it, saying that Mum forgot to water me. Mostly we all got along, though David still had an awful temper when we would tease him about his freckles. Shaye and David were just as smitten with Bryde as I was, and we all jumped at the chance to change her, bathe her and comb her hair. Every day, I made sure her golden locks were clean and brushed. I was fascinated by the way they shone and bounced and felt in my hands. As she grew, she was a light in our home. Izzy still came and went, often drunk. A smudged rainbow.

At first, we lived with his mother, Dorothy, in a tiny house on Churchill Avenue. I had my own room to retreat to, which was wonderful after being on the boat and always sharing space. I was allowed to light candles and burn incense, and I created a sanctuary, a cocoon. I began to recognize in myself a deep need for solitude. Mum gave me a journal and a pretty pen, and my poetry began to flow. From heart, through arm, out fingers, into pen, onto paper.

I went back to West Kent for the rest of Grade 5 and was shocked that some kids didn't believe I had been to the Caribbean. All my stories seemed too far-fetched. I was probably paying for the time in Grade 2 when I had told everyone that I was an alien. They would not be fooled again by my wild imagination. In a small town, all embellishments must be saved for people to talk *about* you, not for you to talk about yourself. Small-town folks can smell bullshit from a mile away, but sometimes they have a hard time wrapping their heads around things they haven't seen and are naturally suspicious.

One summer evening, Mum asked if we could go for a walk together, just the two of us. She was quiet as we strolled toward the boardwalk in Victoria Park, where the sun was just beginning to think of going down. This was the time of the crows. Their vociferous gathering at the park announced the end of the day, when one black wing would extinguish the sun. A nightly murder. Some of the First Peoples say that crows are shape-shifters. The Celts say they symbolize change and are the guardians between this world and the next.

I was about to step from one world into another.

"I have something to tell you because I know you'll understand now, and I didn't want to leave it too long," Mum said. I had my hands in my pockets and kept looking at my feet, listening to the birds.

"Here goes." She took a deep breath. "Marty is not your father. He's . . . he's your daddy, of course, and always will be. And he loves you. But he isn't the one who . . . made you." She was looking at me, waiting for me to say something. I stopped and looked at her.

What she was saying was the truth. The crows flew overhead, fleeting shadows.

"I knew it," I said softly.

"How did you know?" she said, visibly relieved.

"Because Shaye and David look like Dad. I don't look like anyone."

"But you do." She laughed gently. "You look just like Danny.

Your biological father. I knew it the moment you were born. He and I were very in love. We were together for five years from the time we were seventeen, but we grew apart." She was spilling a decade of words at once. "Then I met Marty and went to London. I really wanted to believe that you were his. I was so in love with him and wanted to marry him and make a life. But every day I've watched you grow, and I couldn't lie to you anymore, or myself. The truth of my parents was kept from me until I was nineteen. I didn't want you to grow up not knowing who you are."

The feeling in my body was clear. My cells sang in recognition of it. My DNA danced in spirals. My emotions swirled. I was excited.

"Can I talk to him?" I asked.

"Yes, I think so. His parents still live in Victoria, all the way on the other side of the country. I'll get a hold of them, and they'll help us find Danny."

We walked home, and she got on the phone right away. Within the hour, I had the beige receiver in my hand, the curly cord wrapped around my nervous fingers, the ring tone in my ear.

"Hello?" said a kind, warm voice on the other end.

"Hi. Um. My name's Tara. I'm Sharlene's daughter." I paused and held my breath.

"Yes," he said gently. "I hoped one day you'd call."

We spoke for a while, and he said he'd try to come see me. I liked him right away. He made me laugh. That feeling I always had of being different, separate—this explained it. It explained everything, but mostly it explained my tiny nose. I wasn't Italian after all. My father's people were from the Isle of Man. I was a Viking!

Mum took me to the big theatre, the Confederation Centre of the Arts, in town the next day. She knew the security guard and he let us backstage. All along the walls were photographs of shows from the 1960s onward. We stopped at a photograph of a handsome man in a kilt, doing a sword dance. That was him. That was my father.

Danny mailed me a picture of himself. I wrote him letters and sent him a sculpture of a bird I'd made out of Plasticine. By the time it reached the West Coast, it didn't resemble its intended form, but he loved it all the same and kept it until it was unkeepable. He didn't make it out east that year, or the next. I stopped hoping.

We moved into a stunning house called Westwood, also known as the Old Jones Farm, a sprawling property on the border of the North River in Charlottetown. It was falling apart, had peeling wallpaper and warped floors, but it had twenty-one rooms, high ceilings, a woodshop, a giant barn and so much land to roam. Mum afforded it by letting rooms to all kinds of wild and wonderful people. One sweet friend who lived there was HIV positive, and we knew it was important to give him a home. In the 1980s, AIDS was still vastly misunderstood. Of course, this meant people wouldn't let their kids come to the house. I heard the whispers.

I went to Queen Charlotte, a junior high, for Grade 7, but I struggled, even though my marks had been good in elementary school. Johanna and I were separated, and I was told I couldn't do the music program. One girl decided to make my life hell, and then others joined in. Grade 7 should just be abolished. I did everything I could to avoid going to school, including hiding in a snowbank all morning. My fingers and toes were numb from the cold. I walked home weeping and told my mother. She put me in a warm bath. I cried from the stinging and burning sensations in my hands and feet as I thawed out. I stopped going to school entirely and stayed home to help with the house and with Bryde.

All I did was clean, play with my baby sister and read. I

read everything I could get my hands on. Friends would drop off boxes of books, and I was ravenous for stories. I loved the innocent coming-of-age stories of Judy Blume, the dark mystery of V. C. Andrews, the magic of Narnia, the poetry of Shel Silverstein. I also played guitar. Dad had left one for us, and whenever he came home, he would teach me a chord. It was my job to practise it until he came home again, and then he would teach me another. I'd be a way better guitar player if he'd come home more often!

I told him, one day in the car, that I knew about Danny now. I don't know if I've ever hurt anyone more in my life, because he looked at me with a kind of pain I'd never seen.

"It's not true. You're mine. Do you hear me? Anyone can look like anyone if you want them to. Your mother's wrong. Nothing you could ever say could convince me that you're not my baby." His eyes were piercing mine and tearing up.

But he had taught me how to know what was true. In his eyes, I could see doubt. We never spoke of it again, and until the day he died, he refused to admit any different. And I *am* his baby. He was there. He gave me my name. He taught me to sing harmony and play guitar. He taught me how to write a song. He gave me everything, even the broken heart to pull the songs from.

That Christmas, he came home. We all went to the mall on Christmas Eve to buy gifts. Glimmering in the window of the toy store, Leisure World, was a giant dollhouse. It had electric lights and all the furniture. Everything looked real inside, even the little, Norman Rockwell–style family at the dinner table. It was three storeys tall and was being raffled off. Shaye glued herself to that window. When we pulled ourselves away and went into the store, Dad gave each of us a dollar to buy each other something. Cabbage Patch dolls were all the rage at the time, but my dollar was not going to buy one for my sister. Even if I could have afforded one, it would have been impossible to find on Christmas Eve. So instead, I got her a Cabbage Patch doll pin for thirty-five cents. As I approached the counter, the smiling cashier gave me a ballot to fill out. I wished really hard for a Christmas miracle, wrote down Shaye's name and popped it in the box.

On Christmas morning, we descended the staircase and found, beside the tree, that beautiful dollhouse. My heart leapt in my chest. It was proof that wishes come true. I'll never forget the look on Shaye's face. Mum figured it was the spirit of her grandfather Lou MacLean, still wearing the Santa suit, granting Christmas wishes to his great-grandchildren.

In the spring, Nana came home from a trip and dropped in to see how we were. When she learned that I had quit school, she hired someone to help Mum and took me to live with her. My grandfather had moved to the motel full-time, and I was given his room. His photos and medals were still on the wall, but he was nothing now. My little slingshot had hit him right between the . . . you know. I happily stayed in his room and let Nana teach me good study habits and make me a lunch every day. We lived across the street from my brand-new school, Stonepark. She bought me clothes so I would look like I belonged, and I made new friends. Since I was starting after the spring break, the faculty wasn't certain that I would pass, but I aced it. I couldn't believe how fun it was to learn when I was rested and had the comfort of coming home to a full fridge and a quiet place where I could study. With steadiness, routine and peace, I was able to succeed.

Nana, fancying herself a private investigator, took on some jobs, and she would take me with her on stakeouts. We'd sit in the car in the shadows, crouch down and watch a house. My job was to keep detailed notes of the comings and goings on a little pad in the dim light. She'd look through her binoculars and dictate what to write down: "Twelve thirty a.m. Tall man leaves residence through front door. Baseball cap and jeans. Light stays on inside. He drives away in a Toyota headed south. Licence plate . . ."

We were detectives. We were partners.

Summer came, and I moved back home with Mum.

I heard our landlords sold the beautiful Westwood house and all its acres for $100,000 to developers who eventually tore it down and built subdivisions. We moved back out to the country, to a place called Mermaid. Someone had gifted us with a dog, a Doberman named Tasha. Tessa had died many years before. Thankfully, the new place was an old farmhouse on a large piece of land and Tasha could run free.

These were happy years on the Island. Mum was working regularly in the theatre, and I would look after Bryde while she was onstage. When Bryde fell asleep backstage, I'd sneak out and watch Mum's rehearsals. She was incredible. I would completely forget she was my mother. She could shape-shift like a crow. I was twelve now and had grown out of my distaste for all things theatre. In fact, I was growing to love it. Our brand-new theatre, Kings Playhouse in Georgetown, still smelled of fresh cut wood. Some nights, I was trusted to hand out the programs. Watching the audience's delight night after night made me feel proud of who we were. Realizing the brilliance of my mother's work was a revelation, and Izzy could be a Romeo, or a comedian, or a George Bernard Shaw. Messes in life, masters on the stage.

Mum, Shaye and I even did a show together at the Confederation Centre, which was directed by the legendary Alan Lund, called *Hooray for Hollywood*. My best friend, Jenny, got a part in it too. To us, that building was our cathedral, a place of worship. The dressing rooms were sacred caverns of glamour, where masters would transform from human to immortal, and when the metamorphosis was complete, only then would they emerge to work their magic on the eager audience. People came from all over the world to see the world-class theatre and concerts, especially the wholesome and beloved tale *Anne of Green Gables* by Lucy Maud Montgomery. Anyone who played in the Anne show was a celebrity. Glenda Landry, who played Diana forever, would come to my school to teach us about stage makeup. I felt very special because I knew her. Gracie Finley was Anne, and she was always so kind to me. I was in with the celebrities.

On evenings when Mum was home, we'd often watch a movie together. We didn't have cable, but we had a VCR and all the Monty Python films. We knew *Life of Brian* by heart. She felt it was an essential film for me to watch because it had been banned by the church. She said, "No one is making fun of Jesus. They are making fun of his followers, and that's what the church finds offensive. This is some of the most brilliant social commentary of all time." I'm so grateful for her love of highbrow British humour. It certainly set my comedy course.

Shaye, David, Mum and I would have dance parties in the kitchen together and make up moves to "Stop Draggin' My Heart Around" by Stevie Nicks and Tom Petty while we cooked and cleaned. Music was always playing, and Mum always had a candle going. She was working hard and doing her best. The first time I saw the film *Mermaids* with Cher and Winona Ryder, I was struck by the similarities to my relationship with my mother. It also reminded me how emotional and impossible I'd been at times, about to turn thirteen, about to be flooded with hormones. One day, I had a meltdown and broke a giant mirror that was a family heirloom. Mum wept. I do not wish a first-born teenage female on anyone.

One weekend morning, I was listening to my new favourite record, *Graceland* by Paul Simon. I was washing up the dishes and shaking my bum to the rhythm of the songs. My bum has a mind of its own when music comes on. In fact, many drummers I have played with have noticed that they automatically set their rhythm to the movements of my hips in order to know where to land with the tempo. It's more reliable than any click track or metronome. It's the "buttronome."

Mum had gone to an early rehearsal, and Izzy woke up and told me to turn the music down. Hangover. After opening the fridge door and studying its lack of content, cigarette hanging from his mouth, he proclaimed in his deep, gravelly morning voice that we needed to go to the store. Since he was still too drunk to drive, I would have to do it. I had just turned thirteen.

He packed Shaye, David and Bryde into the back seat (it would have been irresponsible parenting to leave them behind), put a few beers under the passenger seat and set me up to drive. He moved the seat forward so my short little legs could reach the pedals, adjusted the side mirror and the rear-view mirror so I could see properly, explained the pedals, the gearshift and the speedometer, and told me to start the car. Thankfully, the Skylark junker was an automatic.

The key in the ignition turned and somehow it was my hand doing it. The engine turned over and the old car hummed. Izzy cracked a cold one and told me to put it in drive. Slowly, we pulled down the long, tree-lined driveway. This was my first time behind a wheel, except for bumper cars and that had never ended well. I was terrified.

He coached me onto the road and continued to reinforce the need to check the mirrors and my speed while simultaneously staying between the lines. The drive to the store went smoothly. We didn't pass another car and pulled into the parking lot. I pressed the brake a little too fast and we stopped with a jerk. I put the car in park and felt myself breathe for the first time. I turned to look in the back seat, and the kids were all still there, wide-eyed and silent.

Izzy hopped out of the car and went into the store bare-foot, staggering a little. I sank down in my seat, afraid someone would see me from inside the store. Izzy emerged with a brown paper bag and got back in the car. He offered each of us a soda, which we took happily. There's nothing quite like the taste of Seaman's Lime Rickey on a sunny day, especially when you're probably about to die.

Reverse was an experience, but since there were no other cars around, I manoeuvred well enough to point the car back toward the road and pull out in the direction we'd come. Izzy opened another beer and smiled proudly at me. Suddenly, a car appeared in the distance, moving quickly toward us. I freaked inside but didn't want to scare the kids. Izzy must have seen my knuckles turn white and the look on my face as I gripped the wheel.

"Easy does it. Stay in your lane. Watch your speed." He used his calmest voice.

"But I'm a kid. They're gonna see me and call the police."

"Then don't look like a kid."

"But I am a kid!" I was panicking now.

"No. *Act* like a grown-up. It's acting. You can do it. Just be older than you are."

"How?"

"It's magic. Jedi mind trick. Just breathe." He spoke slowly as the car got closer.

I sat up as tall as I could, pretending to be poised.

"That's it. You've been driving for years. Sit back. You're twenty, just driving with your family on a country road."

The Glamour Spell. With this spell, you can make yourself look like someone else. It's powerful magic, but not a hard one to master, especially under duress.

The car drove by without them even noticing me. It worked! I laughed out loud in relief. Izzy lifted his bottle and nodded in approval.

"Cheers to you. Excellent driving. Better not mention this to your mother," he said, slurring slightly. We all nodded in agreement. I gratefully turned into our driveway, pulled up to the house, put the car in park and turned off the engine. My entire body was rigid, my heart pounding. Izzy opened the door and fell out, causing all of us to laugh hysterically. To this day, I don't know if he did it on purpose or not.

Clowns.

Drama In Real Life

Determined to ensure
that no one remained
in the blazing home,
the young Charlottetown
policeman defied the flames
again and again.

By PARKER BARSS DONHAM

**INFERNO
ON
QUEEN STREET**

8.

The Tower

*Lightning strikes and flames rain down. These are symbols
of creativity and inspiration. The Tower proclaims a
change is gonna come, a physical, emotional or spiritual
event. Cathartic, traumatic, abruptly life-altering, terrifying.
Revelation. You must decide how to face it.*
—THE TOWER TAROT CARD,
INTERPRETED BY SHARLENE MACLEAN

We left the house in the country for a project townhouse on Queen Street in Charlottetown. I'm not
sure why we had to pack up the house so quickly.
Mum said she didn't want certain people to know where we
lived. We were to give no one our address.

Our farmhouse furniture looked so out of place in the small rooms of the cheap, ticky-tacky townhouse. I'd never lived anywhere with such low ceilings. No matter how rundown our farmhouses had been, they'd felt spacious. At night, a street light shone right through the window into the room I shared with Shaye. I pinned up a yellow towel to cover it. You can't pretend a street light is the moon, no matter how good your imagination is.

My boobs officially arrived the summer before Grade 8 and they were amazing. There were lots of boys who wanted to touch them. What a feeling it was to be the first girl they explored in this way. Some of the boys had a natural gentleness and a desire for eye contact and slow movements, but my experience was that they could be clumsy, and most didn't yet know how to unhook a bra or connect their breathing rhythms to mine or to the movements of our bodies. They didn't know how to touch me. There was a sweet innocence to this, but it was also frustrating to feel the pulsing places begging to be pushed into. I was often left feeling emptier. I never asked any of them to do more than kiss, but I definitely had my foot on the gas pedal, and they had theirs on the brake.

Perhaps because my sexuality had been ignited earlier than others my age, I yearned for erotic touch, or maybe it was just who I was. How can we ever know, once innocence is broken, who we would have been had it been left intact? All I knew was that it felt good, sweet and healing.

I loved knowing I was a new, sensual frontier for the boys. It gave me a sense of power and pleasure. I loved the look in their eyes as I gifted them with new sensations.

I made close friends with girls—beautiful, vibrant girls— and all we cared about were boys. And makeup. And hair. And music. And boys. I became a cheerleader so I could watch the basketball players. Go Tigers! Was I experiencing a normal life? I was deeply attracted to the girls too. Everything was blossoming all around me.

It was wonderful to be liked at school, to be thriving academically, to be coming into some kind of physical beauty. The only thing I got teased about—and only lightly—was the way I spoke. With Mum being an actress, she maintained a "middle Canadian" way of speaking that didn't pick up the Irish-influenced East Coast inflections. If ever a sentence came from my mouth that sounded like a PEI accent, I was corrected and made to repeat it "properly," thus resulting in some comments from my peers about my funny way of talking ("You tack fooney"). They said I sounded too proper, too posh. That didn't bother me in the least.

Then I went and fell in love with a boy and got my heart broken into a million pieces. That's when I wrote my first song.

His name was Graham. He was smart, handsome and a great kisser. The boyfriends before him were sweet: Ted, Michael and a really special boy named Cory, who I started dating at my thirteenth birthday party. These boys cared for me, but I felt frustrated by their lack of desire to go further when we were making out. My body was on fire. I had a superpower and I wanted to use my understanding of the male body. I was hungry to be touched by someone of *my* choosing.

Cory broke up with me to be with a much more wholesome girl who didn't want to go so fast. She was perfect for him, so I couldn't be mad, and we stayed good friends. He understood me and respected me. In hindsight, I must have been terrifying to a good boy with solid morals. But I was ready to explore. I felt like if I could excel at anything in life, it was at being a lover.

Something about Graham felt different. He was older, tall, smart and popular. He played hockey and guitar. Athletic, academic and artistic, he ticked all the boxes I knew existed at the time—a hat trick of perfection. He was fourteen and, therefore, a man. He kissed me for hours at a party in a barn until my lips went numb. Still, he wouldn't put his hands on me except my bare waist. I kept trying to encourage him to move up inside my blouse, but he preferred closing his eyes and locking lips. Boring.

After the party, I called him to tell him we should find somewhere to go soon so we could be alone. He seemed amenable to that suggestion. The next day at school, he avoided me, and I was informed by a mutual friend that we weren't together anymore. It was humiliating. I had no understanding of the subtleties of seduction, of letting boys move toward me and, more importantly, of having them earn my love.

Unfortunately for my thirteen-year-old self, all that kissing and watching hockey had lassoed my heart into the situation, and I was crushed by Graham's rebuff. I cried myself to sleep for weeks, listening to '80s ballads on the radio. "(I Just) Died in Your Arms" by Cutting Crew made me cry the hardest.

Shaye tried to console me but ended up just sitting with me, witnessing her first up-close heartbreak. She'd climb into bed with me at night and be the big spoon while I cried. I knew she was there, but I felt so alone.

My grief triggered a landslide of unreleased grief, and somehow I knew that the only thing to do was feel it, and I was doing that in a most amplified way. The despair I was experiencing seemed out of proportion with the amount of actual closeness I'd had with Graham. Of course, it was more about being left, without explanation, without a goodbye. I was left to wonder what I had done wrong. Abandonment Issues, master's program.

I finally found my way to my guitar, which became my oar in this suddenly not so gentle stream. A song came through, and somehow it felt like it was keeping me company. One moment, I was alone with nothing but heartache, and the next moment, I was accompanied by what was created from the hurting.

The song had a shape, like a sculpture, and it had an energy. It was . . . alive. It was proof that some kind of love had existed, even if it had just been for a moment. It wasn't over—so long as I had the music, I had a permanent record of "us." Eternal love. A pin on the map on the journey of my heart. The more I sang the song, the less devastated I felt. The song was a siphon for the pain, an antidote for the loneliness.

I put this boy in a pocket of my heart shaped just for him, near where my love for the others was kept. I thought, *My heart is going to have to get very big if I am going to carry all this love around and add more as I go.* Like Dolly taught me, love is always. If it was true that love is infinite, then perhaps so too was my ability to love, even when it hurt.

That was my first experience of music as alchemy, of turning pain into song, suffering into beauty, lead into gold.

I spent a lot of time in our little bedroom, working on that first song. I called it "One More Time," and it changed ever so slightly each time I sang it. It was evolving, refining itself, like when condensation turns to rain, an invisible transmutation. Shaye would sing harmony. She told me it was a good song, and that was high praise coming from her.

Tasha, the Doberman, lay on the floor between our twin beds while we sang about heartache. Our dog was sweet, but she was also incredibly protective and would terrify anyone coming to the door. Our black cat, Cinder, stayed away from Tasha and slept mostly in Bryde's room.

David was nine and obsessed with Elvis's music and Michael Jackson's wardrobe. Bryde was three and just the sweetest thing. Her hair had never been cut (as per my instructions), and her blond ringlets bounced as she walked. I was the keeper of that treasure, the family gold.

Mum was working hard, but she still didn't bring in much money from working in the theatre. She was getting standing ovations every night and coming home with her heart full and her pockets empty. Uncooked spaghetti was something in the cupboard that we could snack on. There always seemed to be money for Tim Hortons coffee, though. Times were lean, but we lived around the corner from Dairy Queen, and Nana would take us for Skor Blizzards, so that was a bonus. She believed ice cream was the answer for everything. Every joy should be celebrated and every sorrow comforted by crème glacée.

Izzy would still come and go, though he and Mum didn't seem to have a romantic relationship anymore. Sometimes, he'd pass out in Mum's basement bedroom, and I'd come home from school to find him there, with Bryde asleep in his arms. I'd carefully extricate her from her snoring, wasted father and bring her upstairs to cuddle with me.

Izzy would wake up eventually and come groggily up the stairs, his rainbow wig askew. One day, he sat recovering in an armchair and listened to me play guitar and sing the song I'd written. He loved it. He looked at me in a way that I would later recognize often in my career when certain people first heard me sing an original song. He assured me that I was on to something.

Izzy didn't come around for a few days after that, and Mum told us to be careful of what we said on the phone because the police were listening in. She pointed out the "ghost cars" outside the house. She explained that two members of our extended family had just gone down for selling pot, and that the police assumed she was involved.

A darkness was falling.

One Friday at school, I couldn't shake the feeling that I wanted to go home. I called Mum from the office and asked her if she could come and get me. She told me to take a taxi. Tasha, our dog, had run onto the road and was hit by a car. She was dead.

I got home as fast as I could and found Mum, Shaye, Bryde and David all there, sobbing. We huddled together on the couch, grieving and sharing stories. Mum said the woman who hit Tasha with her car was crying as Mum held the dog's limp, brown body in her arms in the middle of the road. Tasha had been used to having space to run. We had a quiet dinner and went to bed.

The next night, we were all in our rooms, still a bit shocked from Tasha's death. There was a knock at the door downstairs. I noticed that no dog bark accompanied the visitor's appearance. Mum sounded irritated with whoever she was talking to. She yelled upstairs that she was leaving. I gave Bryde a bath and put her to bed, and eventually, Shaye, David and I fell asleep.

I woke in the dark. There was no air. The only light coming in was from the street light, through the towel I'd hung as a curtain. I started coughing. I heard voices. David was yelling. Where was Bryde? I couldn't breathe.

I got off the bed, but the floor was sizzling hot. I jumped back on the bed, crawled to the foot of it and reached for the door handle, shouting, "Shaye! Shaye! The house is on fire!" Gasping for breath, I screamed, "Bryde!"

When I opened the door, a wave of smoke rushed in.

In the dim light, I saw a hand coming toward me. I reached for it and collapsed. The next thing I remember, I was being carried over someone's shoulder. Shaye was there too, under his other arm. We were on the landing of the stairs. The man carrying us yelled, "On the count of five we're gonna run. Ready?"

On five, we bolted down the stairs. It was all in slow motion. I turned my head and saw the living room in flames. We were running through a tunnel of fire. A burning threshold. As we burst through the front door, officers were there to quickly take us as far away from the house as possible. The man who'd been carrying us fell to the ground. Seconds later, the house exploded. *Seconds.* We would later learn that flashover happened when the house reached 538 degrees Celsius. It caused an ignition point, and a fireball tore through the house, crashed through the windows and out the door. We had just gotten out in time.

I didn't see the ball of fire—my back was to the house—but I felt it behind me, like my Mum had felt that presence in the woods that night.

Our Father, who art in heaven.

Deafening, smashing sounds, like when the bottle hit Dad in the head, but a million times louder.

Hallowed be thy name.

Screams and sirens.

Thy kingdom come, thy will be done.

Thy will be done? Mum? Where are you? Who did this?

Yea, though I walk through the valley of the shadow . . .

Is everyone alive?

I fear no evil.

I'm so afraid.

On earth as it is in heaven. On earth as it is in heaven.

As above, so below . . .

Forever and ever, amen.

Bryde had been found just before Shaye and me, and had been unconscious on the floor when the man picked her up and carried her out of the house. A rag doll. She was now wide-eyed and awake in the arms of an officer. David, who had jumped out of a second-storey window, was standing beside us, facing the burning house. All our faces were covered in soot, the fire reflected in our teary eyes. Bryde whispered, "My toys."

We were put in a police car along with our young neighbour Jason, who was a sweet friend. We were driven by Detective Mike Quinn, whose deep kindness and care was essential as we trembled in the back seat on the way to Nana's.

She was calmly livid as she got the details from Detective Quinn. She thanked him profusely and told him she would take it from here. I could tell that Jason wanted to stay and protect us, but Nana just wanted everyone to leave. Detective Quinn led Jason to the car and drove him home, to his own smoked-out townhouse next to ours. Nana put us in the tub to clean us off and tried to locate Mum. The soap smelled so good. It would take weeks before I wouldn't smell the smoke, and years before I wouldn't wake up in the middle of the night gasping for air. Trial by fire.

Police suspected arson. The same person who had knocked on our door earlier that night had bragged around the town that he had set our house on fire. It couldn't be proven—the police didn't even try—but everyone knew who it was. He never would have gotten in if Tasha had been alive. Had Mum been home, she would have died in the basement bedroom.

Constable David Cheverie just happened to have been driving by with his partner. He noticed wisps of smoke. He jumped from the car, broke down the door and entered our burning house four times to save us from the fire. He risked his own life for us. He was the guardian angel that had been summoned to watch over us as we slept.

Mum arrived home around two thirty in the morning to find fire trucks on the street, hoses spitting water through the windows, all her belongings burned and soaked, her children gone. Every photograph, every book, every Elvis tape, every toy, my guitar and our aptly named cat was turned to cinder.

Our angel received a medal of honour in Ottawa for his bravery, while the ashes of our lives blew away in the Atlantic wind.

Though I'd already received many teachings from life on the temporal and impermanent nature of things, the fire was the one that taught me what can be left behind and what needs to come along. What can be torn away and what remains. What can and what cannot be destroyed. It taught me to always reach for that hand in the darkness. It also taught me that Death sits right beside us, waiting, twiddling its thumbs and humming a song about heartbreak, the practice of loss, the end of the world as we knew it, as we built it, as we watched it turn to dust.

9.

Impenetrable

*Let your plans be dark and impenetrable as night,
and when you move, fall like a thunderbolt.*
—SUN TZU, THE ART OF WAR

E verything is remembered as before or after the fire. That was ground zero, the demolition.

We had no insurance. The community came together as they do in times of difficulty. Nowhere does this better than Prince Edward Island. With the same ferocity that we could tear someone apart with our bare hands for being different in those days, we could wrap our protective power around them in times of tragedy. The wave of love that washed over our family was like nothing I'd ever experienced, having spent my whole life on the periphery of acceptability in a conservative town. Instead of being the object of sideways glances and whispers, we received empathetic eye contact from people and were told that they were there for anything we needed. The tones in their voices were soothing and showed genuine care, like we had suddenly become their family. Stacks of boxes arrived on Nana's doorstep, filled with clothing, food and other basics. The newspaper called. The school raised money. CBC interviewed us. The story was all over the news about the daring rescue, the hero police officer, the lucky children.

From the safety of Nana's couch, we watched the footage of the aftermath, of witnesses telling their stories about the fireball that shot out of the house right behind us as we narrowly escaped. We were grateful for our lives, but bewildered and in shock. I didn't want anyone to touch me; my shoulders were up to my ears. Mum was a mess. Her hands were shaking.

We had to assume that the arsonist had been trying to kill us. He had lit the couch on fire knowing that four children were asleep upstairs. The police said they couldn't prove who had burned our house down. If the arsonist wasn't going to be arrested, we had to get out of there.

Over the next few weeks, we stayed in a hotel and then were moved into temporary housing as plans were made for us to go live with our fathers for our protection and to give Mum a chance to recover. A man from *Reader's Digest* came to interview us about the fire, and the story appeared in the "Drama in Real Life" section of the magazine: "Inferno on Queen Street."

Izzy came to pick up Bryde. We watched them drive away. He got sober soon after that and married someone who cut off Bryde's hair and changed her last name to theirs. They didn't even ask me. I wondered if they'd even considered who'd made it their life's work until then to protect her, to comb her tangles, to wipe her tears, to be there when she had nightmares. She was stolen from us, and no one even mentioned it.

Shaye and I made a pact that one day, we would rescue her and take her back.

Dad came to pick up Shaye, David and me. He had a new fiancée. He was forty-six and she was twenty-four. She was from France and beautiful, elegant with short, black hair and a tiny frame. We'll call her Sylvie. I don't suppose she imagined she would be mothering three kids, one a teenager, when she signed on for a relationship with him. She seemed nice enough at the time. She and my dad decided we would all go to Paris to live. I was elated. I was obsessed with Paris, even though I'd never been there, and had gobbled up all the books and films I could find that were set there. I told everyone that we were going.

Dad had a summer gig in Parrsboro, Nova Scotia, playing Hank Williams, so we spent the summer there and planned to leave for France in the fall. While Dad and Sylvie searched Paris for a home for us, Shaye, David and I flew with Nana to London. From there, we boarded a train to Scotland and landed in Oban. A short, chilly, misty ferry ride later, we were on the Isle of Mull. Rainbows greeted us like banners welcoming us to Duart Castle, home of the MacLean clan. I felt instantly connected to the stone walls my ancestors had built and rebuilt since the thirteenth century. I knew what it was to be blown to pieces and to reassemble. The walls held my history, my name, my courage. As I touched them with my little fingers, something within me fortified. The bagpipes played in the distance, making the hair on my arms stand up and my heart swell in my chest until I thought it would burst. I was home.

When we arrived in Paris, I began to miss Mum terribly. The shock from the fire had worn off and my grief was beginning to surface, like hot lava emerging through cracks in the earth. I hadn't spoken to her in a month, and I didn't know where she was. When I shared this with Sylvie, she yelled, "Then why don't you go home to her?" and stomped away in fury. I stood there in shock, tears stinging my eyes, but I refused to let her see them. I was a fortress now. Uninvadable. Impenetrable.

We all ended up going back to Canada the following week. I don't know why they couldn't find a place to live, but I think that having three kids foiled Sylvie's plans of living in her hometown, and she took it out on us, mostly me. One minute she was moving to Paris with her troubadour fiancé, and the next she was back in Canada, stuck living in an ugly, dark subdivision in Dartmouth, Nova Scotia, with three kids. It was the opposite of the City of Lights.

All I wanted in the world was my mother. I ached for her night and day. I called Nana and she told me that Mum had flown to London, expecting that we would be in Paris and close to her. She wasn't coming back to Canada because it wasn't safe. The man with the matches still prowled the streets and dirty midnight bars, still watched for her from the shadows.

I insisted that I had to join her, and Nana let me know in no uncertain terms that I couldn't do that. Mum wasn't well and needed some time on her own to heal. She was making money singing on the London trains and taking shifts in pubs. She was drinking—a lot. It was no place for a child. As if anywhere was.

Mum called me from a pay phone, which she said was just like the ones from *Doctor Who*. I cried and begged her to let me come to London. She said she was working to build something for us all there. She had to stay in London. She'd left once to follow Marty, and her life had fallen apart. She wasn't leaving again. Six months, she said. Just give her six months.

At least I had a guitar. I had one of Dad's in my room. He didn't give me any more guitar lessons, and there was no more singing at the foot of the bed. Something inside him seemed to have withered. He didn't laugh much anymore, and he couldn't look me in the eyes.

By this time, I'd learned enough from him about how to use music to navigate my inner life. If I could write a song, I could stay afloat, no matter how much it felt like I was going under. Songs were my rowboat. I could sing myself to sleep now, and my guitar would sleep beside me. Life is but a dream.

In October, a few weeks after we arrived in Nova Scotia, Dad and Sylvie bought me a bus ticket to PEI. They said it was so I could have a visit with Nana, who was just a few hours away. What they didn't tell me was that on the day I was gone, they were getting married. She didn't want me there. When I got back, I saw a wedding cake top in the fridge. She looked at me with a satisfied smile, her wedding ring gleaming. That night, I went to the fridge and turned the wedding cake upside down and pushed it through the grate. It was incredibly satisfying to watch it fall in thin ribbons down to the next shelf.

I woke to a big, empty suitcase in the middle of my floor and Sylvie standing over me, screaming at me in French to pack my things. I got up and began frantically emptying the dresser. Shaye came in and started sobbing on the bed, while Dad cowered in the living room.

They drove me to the bus stop, and Dad stayed behind the wheel, silently looking ahead, a cold chauffeur in an old, rusty brown Mercedes. Sylvie got out of the car and took my suitcase out but left the guitar in the trunk. I got out and stood beside my bag, looking at Dad and hoping he would turn his face toward me and see what was happening. I wasn't going to scream and cry and beg for him to keep me this time. She handed me some money, enough for the bus ticket back to PEI, and said six words that I can still hear: "Never interfere in our lives again." She got into the car, slammed the door and drove away with my facing-forward father. I watched the car until it disappeared like a dandelion seed in the wind.

It was my fourteenth birthday.

It would be eight years before I laid eyes on my father again. She kicked Shaye out next and then David a few years after that. Then, I assume with no one to blame for her dissatisfaction, Dad got the boot. The next time I saw or spoke to my father, we were backstage at an arena, three hours before we had to go onstage to sing together in front of thousands of people on national television.

What is it in the heart of a man that makes him a devoted father or a lost boy? What makes them run? What makes them stay?

I remember that bus ride to Prince Edward Island. Never had I felt so untethered, alone, disposable. I took a taxi to my grandparents' house. Instead of me feeling the welcoming arms of home, everything felt wrapped in razor wire. I had almost escaped, but here I was, back at the door of the lair of the monster.

But I had armour now.

Nana opened the door and I didn't smile. I had always had a smile for her, all my life. The one good thing that I inherited from my grandfather was that no matter what was happening inside me, I could light myself up by smiling. It wasn't a mask really; it was a way of going to battle with despair. A bio-hack. Smiling was also contagious. As a kid, I would walk around smiling at people to see if I could cheer them up. I would look them right in the eyes and do my scientific research.

I once overheard a young cousin ask Shaye, "Why does Tara smile so much?"

She answered dryly, "She was hit by lightning."

Then she came to me and said I should dim it down or people would think I was missing something upstairs.

But I was a "smile though your heart is aching" kind of girl. It was my sword and my shield.

On this day, I had nothing to smile about. I couldn't even fake it. Nana knew me better than anyone. She knew me by heart, every gesture, tone in my voice, sparkle in my eye. She knew my laughs, my posture, the angle of my head, and she knew exactly how to wrap me in her arms when I needed love. She didn't know the hollow girl on her doorstep that day.

I didn't hug her. I just pushed into the house, hauling my bag. There were no balloons, no birthday cake, no presents. The word from Dad and Sylvie was that I was being difficult. When I asked if I could stay with her until Mum could take me, she told me that my grandfather wouldn't allow it. He hadn't been well and had moved back into his room. He was spending most of his time at home, and he didn't want me there. I had nowhere to go.

When I heard he was denying me sanctuary, I felt the crimson blood in my body boil over. It was a volcanic eruption. My cheeks burned. How dare he. Did he not know how much power I still held? If he wanted a war, I'd give him a war. I still had ammunition and I outranked him.

I was allowed to stay for a few weeks while Nana came up with a solution for where I was to go. I was not to disturb my grandfather. One suggestion Nana had was that we try to locate Danny, my biological father, to see if he would take me for the six months until Mum was on her feet.

Nana had to go away for a few days, so my aunt came upstairs to fix my grandfather a sandwich. She and my uncle lived in the suite attached to the house. Their daughter would toddle around, and we were all smitten with her. She looked like one of those antique porcelain dolls, with impossibly giant blue eyes and black curls.

My aunt was being very kind to me and asked where I was going. I shared that we were trying to find Danny and that maybe I would go to British Columbia. Her eyes were full of compassion.

"You don't leave your daughter alone with our grandfather, do you?" I asked.

The look in her eyes changed to confusion. "What do you mean?" She kept making the sandwich.

"You know, because of . . . the way he is."

"No, I don't know. What do you mean? The way he is?" The sandwich-making stopped.

"He's not someone you leave with little girls." I held her eyes. She stared at me, and I witnessed the comprehension dawn across her face. I had the weapon Smiley didn't have. When truth lands, it can decimate. How many times had that beautiful, black-haired baby sat on his knee, his hands around her little waist, bouncing, laughing, unaware of the claws and drooling fangs? He could not have her. For over fifty years, he'd taken whatever he wanted from the women in my family. Now I would be collecting on our behalf.

My aunt dropped the knife on the counter and turned around and went quickly downstairs to her apartment. I knew I was doing the right thing by blowing the whistle, but my heart was sinking straight to the bottom of the river. I was causing pain. Maybe I was bad after all. Or maybe he'd just finally crossed the wrong MacLean. The one with Viking blood.

The next day, crashing noises started coming from my grandfather's room. My aunt came tearing up the stairs and opened his door. I heard her speaking to him firmly. I slowly walked toward the door and looked in. I could see his feet thrashing. Stroke.

"Call an ambulance!" she yelled to me.

I stood there, detached, watching with cold curiosity. Frozen. Drawbridge up. Death stood beside me, silently waiting, its hand on my shoulder. I saw Shaye, sitting shirtless on the edge of the bed in the motel. I saw my young mother in her nightdress, my beautiful grandmother, discarded. I saw his shadow standing over me. Time was still. There was no air, no breath. My aunt yelled again, but this time, her voice was muffled and distant, like I was underwater.

A time to live, a time to die. Where was that from? The Bible? King Solomon. Yes. A time to die.

My aunt came running past me to grab the phone, giving me a well-deserved what-the-fuck-is-wrong-with-you look. I watched from my submerged suit of armour as his feet continued to jolt. The ambulance came. I looked out the window as he was taken away. He was still alive, though barely. My aunt looked at me from the driveway, her eyes filled with tears. Salt met steel. I closed the curtains.

Nana returned home and went straight to the hospital. He couldn't speak or walk anymore, but he could still smile with half his face.

She came home and met with her son and his wife, who told her what I had divulged about the monster he was. Nana swore to me that she didn't know and begged me not to call the police; it would "ruin the family name," and he couldn't hurt anyone now. There were rivers of tears.

How could she not have known? She must have felt it. But she had just been a child too when he lured her into his lair. If the lair has velvet furnishings and shining silverware, it's hard to know you're in hell.

She was right that he couldn't hurt anyone now. He was imprisoned in his own body, which was worse than death. Justice served? Almost.

I always appreciated that my aunt didn't tell anyone how catatonic I became in that moment. Maybe she didn't remember—the event was highly traumatic. Or maybe some part of her understood, and without judgment, this was her silent thanks for trying to protect her daughter.

It was the beginning of a long journey for their family as they came to terms with the horrible truth of a man who had been their hero. Imagine a son thinking his father was the epitome of greatness, and learning in a moment that he was actually the lowest, most dangerous form of parasite. How do you ever recover? It could become a lifelong pilgrimage to affirm your own goodness.

Nana found Danny's number in British Columbia and called him. She told him the situation and then handed me the phone.

In the calmest, kindest voice I'd ever heard from a man, he said, "I guess it's my turn." A few days later, social services came to pick me up and put me on a plane headed west. Escape velocity. I was nervous. The trip was eight hours, but it felt like days. Where was I going? Would they like me? Would they want me?

I landed late at night, picked up my bag and, heart pounding, walked out into the Victoria airport. I was the same age my grandfather had been when he left Ireland alone. I could do this.

I was greeted by a clan of people who looked just like me. They stared at me with fascination, then looked at each other with excitement and tears in their eyes, then stared back at me again.

"We knew it was you right away," said a sweet old man who looked like Colonel Sanders. I guessed he was my grandfather.

I was able to smile, though inside, I was numb, battered and disfigured.

A Plasticine bird.

10.

Little Viking

Quocunque jeceris stabit.
(Whichever way you throw me, I shall stand.)
—THE MOTTO OF THE ISLE OF MAN

I looked around the crowd at the airport but didn't see my father. He wasn't there to greet me.

On his way to get me, he'd had an appendicitis attack in the car. He ended up in emergency surgery just as I landed, and so my aunts, uncles, cousins and grandparents were my giddy welcoming committee.

They had only learned that day that I existed.

The only choice I had in the moment was to trust that I was safe. Their enthusiastic welcome helped to melt my fears. They hugged me tightly and with such deep love that I couldn't help but smile. Their voices had a softness that I recognized. We looked alike. This was my flock. Still, part of me was in shock, and I was moving breath by breath, step by step, shoulders back, chin up, like Nana had taught me.

I was taken straight to my "new" grandparents' house and told that I would see my father in the morning. I was exhausted and four hours ahead, on Atlantic time, in my body, but still I was sharp as an animal in a new environment, taking in every detail, on alert for danger. My grandmother Kay showed me to my room. She was warm and petite and gave me a hug good night. She held me for an extra moment that told me I was welcomed by the matriarch.

I stared at the ceiling in the dark. It smelled different here. I was alone, and yet I had the feeling that I had never been less alone in my life. It was like a soft nest had been built for me, filled with down. I fell asleep quickly, and the next thing I knew, it was daylight and someone was knocking at my door.

My grandfather Ernest poked his smiling head in. No part of that gesture felt invasive.

"Good morning. Would you like some toast and tea, dear? They are expecting you at the hospital shortly." I loved that he called me "dear." His voice was gentle and friendly and tinged with excitement.

"Yes, please. Thank you." I was disoriented in this strange house. I got dressed quickly and checked myself in the mirror. I pulled my hair back in a low ponytail and clipped a bow on it. I wore a long khaki skirt and a white blouse. I felt like I looked pretty. We had breakfast in a bright kitchen overlooking a golf course and a huge duck pond. My grandparents were curious and kind, though I noticed my grandmother asked the same question twice.

The drive to the hospital was fascinating. My face was glued to the car window in the back seat. British Columbia is beyond description. It was like a different planet. There were *palm trees* in Victoria. The majestic cedars, the mountains, the Pacific Ocean were worlds away from my tiny island of sandstone. Where things had once felt easily eroded, sand shifting beneath my feet, I now felt the stability of Jurassic granite, of volcanic rock. It seemed like everything was solid in a way that I had never known.

On Vancouver Island, most of the houses were built of stone or stucco. Fire resistant. No Big Bad Wolf could huff and puff and burn our house down here. I felt safe—an old feeling I remembered from the cabin. A feeling of belonging.

But unbeknownst to me, far beneath my feet lay the Juan de Fuca tectonic plate. The Cascadia Subduction Zone runs from where I was all the way down to Northern California. This zone is actually one of the most unstable on earth, for if it moves, not just a little sand will slip into the sea, but everything will be swallowed whole. In time, even the strongest foundations crumble. This is the nature of all things. Everything is collapsible, except for the basic elements. That's why we must be elemental. Fundamental. Indestructible. Immutable.

I'd had to grow up so quickly to survive, but the child still left in me desperately wanted to imagine there was a safe place in the world.

We arrived at the hospital, and when the elevator opened on the floor where my father was, the hallway was lined with doctors and nurses, all looking at me. A lovely nurse approached me and said, "You must be Tara. Your father is just down here."

Everyone in the ward had learned that I was meeting Danny for the first time and had come to witness the moment. Many of the hospital staff were wiping tears from their eyes. I just put one foot in front of the other, shoulders back, and reminded myself to breathe. I could feel my grandparents behind me.

I turned the corner into his room, and there he was in the hospital bed, smiling at me. He had short, chestnut hair, the exact colour of mine; sky-blue eyes, just like mine; a nose just like mine; and a beard. I didn't have a beard. I studied him silently for a long moment. For the first time in my life, I had no words. I walked slowly over to the bed and sat down near his feet. I noticed a nurse in the corner of the room, wiping her eyes with tissue. Grandpa Ernest and Grandma Kay stood in the doorway, giving us space.

"Sorry I wasn't at the airport," he said gently. "I was on my way, and this happened. Strange timing."

"Can I see your feet?" It was the first thing I thought to say. Then I realized how strange it must have sounded. I added, "Everyone says we have the same feet. Dancer's feet. I can't dance, though."

He said sweetly, "Well, we'll have to do something about that then." He pulled the blanket up and let his left foot peek out. He pointed his toes. His high, elegant arches were identical to mine. I took off my shoe and pointed my toe. He smiled with tears in his eyes, and I smiled back, my heart in my throat. From head to toe, from stars to earth, there was no doubt we belonged to each other.

I have often wondered about the timing of that appendectomy. I'm not one to think that everything happens for a reason, nor do I look for signs or meaning. I tend toward an acceptance of chaos and randomness, which make more sense to me. But I couldn't help but think about how a vestigial organ, a remnant of some past ancestral function, chose that exact moment to leave my father's body. Life kept demonstrating something that I could see out of the corner of my eye. I was beginning to notice a pattern. In order to make space for the new, something must be sacrificed. The outmoded must fall away. If the sacrifice happens first, the brutal emptiness, terrifying as it is, is only a temporary state. Facing that emptiness in free fall is how we learn to fly. Every sparrow knows that.

I felt something beneath me that would hold. I had landed on the West Coast in the arms of a loving family, a nest I hadn't even known was there.

I loved my father immediately. He had a lightness and a sparkle that was elfin for sure. He was smart and fair, kind and calm. And he was funny—in a cheesy dad kind of way.

He was a dancer like Fred Astaire and could sing like Bing Crosby. We would sing together and harmonize, and it was a completely different experience than singing with my other dad. Marty's voice had a folky, old country vibrato, whereas Danny was a tenor and musical theatre was more his style. And he could whistle.

My grandfather walked around whistling too. I was surrounded by other birds. Grandpa Ernest knew everything about every bird in the area, and we would sit on the deck with binoculars and he would tell me all about their behaviours, their songs, their migration patterns. I would watch him watching the birds and think that this is what a grandfather should be like. His feathers were like mine.

Danny was also a carpenter, a set builder and a union man. His motto was JFDI: just fucking do it. No excuses. If he wasn't onstage, he was behind the scenes, making sure everything worked. He could engineer anything, rig anything, invent systems and create entire worlds that folded up, turned around and became new ones. It was all about the show.

Though he came from very stable parents, he was a nomad. He loved nothing more than to live simply, alone in a camper van, and go from show to show. He was a bit of a ladies' man, but now he had a girlfriend. She was away on a trip when I arrived, so I didn't meet her right away.

Staying at my grandparents' house was temporary until we found our own place. I was only going to be there for six months, until Mum figured out our situation in London, but Danny took setting up a life for me very seriously. He was able to effortlessly turn one world into another, a sturdy set I would not fall through.

Danny put me in a dance class. I was connecting to my body in a new way, moving in beauty, reaching and stretching into places I thought were dead, too run over and deflated to reanimate. Bent feathers shuddered in the wind. I wasn't as coordinated as I'd hoped, but just moving was enough. I didn't have to be good; I just had to find where the music met me.

Grandma had been a highland-dancing teacher, but her mind was being slowly wound backward in time by the hands of Alzheimer's. She kept asking who I was. I wasn't able to know the strong woman she had been, but I did witness the love and closeness she and Grandpa Ernest had. He adored her. He wrote her love poems his whole life. Perhaps he was where I got my romantic streak and my poetry. He spoke fluent Gaelic, Latin, French, German, Italian, English, Japanese and Spanish. He used Coast Salish phrases daily with his children, immersing them in the original words of the land they lived on. This would have been almost unheard of in the 1960s. He was a brilliant man with a deep sense of honour and had been a pilot instructor during the war.

There was a wall lined with photographs that Grandpa Ernest called "History Hall." He walked me down the line of framed pictures that seemed to be in chronological order. There, proudly frozen in time, stood his parents and grandparents on the Isle of Man. He explained that Costain, the family name, used to be Thorstein, meaning "son of Thor." We were direct descendants of a Norse god! That explained a lot.

I stopped at every picture of my father as a child. We could have been twins. My mother must have been shocked by the likeness when I was a baby.

At night, Danny and I would curl up together and watch *Star Trek: The Next Generation*.

He was a science-fiction buff like me.

One night, I could tell that he had something to ask me, but he was squirming a little. He was usually a direct and open person. Finally, I got it out of him, and he took a deep breath and asked if I'd had sex yet. I told him no. It felt too soon to tell him about the hard things. I think he sensed I'd had a time of it. He wanted to make sure that when the time came, I would be ready.

The next day, he brought me to Planned Parenthood, and it was decided that I would go on the pill. It was his first time being a father, and the stork had dropped a young woman into his life. This was his way of protecting me. I felt very grown-up.

On my first day of school, Danny dropped me off on time with a packed lunch. I walked into the office where my uncle Kevin sat behind his desk. He was the vice-principal. He gave me a huge hug and welcomed me to the school. He put some paperwork in front of me to fill out so I could register there. For a long moment, I looked at the space that asked for my name. I realized that this was my chance to start over. Martirano and Reno were vestigial to me now, and it was time for them to fall away. When my last world was burned to ash, so was the girl whose life kept happening to her. The person sitting there in her place was someone who was going to happen to life.

Also, that arsonist who tried to kill my family was over five thousand kilometres away. He wouldn't be able to find me now, especially with a different name.

I wrote "MacLean" on the page. Tara MacLean. It was my first time seeing it. It instantly surrounded me like fortress walls. Armed with this name, I walked confidently down the halls of my new school as my uncle introduced me to my teachers. I was put into a special program called FLEX, which would allow me to finish my year in six months, because London was waiting. But for now, I was safe here, beginning again. A girl reinvented.

I made a friend named Stephanie. She was probably the most beautiful girl I'd ever seen, the daughter of a Chinese mother and Trinidadian father. She exuded a confidence that I had never witnessed. The boys would fall over themselves when she walked by. One boy who caught my eye was a tall, blue-eyed beauty. Stephanie coached me on how to be cool around him, because I had no game. I sent my most seductive smile his way, and in no time, we were in bed.

He was my first, but I wasn't his. I really wanted it to be magical, and I told myself it was because I had chosen him. It was a miracle I had kept my virginity with all the predators around, so I was empowered by that. However, after a couple of encounters where my pleasure wasn't considered, he decided to move on to another girl. I was gutted. Why did this keep happening? Why couldn't boys communicate? Why did they run off? What was wrong with me? What made me disposable?

When I look back on the hurt I felt in that moment, it deepens my conviction that there are two things that every teenage, cisgender, straight male should learn: first, how to give a woman an orgasm, generously and without expectation; and second, to never, ever ghost her afterward. It is the height of disrespect, ignorance and theft. Teach young men to give, to honour, to worship. Teach them to know what has been sacredly given to them. Teach them to kneel at the feet of a goddess.

In time, that boy grew into a generous, kind man who learned all these things, and our lifelong friendship is precious to me. As an adult, I asked him about what had happened in high school, and all he could say was that he had been so young and didn't know anything at the time about the value of what he was being given. This is a common story. Teach them young.

The pill made my body fill out, and my already ample breasts went supernova. I noticed that when the boys walked by me, their first glance was at my boobs, and then my face. With all the food in my dad's cupboards, I was filling out all over. I didn't know how to regulate my eating because of my previous feast or famine existence. It didn't take much for my tiny frame to accumulate padding.

A boy in one of my classes told me that I could be the prettiest girl in school if I lost ten pounds. I thanked him for the compliment and went to war with my body.

Shortly after, another boy in that class came to school with the *Reader's Digest* issue that featured the story of the fire. He brought it to my desk before class started, and I saw that he had underlined my name in pen, and my mother's name as well. He'd put together Sharlene MacLean, Tara Reno and Charlottetown.

I'd been found. My walls had been scaled. My fortress invaded.

The artist's rendering of Shaye and I being carried out of our burning house by Constable Cheverie sat in front of me. I fell into the picture. I could smell the smoke and hear the fire engines. Embers of that old life heated me with rage from the inside, and my cheeks burned. I looked at him, stunned, and slowly nodded in affirmation, handing him back the magazine.

Wide-eyed, he said, "I knew it! My mom showed me. It made her cry. I told her I was pretty sure I knew who it was. That musta been scary, huh?" He had black, feathered hair like Ralph Macchio in *The Karate Kid*.

I nodded again and looked away. He took the hint and left me alone. My body started to shake. I got up and went to the bathroom, trying to breathe. I looked in the mirror, but I couldn't see myself. All I saw was a soot-covered shadow, dispensable, unwanted, unworthy. I had to take control. I saw my grandmother behind me, telling me I would end up alone. I went into the bathroom stall and made sure I quietly threw up everything I had eaten that morning. I went back to the mirror to wash my face, and I could see myself again. I was blurry, but I was there.

Control.

When things feel out of control, we grasp for anything that feels solid. We secure the perimeter, find safety. When we don't know what that looks like, we can delude ourselves into thinking we have gained some kind of foothold when, in fact, we are spiralling further.

If I could control my size in the world, if I could be smaller, I could avoid detection, or at least I could be recognized for my discipline and not my weakness. To nourish myself when I was undeserving was weak. Feeding my desires made me a monster like the rest of them. I would starve the demons out of me. But little did I know, I was opening the door for them, reversing the natural flow. An esophageal entrance.

Women wore the corset for so long, it wove its way under our skin.

Every day at school, I found reasons to excuse myself and go to the bathroom when no one would be in there, to make sure I remained empty, to make sure I would reappear. I became the hungry ghost. There was some kind of power in denying myself what I didn't deserve. What was my body for anyway? It was a useless, imperfect waste of space. I had to take up as little space as possible. Maybe then I would be worthy of love?

Danny, his girlfriend and I moved into our own two-bedroom apartment. I came home from school one day to find a guitar in my new room. Danny had bought it for me. I picked it up and cradled it on my lap. The feel of the wood against my body and the sound of the strings made me so happy. I tuned it to the best of my ability and began the picking pattern that Marty had taught me. I had about five chords to choose from and remembered that one song I had written. It turned out that the song could be applied to the latest boy who had broken my heart. The song comforted me. Every day after school, I went straight to my guitar. It would lie beside me in my bed, a little raft to cling to. More songs were coming through. The more broken I felt, the more the sounds sutured the wounds, weaving in and out and pulling together the disparate parts of myself, creating scar tissue.

We had arranged that I would talk to Mum every Sunday. She would call from the TARDIS, the *Doctor Who* phone booth, collect. She would tell me all about the life she was building there for us all. Shaye and David would stay with their dad for now, but in a few months, I would fly from British Columbia and meet her on Prince Edward Island, and then we would fly to London together to start a new life.

She was on the list to get a council flat in West Kensington, which meant we could have a nice place in a nice neighbourhood for very little rent. However, that would take about eighteen months to be available. For the moment, Mum was living in a nightly rental room. She would go to work during the day, singing on the Tube with her hat out to make enough for a place to sleep, a meal and a drink. One night when she didn't make her rent, she slept in the council office. One night, she was attacked and robbed.

During one of our Sunday calls, I decided to tell her about losing my virginity. She wasn't pleased at all. She felt I was too young. Too young? Now, she was going to parent me? I let her rage over the phone for a while, holding the receiver away from my ear. Sometimes, I could tell she was drinking, and other times, she seemed so strong and solid. There was a subtle difference between sober Mum and drunk Mum. It was in her cadence. I knew her voice better than anyone.

My dad's girlfriend, though well-meaning, had a lot of opinions about my weight and about my mother's inability to keep her children safe. I found myself becoming defensive of Mum, and the assessment of my physical failure drove me more deeply into the dysmorphic view of my body. She confirmed my suspicions that I was deeply flawed, and since I was getting heavier, I must be taking more than I deserved. The messaging went deep. I continued to accept the regularly scheduled programming of the current beauty standard, something that was ingrained in her as well.

This wasn't my first rodeo with a stepmother. Fortunately, this father defended me and told her those comments weren't helpful. Danny was my champion. I finally had a champion.

He came into my room and dried my tears.

One day, I told him about all the things that had happened to me, and who had done them. I watched him clench and unclench his hands as he paced, taking deep breaths to stay calm. He had known about my grandfather because he had been a part of my mother's escape.

Danny had met my mother when they were seventeen years old. He had come from Victoria as a singer and dancer to perform in the Charlottetown Festival. My mother, the most beautiful woman on earth, captured the heart of my charming father. Onstage, he was my mother's first Romeo to her Juliet. Offstage, she and Danny were deeply in love for five years. When they were twenty, they bought a farm in Savage Harbour on the North Shore and lived the bohemian life of young thespians. She shared the truth of her childhood with Danny. As a Viking himself, he envisioned how he could avenge my mother. Though he never acted on it, a part of him raged for the woman he loved. When he heard that I'd had to endure that abuse as well, he felt responsible somehow for not taking care of it when he was there. He felt like he had left me to the wolves. And indeed, he had. But he was here now, and that's all that mattered.

In the spring of 1988, when the six months were up and my Grade 9 academics were complete, I hugged him tightly at the airport. With tears in his eyes, he said goodbye and told me that I would always have a home wherever he was. A suitcase in one hand, a guitar case in the other, I went to check in for my flight. My heart was torn but more intact than it had ever been.

My mother had flown to PEI the week before, and she was going to meet me at the airport. I hadn't seen her since the fire.

As the plane flew toward the red shores of Prince Edward Island, I could feel the rush in my heart that I was going to be home. My yearning to see my mother twisted my stomach and sat on my chest. As we landed, I felt the arms of the island wrap around me. The cool spring air on my face as we disembarked let me finally take a deep breath. I was minutes away from holding her.

As I entered the airport, I saw my grandmother with a stern and worried look on her face. I looked around for my mother. My panic was rising.

"Where's Mum?" I asked anxiously.

"She's in rehab."

II.

Holes

There's a hole. There's a hole.
There's a hole in the bottom of the sea.
—TRADITIONAL FOLK SONG

The road from the airport to my mother was full of potholes. The spring thaw had washed away the sand beneath the asphalt. The road was my mirror. I was caving in. With each bump, my stomach would lurch. I couldn't breathe.

Nana pulled into the parking lot and turned off the engine. She stared ahead, took a deep breath. Turning to me, she held my eyes and then, with a subtle gesture, lifted her chin, silently instructing me to do the same. I copied, opened the door and walked into the building.

The rehabilitation centre was depressing. The blanket on Mum's bed had holes, and while there was a small window in her room, it was really just a hole in the wall.

There were holes everywhere, mostly in her.

Mum was quiet. She looked thin as she drank her coffee. The beam of sunlight that came through the window was hazy with smoke from her burning cigarette. The ashtray was overflowing. Beauty for ashes, Isaiah says in the Bible. That's the deal. You bring me your burned-out life and I'll give you something to live for. Sounds like a good trade.

My grandmother sat quietly with us. She had brought grapes. I looked at them in the bowl: ten calories per grape. Nana got up and said she'd leave us alone to talk.

Once she was gone, Mum looked at me and smiled weakly.

"She put me in here. Do they honestly think alcohol is my problem? You listen to me: drinking isn't my problem." Her eyes became wide and scary, and she moved her face closer to mine. "Men are the problem. It's always been men." She took another drag of her cigarette, lay back and looked into the distance. I nodded in understanding and twisted the thin, shabby blanket around my fingers, wondering if I could cut off the circulation in them.

"We're going to London as soon as I get out of here. Don't unpack. It's not safe for us here."

She imagined someone in the room with a lit match when she tried to fall asleep. She heard the whispers in town that she was a mother who abandoned her children. This town was a minefield, blowing holes in our lives.

As I got into the car with my grandmother, I looked over at her. Her chin had fallen and she looked tired. She said, "Your mother wrote to me from London saying she was depressed and drinking. She got off the plane drunk. I took her here. I can't let you go to London with her if she's not well. I am holding on to some money that Marty sent for her that she will get when she completes this program."

Marty sent her money? He'd owed her a few thousand dollars from many years before and chose that moment to pay her back. We needed it. I still couldn't think of him without seeing the back of his head in the car and his hands on the steering wheel as he drove away from me on my birthday, the sound of the sputtering muffler trailing off as the space grew between us. Shaye and David were still living with them in Dartmouth, though word was coming back that things weren't good. I couldn't imagine it was a happy home. If Mum and I got to London and built a life there, Shaye and David could come and live with us, and perhaps one day, little Bryde, too.

All these thoughts rushed through my mind as we drove away from the rehab centre. The rolling, peaceful patchwork of the landscape tried to soothe me with its beauty, but all I could see were holes. I rolled down the window, closed my eyes and let the wind hit my skin. A life-affirming collision.

Then Nana dropped a bomb. A crater opened in the earth. She told me she had to stop at the nursing home to see my grandfather. My blood ran cold. He'd had a second stroke and couldn't speak now. She asked if I wanted to come in. This moment is seared into my brain: the disbelief, then the dawning. This was likely my last opportunity.

"Oh yes. I'll be going in there," I said, barely opening my teeth as I spoke.

"Please don't make a scene." It was a weak request. I was quiet on the outside. My heart pounded in my ears. I was going to see him. The shadow man himself. I would make any scene I wanted—surely, my grandmother, if anyone, knew how dangerous I was.

As we pulled into the parking lot, I had no idea what I was going to do or say. I just knew I had to see him in his diminished state and get him alone. Nana didn't say a word as she walked through the halls a few steps ahead of me. There was nothing intimidating about the door to his room this time, but still, I armoured up. As we entered, I noticed that all the photos and medals from his room at home had been moved in here and hung on the wall. There he was, the dashing young hero, in frame after frame. I wanted to smash them all off the wall. Maybe I would. I hadn't yet decided what kind of damage I was going to do, and I didn't know what I was capable of.

Nana went ahead of me with a bag of clean clothes and cigarettes for him. He made some grunting noises, and as she moved out of the way, I saw him. He saw me too. His eyes went wide.

"Nana," I said, not taking my eyes off him, "can you leave us, please?" He made a sound that seemed like a protest, but my grandmother nodded to me and left the room, closing the door behind her. I suddenly recognized that she had brought me here for this, to give me this. She owed me this.

In a wheelchair sat a melted version of what had once been a strong and strapping soldier. His face poured off his skull on one side; drool dripped down onto a bib. He weighed half of what he had in his prime. He was smaller than I was. I had him now. His eyes were glassy, but I could tell he was afraid. Good. This was the battlefield and the enemy had been rendered defenceless.

I looked at him with cold disgust as I sat down on a chair beside him. I wanted to end him, to humiliate him, to despise him. I was his nemesis after all, was I not?

"Well, look at you." I gestured toward the photographs on the wall. "I guess all the nurses in here think you're a great hero. So brave." I turned back to him. "Do you think you're brave? Fucking little girls?" I wanted to hate him so badly, but hate wouldn't come. He made a moaning sound.

"Are you scared of me right now?" I felt the ice melting as the lava began to surface through the holes. I felt rage for the women in my family, for all the times he'd rendered us powerless. "You should be. I should just smash all these pictures." I saw myself doing it in my mind's eye. I heard the screaming inside myself as I imagined throwing them across the room, glass shattering everywhere. But I just sat there watching him, frighteningly calm.

"You're going to die soon," I said. Tears came to his eyes and fell down his wasted cheeks. "You're going to die and everything you did will die with you. You won't be a hero in the eyes of your family." He began to sob. The sound was primal. I hadn't heard it before, but I knew it. It was the sound of begging for mercy.

There on the field, my enemy conquered, all fury left me. I took off my armour and laid my sword and shield on the ground. Something inside me softened as I witnessed his pain. It was real. It was agony. I saw him lying on the ground in a war zone, wounded by a bomb, his driver in pieces all over the road. I saw him holding his dead father, his dead baby sister. Somewhere in my grandfather was a terrified little boy who had taken beating after beating. I could see his bare feet on the red dirt roads as he ran from the farm, his face bloody, all alone in the world, the same age then as I was now. He was a lost child. All I could feel was pity. All I could see was justice. He was living in hell in his own body, behind his own unsmiling face. Powerless.

"One day . . . one day, we will forgive you. Shaye will forgive you. Mum will forgive you." I paused to be certain of the truth before I said my last words to him. "I will forgive you.

We won't carry this with us. We are free from you. So, when you're dying, I want you to know something." I stood up so that I towered over him, so that he was in *my* shadow. *Do you fear me? Do you fear me now?*

I leaned in close and whispered, "I want you to know that you didn't win. Do you hear me?" Defeated, he nodded through his tears.

I left the room, closing the door behind me, leaving him alone with his decimation.

It was the last time I would ever see my grandfather, and I had said all there was to say. I hoped it was true, that we would forgive him in time. Compassion is not absolution. A line I learned in Sunday school kept ringing in me: "Forgive them for they know not what they do." If Jesus had existed, and if he could say that as nails were being hammered through his hands and feet, certainly I could forgive the sick old man. I didn't know what forgiveness entailed yet—it was still just a concept in my mind at the time—but I knew it had power. Real power. Not money, or weapons, or force. Not political, or religious, or hierarchical. The kind that is a universal law; the kind that, though unseen, is a spark that ignites the heart of the world; the kind that, like gravity, holds us in place and gives us clues about the true nature of existence; the kind that teaches us that light comes in waves, but so too does darkness.

As I walked out of the building, something began to form inside me, a flash of a significant understanding. If I could forgive him for committing the most unspeakable crime, then maybe nothing was unforgivable.

I've heard it said that holding on to anger is like holding a knife but gripping the blade instead of the handle. I wanted to learn how to wield this new power, forgiveness, to let go of the things that hurt, so I could be free of the past, so I could stop bleeding.

But the past doesn't let go of us so easily. It can pull us down like quicksand if we aren't careful where we step along the way. *Samskaras*, ancient neural pathways like hidden canyons. Fault lines. Grooves in a record going round and round. A primordial orbit almost impossible to escape. There is no map. We are just spinning here on a ball in space.

Maybe we are all lost children.

Mum ordered a Bloody Mary on the plane as we celebrated our escape to London. She had no intention of staying sober, and I knew that. Nana had given her the money from Marty, and after buying our tickets, we still had five hundred pounds ($1000) to carry us through until we got jobs and a flat. We would prepare a wonderful life for Shaye, and even David if he wanted to come. I was finally on my great adventure.

We landed in London in the morning, took the Tube to Barons Court and went straight to a pub. This neighbourhood was where my mother had been living. Here, we had the holy trinity of pubs: Barons Ale House (now called The Curtains Up), Three Kings (a few blocks away in West Kensington) and The Clarence, just up North End Road. Everyone knew my mother.

As we walked into the dark, smoky Barons, the owner shouted her name and poured her a shot of whiskey. I got a Diet Coke and was introduced to a round of nice folks with heavy accents, red noses and sad eyes. We got some chips (french fries) and then went to find somewhere to live. Around the corner was a sign advertising a room for rent. It was eighty pounds ($160) a week and had one shared bathroom that serviced ten flats in the building. It was disgusting. We took it.

The ceiling was higher than the room was wide. There were two ratty single mattresses on either side of the room.

There was a kitchenette between the beds, which consisted of a small gas stove, a tiny fridge and a sink. Mum took the bed by the tall window with torn curtains that looked out onto a stone building. To get heat, we needed to put pound coins into a box. (We quickly learned how to break into it and take our coins back.) We needed bedding. With shelter secured, at least for the week, Mum was excited to show me her London.

North End Road was a cacophony of sounds and smells. There was an outdoor food market, clothing stores and stalls, and a kebab shop that would be life-changing. Since neither my mother nor I was inclined to cook, the shop would become a daily stop. The brakes of the streetcars squealed and scraped in my ears. I was learning this auditory landscape. It was loud and exciting. I realized what Mum loved about it. If you can't hear yourself think, then you've escaped.

We picked up some sheets, blankets and pillows at the market and went home to make our beds. Mum's way of turning any dump into a palace was most useful in this situation. I bought some cheap posters for the walls and laid my guitar on the bed, headstock on the pillow. There. Home.

We had to find jobs fast. Mum told me to put on my most posh outfit and to say I was eighteen. I could easily pass for that with my boobs and my poise. I knew the Glamour Spell.

We walked to the Queen's Club, a fancy sporting club in the neighbourhood. There was a tournament going on, so we followed the signs to the catering department and found that they were hiring. They didn't ask for ID but inquired if we had Silver Service training. Mum had told me to answer every question with an enthusiastic yes, even if I had no idea what they were talking about. I could do any job requiring customer service. We were hired on the spot. Thrilled, we headed back to North End Road to buy black flat shoes, black skirts and white blouses.

Thank goodness, Nana had taught me what cutlery was what, because I had a head start there. I learned to fold napkins into swans, and I loved the ambience of serving all the fine people in their beautiful clothes. I studied them, but I didn't envy them. This was the highest echelon of London society. It was called the Queen's Club for a reason. Many of the attendees at the tennis tournaments took me for a curiosity because of my accent. I loved that they would stop me and ask where I was from, ask why I was there. This would irritate the other servers because it would slow things down, but the manager insisted I "chat up and charm" them if they inquired. We were allowed to take home the extra scones, cream, cheese and meat at the end of the day, and that was always our breakfast.

With all these treats to nibble on, I needed to be careful about my weight. I bought eggs, grapefruit and popcorn and started living on that. I began a nightly regimen of exercise in our flat: one hundred sit-ups, thirty push-ups, stretching. I only drank Diet Coke. I started shrinking in all the ways I wanted to (which meant everywhere except for my boobs). There was something about living with my mother that made me less hungry and more determined to be disciplined.

Mum and I decided to get jobs at the Wimbledon tennis tournament, but we only lasted a day. We were excellent at Silver Service by then, but it was a different company, and everyone was unhappy. The management spoke down to the staff and there were no extra scones. We weren't going to live like that. At the end of the day, we went home and came up with a new plan. Mum would work at the nearby pub, and I would go to the temp agency and see where I could be placed.

A few days later, I found myself on a 6:00 a.m. bus that travelled to the outskirts of London, where I would be working in a coffee and sweetener packaging factory for less than four pounds an hour. It took forever to get there. I was the only white person on the bus.

When I got to the factory, I learned how to clock in, got a hairnet and apron, and went straight to the assembly line. My first job was to stamp boxes. After a few hours of the repetitive movement, my shoulder ached. The woman beside me leaned in gently as I rubbed it and said, "You get used to it." All the managers were men. All the workers were women.

Mercifully, after what seemed an eternity, we got a lunch break. I went into the cafeteria and sat down. Immediately, I was swarmed by Indian women asking me all kinds of questions. They circled me closely like a wreath of marigolds. What was I doing there? Who was I? Where was I from? Why on earth was I working in the factory? I learned that many of them had been there for over twenty-five years. Almost all of them were mothers, some were grandmothers, and many were sending money back to India. I introduced myself and explained that I was really just fourteen and needed a job.

A very large, powerful and intimidating woman with kohl-rimmed eyes moved forward through the group, which parted to let her through. She sized me up. She was clearly the matriarch.

"Your name . . . is an Indian name. Tara. But you don't belong here," she said calmly, in a thick accent. "You need to go." I was confused. Reading the look on my face, she softened, realizing she may have scared me. "You should be doing something else. Let me look at you. Stand up." I did as she asked. She made me turn around. She gave me an approving glance and said gently, "You won't last here. This is not the place for you. You should get out while you can."

The crowd around me all nodded in agreement. I understood that they had no malice toward me; it was just how it was. Then they put the most delicious food in front of me.

The afternoon shift was different. I had to push full jars through something that covered them in a plastic wrap. I was terrible at it at first, but then I got the hang of it.

I returned every day for a week. My body hurt badly from the work. My neck and back and feet ached, but I never dared complain. My fellow workers had given me kindness immediately, but now I wanted to earn their respect. I learned about them and loved sitting quietly as they shared their thoughts and stories of their children. They laughed a lot. They sang.

On Friday, at the end of my shift, I said goodbye and told them I wouldn't be coming back. They hugged me tightly. I see now that my being there was giving them a job on top of a job, looking out for me, which they didn't need. I often think of them on the assembly lines, proudly working to support their families. Now, when I open a jar of anything, I silently thank whoever sealed it. I look at the labels, the box, the wrapping, and I wonder whose hands touched it to bring it to me. What brought them there? Who were their families? Did their hands blister and bodies ache? What songs did they sing?

Next, I tried my hand at waitressing, working in a clothing shop and, believe it or not, cooking pub food. Mum was able to secure a new room above a pub for us. We shared a bed and had a private washroom. The publican paid me to clean the kitchen, prep food and iron his shirts. He was kind to us.

Mum introduced me to the music of Pink Floyd, and it was all I listened to. "Comfortably Numb" had the most beautiful melody I'd ever heard. It held a kind of existential sorrow that I had felt but never heard described. I let that song become an internal anthem.

Mum was drinking more because patrons would tip her by buying her shots of whiskey.

I went off birth control and became very thin. My food and exercise regimen was how I was trying to control my life. The more my mother drank, the more I felt I had to pull myself together. The more out of control she got, the more meticulous I became. I was running a race against her decimation. I felt her crumbling.

There is a way of looking at a family like a constellation. Everyone has their place to create the formation. When addiction takes down a parent, the constellation changes, and the child often becomes the adult. I was watching my mother drowning in a sea of Irish whiskey, trying to navigate by obscured stars.

My lifeboat was discipline. My sextant was my songs.

Soon, Shaye flew to London, and I was so happy. Marty's wife had kicked her out, and she had gone to live with a family friend until we could afford her ticket. I had missed her desperately. Just like I had introduced her to the woods around the cabin when we were small, I showed her around the streets of the epic city, pointing out the essentials. The three of us slept in the bed above the pub, though Mum was staying up later and later every night.

Shaye and I began school in Hammersmith, which was one Tube stop over on the green line. The rush of bodies moving together every morning was exhilarating. We wore a uniform. I immediately felt out of my depth: the history, the math, the science was all miles beyond what I had learned. I was smart, but I felt overwhelmed. The school was racially diverse, but all the groups seemed to segregate themselves. There was a break in the day that was scheduled around watching *Neighbours*, an Australian soap, on the telly in the cafeteria. This seemed to bond everyone.

I made a friend, a Muslim girl with a diplomat father. She was deeply religious and explained to me how, after we die, a piece of our hair is strung from one cliff to another, with a chasm between. For every sin we commit on earth, we are heavier. If we can walk along this tightrope without breaking it, then we are safe. If our sins weigh us down, the hair will snap, and we will be lost for eternity. I imagined falling— terrifying. It was definitely up there with the Christian version of Judgment Day. I began to cut school. My hair was thin; there was no way I'd make it across anyway.

Even with a few friends and my sister in London, I knew that staying there wasn't good for me. My beautiful mother, a goddess of the stage, was wasting away in a dark pub. The bar stool seemed to be the destination that everyone aspired to reach at the end of the day. This was not my place. I would drown here and so would Shaye. I wasn't able to balance my mother anymore. All of it was falling into the chasm. The threads were snapping.

I told my mother that I had to go back to Canada to be with my father. This went over like a lead balloon. I hadn't been sure whether to tell her I wanted to leave when she was sober or drunk. In the end, I chose drunk. It was the wrong time.

She screamed at me. "We came here together to build a new life! You are NOT leaving. This is home now."

I looked around the small room we all shared, the mattress on the floor, the overflowing ashtrays I kept emptying, the stains on the carpet. Shaye cried in the corner as we fought.

"But Mum, there is nothing for me here. I'm dying. This isn't my life!"

"What do you know about life?"

"I know a wasted one when I see it," I spat back. I grabbed the alarm clock we had bought to wake us up for our shifts when we'd first moved there, and I threw it out the window. It smashed in pieces on the street.

Mum went to the closet, took my passport and showed it to me. "You aren't going anywhere." She put it in her purse and walked out of the room, down to the pub. A primal scream, the sound of a caged wild animal, escaped me. I ran down the stairs and out the door, passing the smashed clock, a mess of cylindrical metal gears, face down, hands on the pavement.

Close by was the Three Kings pub. I went in and ordered a double Jameson and knocked it back. I left and kept walking. I had no idea where I was going. I was just running. I knew I wouldn't get far without my passport or money. I felt rage like I had never felt. I purposely walked down dark alleys, took turns onto sketchy streets where I was told never to go, walking by dodgy-looking people. I was daring life. *Come and get me. I'll fight you with my bare hands.* I was wild. What could anyone take from me that hadn't been taken, besides my life, and what was that even worth?

Exhausted, I made it back to the pub. But I had a plan. I climbed into bed. The next morning, as Shaye and Mum slept, I took all the tips I had saved and slipped my passport from the purse. We had return plane tickets that we weren't planning on using. I took the Tube to Oxford Street and paid eighty pounds to change my ticket to leave the following week for Halifax. The Air Canada agent didn't bat an eye. I was calm and steady. Glamour Spell activated. I went back to a still-sleeping mother and put the passport exactly where I'd found it.

That week, I played nice with Mum. Every time I looked at Shaye, I felt desperate that I couldn't get her out. I was worried she would hate me for abandoning her, but I didn't know how to create an escape plan for both of us, not this time. She was too young, and we would have been overly conspicuous together. I would have to come back for her somehow, once I'd saved myself. I couldn't meet her eyes. Every time I played my guitar, I realized I had to leave it there. Shaye would need it now. She knew how to play and write, and it would save her.

I ironed shirts for extra money and I sold a few of my nicer things. I told one of my friends what I was up to and asked if I could stash my belongings at her house throughout the week so Mum wouldn't notice me leaving with too many things at once. I didn't go to school all week. I walked around London alone in my uniform. The city is full of statues.

The night before my flight, I made sure I had an eye on my passport. Mum had put it back in the wardrobe, in a box on the shelf. I told her I was going to a friend's house for the night, nicked my passport, kissed Shaye goodbye and left. I turned my heart to stone. A dangerous spell. This is what you have to do to save yourself sometimes: turn into a moving statue.

I hardly slept at my friend's. When the first light came through the window, I packed all my things and went to the airport. I wore heels, a skirt and a blouse, and no one noticed anything amiss. By this point, I was quite thin, but I still had breasts enough to make me look older. I boarded the plane and smiled at the flight attendant. I didn't seem nervous, but inside, I was freaking out. *Get to the seat. Just get to the seat before you collapse.*

Once we took off, I went to the toilet and closed the door. My body started shaking. I looked at myself in the mirror as the spell wore off. I would be fifteen years old in two weeks, but I felt ancient. Exhausted. To achieve escape velocity, you have to run fast and it takes everything you have. And stone is heavy.

I went to my seat and fell asleep. I dreamed of Shaye. I heard my mother screaming. I woke as we were landing. *Canada!*

I had no idea how I was going to get from Nova Scotia to British Columbia, but I would figure it out. I had a little money and thought I could buy a train or bus ticket west. As I came off the plane, an RCMP officer approached me. She was huge. She identified herself as Constable Horse. She asked if I was Tara Martirano.

"My name is Tara MacLean."

She took me by the arm and spoke into her walkie-talkie: "We have the runaway in custody."

She led me to a room and explained to me that as a minor, I had no right to be in Canada. I was illegally in the country. When my mother had found out that I was missing, she'd called the airline. I was to be sent back to London immediately. Dread filled me. According to the officer, my mother was livid, and I was going to military school. For the night, however, I would be put into a safe house under lock and key, because I was a flight risk.

That night, as I sat on a clean bed in a small, windowless room, without even the smallest hole to crawl through, a man from social services knocked on my door. He unlocked it with a key and came in and sat in a chair by the bed. He was kind and approached me with openness. I wish I could remember his name.

"I have a few questions for you, if that's okay," he said.

I nodded.

"Do you think you will run away if I leave your door unlocked?"

"No," I said. "I'm tired and I have nowhere to go."

"What are you running from?"

"I can't live in England. It's not a good place for me there. My mother drinks so much and I just want to be with my dad. He lives in BC, and I was hoping to get back there. He doesn't know I'm coming, but he told me I would always have a home with him. Please don't send me back to London."

"So really, you're running *toward* something," he said.

He got it. He saw me. Another angel had been sent to watch over me. He left the room and didn't lock the door. No part of me had the strength to run. I fell asleep, waking with a jolt a few times from the feeling of falling into a hole. I woke up to breakfast being brought in by a nice old lady. She asked me to get dressed, packed, and to come downstairs. I had no idea what was happening. *One breath at a time.* When I got to the office, the kind man who had spoken to me the night before was there. He smiled as I came in the room and told me to have a seat.

My angel explained that he had spoken to both my mother and my father. Danny had said he would take me, and Mum had decided to let me go. In a few hours, social services had me on a plane to British Columbia. Air Canada sat a chaperone next to me to make sure I would be handed off to my father safely. By the end of the flight, after I'd shared my story with her, she was in tears. I just looked out the window. I couldn't feel much. I didn't know how to dissolve the stone that had entered some part of me. Uncomfortably numb.

From the air, as we passed over the grey and white Rocky Mountains, British Columbia was a sea of trees, with giant scars in the hills, holes in the green mountains. I saw myself mirrored in the landscape. The coastline came into view, and soon, I was in the arms of my father.

It was my ability to turn to stone that had gotten me out of London. It was self-preservation. But I had left behind a trail of devastation—a sister abandoned, a mother distraught. I had torn holes in the fabric of the lives of others to ensure my own survival.

12.

Slashes

Mary, you're covered in roses
You're covered in ashes
You're covered in rain
You're covered in babies
Covered in slashes
Covered in wilderness
Covered in stain
—PATTY GRIFFIN

landed on my father's doorstep in pieces. I was battle weary, threadbare, barely audible. He welcomed me and gave me sanctuary, a new guitar and nourishment. He gave me love.

Soon, I was back in school, back in dance class, back in the arms of the Pacific, mountain mothers watching over me.

My dance teacher commented on how thin I was, but not in a congratulatory way. She was worried. My breasts were still big, and that was all I could see when I looked at myself in the mirror in her class. She told me that I wasn't inside my body, that I could only remember movement when I was looking in the mirror. My body had no short-term memory. It couldn't hold moves the way I could hold melodies. The other dancers had a freedom I didn't have. They inhabited their bodies. I dissociated. My moves were hesitant, and no matter how often the choreography was repeated, my body had no recall. Where was I? I was in the mirror, but I wasn't in me. The hungry ghost of my grandmother followed me into every reflection. All the men who had touched me without my consent had left their heavy, greasy fingerprints.

I began to use Tensor bandages like a corset around my chest, to hide my voluptuousness, not just in dance, but during the day. I still didn't eat much.

I turned fifteen.

I dated a few boys, fell into bed, excelled academically, but I was empty. Songs were emerging from this forsaken place, melancholy songs, gripped by longing and despair. I knew when a song was coming. It would push at me from the inside, claw around beneath my ribs. Sometimes, it would crawl up my throat, trying to get out. It was a pressure that could only be released when I had my guitar, paper and pen. As the song was emancipated from my body, the sensation would ease, and I would be unburdened of the weight of it.

What is the weight of a song? There is a neutron star that is twenty-five times the mass of our sun, but the size of a city. Some songs are more dense than this. Some are but a breath.

Every song will save you bit by bit if it is exorcized. If not, it can hold you down and choke you. It isn't always easy to open, especially if the song tears a hole on its way through.

But there's no choice. Otherwise, you can die slowly with your song trapped inside of you.

My father's girlfriend was more sensitive to me after I ran back to them. She told me I should go see a counsellor after all I had been through. She set up an appointment.

I sat in the grey, comfortable chair, and the counsellor looked at me warmly. She asked me to tell her what had happened to me. And so, I opened my mouth and out came the details, unedited, unfiltered, true. I looked at her when I was finished, wondering what she could possibly say. Then she asked me something extraordinary.

"Have you cried leaving Shaye and your mother?" She must have perceived that the Stone Spell was still activated.

"No."

"You just told me your story like it belonged to someone else. I invite you to make room to feel what you told me."

I laid my head back in the chair and looked up. It hadn't occurred to me that I had to grieve, that I could grieve. Statues don't cry. The holes had been plugged. The songs were moving something. What more could I do?

But the tears came easily. I gave myself permission to let them flow. They ran in rivers, the kind that try to drown you. She passed me a tissue box, and I wept and wept. I went home, went straight to my room and cried for days. I hadn't cried like that since my other father had left when I was small.

Perhaps the moment a child is abandoned, a protective shell begins to form. All our raw and exposed places require some kind of covering that is no longer provided for us. We reach for anything that looks solid and pull it toward us, like an octopus hiding from a shark. We draw a pallium of shimmering abalone or a matte white cloak of calcium around us. An exoskeleton of our own design.

This mantle can only be removed when we feel safe enough.

Danny made me feel safe. I slowly uncovered. I could barely look at what I'd been hiding. How unlovable and disposable this thing must be beneath the mosaic created from the broken pieces of my world. But the tears were a start. I had tears and I had music. Instead of putting a knife to my skin, I let myself bleed songs when I thought the sharks might be gone.

My mother still wouldn't speak to me, and late at night, I would ache for her and for Shaye. David was still in Nova Scotia, enduring the neglect of that situation. Shaye was furious with me for abandoning her in London, but we spoke as often as we could. I promised her I would build a place for her to come to.

For years, I carried the pain that I'd left her, but someone once told me about the analogy of the airplane oxygen masks. You have to put one on yourself first, and then on your children. If you can't breathe, you are good to nobody. That understanding helped me to let go of that weight and realize that running away was the only way I could save myself.

It was a year before my mother would take my call. She was descending more deeply into addiction. I could hear it in her voice when we finally began to communicate. We could only speak on Sundays, when it was cheapest for the call. I spoke to Nana every week. I was allowed to call her collect, and she never missed my call. Her voice had a loving, musical tone when she talked to me. We would sync our spoken notes, and it was always obvious to others when I was speaking with my grandmother. Our birdsong had an original melody.

Safe in Danny's house, I would play my guitar softly until I fell asleep, instrument beside me.

In Grade 11, I ended up at a new school, Mount Douglas. I created a beautiful bouquet of girlfriends, all exquisite and smart. We lifted each other, danced together, held each other. We created the Girl Code. No boy was available if one of us had been in love with him, unless that friend was consulted and all feelings were completely done. We had each other's backs. We didn't talk much in this group about attractions to other girls, but it was just understood and accepted that I liked girls too, though I didn't date any in high school. We went to school soccer games and painted our faces in the school colours. Sometimes, we'd skip class and go somewhere, and my friends would have me sing them my latest song. I wrote songs for them, to help them navigate their own hearts. Most of them came from wonderful families, and I felt safe in their homes, marvelling that they had always lived this way, with fridges full of food, closets full of clothes. Fullness.

They'd been Brownies and Girl Guides and had had a lifetime of dance classes and piano lessons. Someone had kept them safe and warm. Some of my friends had it tougher, with difficult relationships with parents, but regardless, we were a band of pretty badass girls. We knew each other's secrets and we were vaults. But almost all of us, no matter how beautiful, how thin, how accomplished, hated our bodies. We'd all been conditioned by the current cultural beauty standards to feel imperfect, lacking, incomplete. No matter our cultural background, upbringing or shape, we were female, and so we weren't good enough. Eating disorders were rampant. They were discussed. We knew who among us was bulimic or anorexic, or just aspired to be one of those. It depended on willpower and discipline.

Around this time, the most thin and beautiful girls in the school were plucked from class and sent away to Asia or the United States to model. Being a model was seen as very prestigious, as they appeared on magazine covers and starred in commercials. Being beautiful and thin enough to sell a product was the height of accomplishment. Many models came home damaged but wealthy. Some went straight to rehab or the psychiatric hospital. Many had stories of severe assault. Still, the less beautiful of us, who had stayed home, felt some envy. We just weren't pretty enough to be exploited.

I decided I had to be rid of my breasts. I was still dancing and taping them down. They always gave me away, ruined my outfits and pictures, and brought attention from every boy. I found a doctor, and he told me to wait a year, and if I still felt the same way, he would help me. The countdown began.

Then I met a boy. We'll call him Jake. I loved him. He was dark, gorgeous and sexy, and he loved me fiercely.

I was working in a shop at the mall that sold Italian music boxes. I loved the ancient design of revolving pins and combs. They'd last forever unless they were overwound. You had to know when to stop putting pressure on the spring. Everything has a breaking point.

I was sixteen now and decided to go back on the pill. I had filled out again, my face rounder, my hips fuller, but I felt great because one of the best things on earth had happened to me: I had figured out how to have an orgasm. Seventy-two thousand nerve endings all meeting one little button to provide pleasure and a happy hormone flood—how fantastic! I taught my boyfriend how to get me there, and we ended up having beautiful sex. There was deep healing and freedom in this for me.

I auditioned for a professional show at Butchart Gardens, and I got the part, so long as I lost ten pounds. I agreed. This was for a variety show that would play nightly throughout the summer, followed by fireworks. It was considered a great opportunity for a young performer. A job singing and dancing? I couldn't imagine anything better. How hard could it be to lose the weight? I had done it before. The prescribed wisdom of the time was to cut fat out of everything, so I only ate carbohydrates and lived on fat-free muffins. No one was getting thinner that way, but it was what we were told to do.

During rehearsals, the director grew meaner every day. He commented constantly on my weight, shaming me for my curves. I just couldn't seem to shed the pounds. I would get calls from the producer telling me to just drink water. The choreographer would roll her eyes at me and whisper to the director. A few weeks before the show was going to start, he called me into his office and told me I couldn't dance and I was a lousy singer. He fired me.

I was devastated. I remember that someone drove me home and I had my head in my hands the whole time. It was humiliating. They replaced me with a stick-thin ballerina. They must have been so relieved to not have to deal with the daily disappointment of my body.

My father was livid, but he didn't intervene—I begged him not to. He had done that same show when he was my age and was considered a legend in the Victoria arts scene because of his incredible voice and magical feet. But he never made me feel like I'd failed him.

"Fuck that guy. You have something he'll never have. You have your own songs."

My boyfriend was less forgiving of the director. He told me I'd feel a lot better if I slashed his tires. So, late the next night, he drove me to where I knew I could find the director's car. At that moment, it felt like the only power I had. I imagined him waking up the next morning, calling the police, knowing deep down that it was me. I wanted him to know it was me, for every knife he stuck into my confidence. Tires are tough, but my fury was stronger. The knife broke in the last tire. No police officer showed up at my door. I think he knew we were even.

What I didn't know then was that he had gifted me with something priceless: a creative wounding that I would have to suture myself. There was nothing better for me as a performer in that moment than to be told I was terrible, because I had to reach deep into that cut and pull out the broken tip of that blade, and what I found under the skin was what I had to give the world.

However, after this experience, my bulimia escalated, and I made the appointment to have a breast reduction. One day at school, I was talking nonchalantly with another curvy girl about how to lose weight, and she shared that she had been severely bulimic but that it had hurt her teeth and her throat. When I told her that I sang, she looked at me sternly and told me that throwing up regularly could ruin my voice. I never did it again. How I felt about my body didn't change, but that behaviour never returned. Once again, my voice saved me. I thought it was the one thing I could never lose, but it turned out I could take it from myself. That girl made me accountable to her, and we spoke regularly for a month, marking a happy face on the calendar every day until we decided I was not going to relapse.

In Grade 12, I moved in with my boyfriend, kept working at the mall and did well in school. Shaye left London and went back to Dartmouth to be closer to David, who was only thirteen and needed her there. They were parenting themselves most of the time, walking on eggshells around their stepmother. This experience bonded them deeply. Surviving in a cold, loveless house, they made their own hearth. I told Shaye I would meet her at the end of the school year and we'd make a new plan.

I starred in the school musical that year, *Bye Bye Birdie*. I wrote a song with the resident punk rock kid, Dave, who also starred opposite me in the musical. It was such a stretch for him to do that, but he was so brave. I had a massive crush. We kissed a little (shhh). He was cool in his long hair and leather jacket. He played the piano with such passion. We would hang out and listen to The Cure, The Clash, the Ramones, and all kinds of obscure punk music. I made him fall in love with Pink Floyd. He told me that he loved my voice, that in all its beauty and sweetness, there was an edge to it that gave away the darkness I had faced. He told me to write from that edge. The song we made together was dark:

All the dreams that turn to stone again,
All the broken glass and porcelain
And the tattered hearts of paper dolls I see
Falling right in front of me.

He ended up being an influential musician in the Victoria and Montreal music scenes. He died, hit by a car. I heard he was lying in the middle of the road, wearing black on a rainy night. I guess he was waiting for someone to run him over. He'd lost a lot in his life, mostly friends to drugs. I guess we'll never know what happened, but everyone who knew him could agree that his heart was tattered.

Before I graduated high school, I got my breast reduction. I remember looking down after I woke from the surgery and seeing my chest looking exactly how I imagined. I felt light and free. I walked into school with a new little bra, a camisole under a sheer white blouse and tight jeans. My shoulders back and chin up, I walked with the confidence of a queen, channelling my auntie Win. Some boys playfully teased me that they would miss the best thing about coming to school.

Though the surgery left me with brutal scars—slashed tires—I felt like I had taken back the power over my own body.

13.

Don't Panic

Each one has to find peace from within.
—MAHATMA GANDHI

When I went to the police with the video of Gilles the monster, who had molested us as children, they believed me. Most of us are not believed, but I got lucky that day with that officer. When they found him, he pleaded guilty and went to jail. I wasn't allowed in the courtroom for the trial, but a victim-impact statement was read aloud, so I know he heard my words. I said that no matter how much jail time he was given, my sister and I got life. He was sentenced to eighteen months. I felt like *some* justice was served, but an uncle of mine got longer for selling pot. What is the value of a little girl?

Ever since I can remember, I've reflected on justice and have been obsessed with Gandhi and his non-violent movement that freed India from the British. I saw the film about him when I was twelve, and my young, impressionable mind was altered by the story of this small man whose heart was so big that he could walk into the political arena and remain true to his people and his purpose, and not his own glory. That fascinated me. Since the church held no interest, perhaps Gandhi took on the role of God for me. He and his followers would take beating after beating and never raise a hand to the enemy. That was power. They took such simple and elegant actions, like walking to the sea to make salt, which drew the eyes of the world to glaring injustice.

It was from Gandhi that I first learned that justice is not always the law, but the law can sometimes be a road to justice. And there is a higher law to fight for, to try to weave into the fabric of our unfolding story: the law of love, which encompasses compassion, equality and deep care for one another and the planet. Gandhi knew how to pinpoint inequality and injustice, how to defy it and how to bring its perpetrators to their knees. And so he changed the world. How many thousands of times have I thought about him being thrown off that train in South Africa? He could have stood up, dusted himself off and skulked away. But he did the opposite.

Inspired by his example, I decided to go law school. I wanted to find the places in the law where love was lacking, where laws were outmoded, where scaffolding was needed.

But first, I needed to go to London and make things right with my mother. How could I make the world right when my relationship with her was still in tatters? How could I embody love when there was a glaring disconnect in my family constellation? The shape was distorted. A star was obscured by a cloud.

As soon as I graduated from high school, Jake and I packed our bags and headed to Prince Edward Island. My mother had a summer job at the Confederation Centre again, acting as one of the ladies of Avonlea in *Anne of Green Gables*. When it ended, we would all head to London with Shaye.

Seeing Mum again felt just right. We held each other and cried for the two years we'd lost and the relief of the forgiveness that flowed through us. We spent days at the beach, and she looked well and seemed happy, clearly a result of her being onstage. Though she was still drinking, she was shining in her role. She had an ability to make her few lines funny, and she never broke character. She was exquisite and beautiful, regal and humble. I must have seen the show ten times that summer. I was proud.

I also developed a fierce crush on Gilbert, the male lead in the musical, as Island girls are wont to do. He was extra cute that summer. He could dance and sing, and I'm sure he flirted with me. I made every effort to shake Jake and go to cast parties with Mum so I could perch on the end of a sofa and wait for him to find me. I was the age my mother had been when she'd met my father, when he was singing and dancing in the Charlottetown Festival. Though nothing happened between Gilbert and me—perhaps he was just being kind to me with his eye contact and dazzling smile—I had a vivid fantasy of running off with him. He was laid-back and funny, and his voice got me. I'll always be a sucker for a man who can sing.

The best part about that summer was that we saw Bryde. She was still so little, only seven, and her father, Izzy, had gotten sober, remarried and added even more children to his collection. There was a whole, beautiful week when David came over from Nova Scotia, and the four of us kids were all together for the first time since the fire. We curled up with Mum like kittens in a box. We swam in the warm waves. We stayed up late telling stories. When finally we drove Bryde home, her tummy hurt when it was time for her to leave us, and we all tried to be brave as we hugged her goodbye. We watched her go into her house, where she was the oldest sister. We weren't welcome in that house, because there was tension with the new wife. We drove away, sobbing. Shaye was the quietest, until finally she spoke: "One day, she'll be ours again."

In September, Mum, Shaye, Jake and I boarded a plane for London. It would be different this time—I could feel it. I was all grown up and Mum felt even less like a parent and more of a friend. We were two women. I had changed, I had a partner, I was finished school, and nothing could drag me down. Now that the relationship with my mother had healed, I could move forward.

Mum went back to working at the pub. I didn't understand why she didn't try to get into the theatre there, but there were lots of excuses, the main one being that she was terrible at auditions. And so, the smell of a stale, dark bar and cigarettes became normal and strangely comforting. It was something you could count on in London, day after day, century after century.

She laughed a lot more these days and had a boyfriend who was quite sweet and funny. He drank a lot too but had a good job. He was from Aberdeen, Scotland, and his accent tickled. He loved football (soccer), but so did everyone in the UK.

It was good to see Mum in love. She liked seeing me as an adult, but she was wary of Jake. When she drank, her truth would fall out of her mouth, an avalanche of barbed wire. He was controlling, she said. He wasn't the right man for me, she said. I could feel my heart contract. Who was she to tell me anything about choices in men?

We all lived together in a tiny flat on Barons Court Road in West Kensington. Mum had secured the council flat, and the rent was cheap. Shaye and Mum slept in the living room on a mattress on the floor, and Jake and I had the bedroom. He went to work at the Waldorf hotel as a bellman, and I got a job at the Queen's Club again, this time as a bartender. Once, I served Richard Branson, who drank an alcohol-free beer called Swan. He didn't really tip me well, but he had a lovely smile.

On one of our days off, Mum said she had a surprise for me. One of her best friends came over and brought LSD. She said it was time for us to do this together, and she wanted to make sure that I knew how to navigate with psychedelics. She would be the medicine woman and guide me. She wanted to be sure I wouldn't bring anything through that wasn't safe—whatever that meant.

Mum's assurance that everything would be fine kept me from getting too nervous. The only rule was that I was not to look in the mirror. She shared a story of someone she knew who looked in a mirror all night at a party, and when it was time to go, he couldn't move because he didn't know which one was him. He was never the same.

With this guideline in place, I chewed on the little piece of paper, my heart pounding with excitement. As it began to kick in, the light in the room changed. Mum's friend decided to tell us the entire story of *The Hitchhiker's Guide to the Galaxy* by Douglas Adams. She began explaining that there was this man named Arthur Dent, and that earthlings had no idea that there was a hyperspace bypass being built and earth had to be demolished, but Arthur's friend knew, and they went to the pub . . .

I don't know if I've ever been more engaged in anything in my life than when I was on psychedelics for the first time and hearing this story. I saw it all. This woman was a genius. She didn't miss anything. After the story was over, Mum sat smiling in front of the window. She was glowing, like Mary in the stained glass. Like Aphrodite. Shaye stayed curled up on the couch watching us. She didn't want to do LSD, but she was fascinated by the whole thing. Jake was tripping on patterns on the wall and the streamers that emerged when he moved his hands. I looked over at him, hoping to profoundly connect, but I couldn't find him. His physical body was there. He was giggling, happy, childlike. I looked at Mum and she gave me an amused look. She saw everything that was happening. She suggested we all go for a walk.

Into the London twilight we went. An ancient city filled with modernity. I could see the air. Waves of light particles, photons, blinked in and out of existence. Where did the light go when it wasn't here? "Mum! Mum! It's all about light, isn't it? If I'm not here to see the light, what is here? Mum! Am I here? Who am I? Who are you?".

She floated beside me silently in the cosmos as I asked her questions, which she answered wordlessly. An understanding began to dawn. This whole thing is so much bigger than our human senses can detect. There I was, almost eighteen earth years old, but I was eternal, stretching through time. I felt like my heart was going to burst with wonder. I laughed as tears streamed down my cheeks.

There was a sound. A low hum. Was it coming from beneath the ground? A sound beneath a sound? I lay on the sidewalk listening, my ear to the pavement. It was coming from everywhere. It wasn't just the city; it was deeper, lower, primordial. Everything disappeared and there was just the vibration. It was in everything. It was all singing together. One Song. Uni Verse. It was a symphony of quantum strings. It was the sound of galaxies spinning, asteroids colliding. It was the blood rushing through my body. It was the sound of starlight reaching the earth after light years of searching. The sigh of relief of light finally home. Om. Waves crashing. The electric language of tree roots. Airplanes. Cries of grief and joy. Orgasm. Birth and death. Breath. All of us breathing together.

The street lights came on and they hummed too. Some were yellow, some pink. I could see and hear everything connected, the web of existence, the harmony. Just as I felt myself drifting into oblivion, I felt a moment of fear. My mother appeared, smiling, and pulled me gently down to earth. Good mothers always know when to take your hand. After all, they brought you through the portal into this life of form. Even when they aren't holding you, they are. Uncut paper dolls.

The moon came out to bless us. She followed us around the city all night, as she does, offering her four and a half billion years' worth of wisdom and illumination. I was the first person on earth staring up at her for the first time. Then I was everyone. Then I was no one. Then I was me, as present with life as I had been as a child. I remembered. I was home. Home was where I was.

The next morning, I felt depleted, achy, but older, quieter, more centred. Different. Deeper. I could never unsee what I had seen. I was still processing. The doors had been opened. Mum made me breakfast with orange juice and then ran me a bath. Post-journey care was important, she said. The experience changed everything for me. There was a new, expansive silence inside me. I knew something I didn't know before. There were places to go within and without that were uncharted, and I could stick my thumb out and hitch a ride at any time. The only rule? Don't panic.

Spring came and it was clearly time to go. Mum and Jake had had a few arguments, mostly when Mum was drinking. Shaye was coming with us to start school in British Columbia, and she had already missed too much.

It was hard to leave London this time. Mum and I had healed so much between us. Still, there was nothing for me there. I couldn't see a way out for her. She was deep in a cyclical world, a slow spiral in a direction I didn't want to go. Though it broke my heart to leave her, I swam hard away from the whirlpool.

Jake, Shaye and I travelled back to BC and got a small place together. Shaye was at the end of Grade 11, and I assumed the role of her guardian. We found it hilarious that I could write notes to get her out of class. We enrolled her where I had gone to high school, and she signed on for the fine arts program immediately. She excelled in theatre and was able to pass enough courses to move on to Grade 12. Smart little cookie.

After the acid trip, I couldn't see Jake in the same way. There was nothing wrong with the journey he'd taken; it was just so completely different than mine. The more distant I became, the more he closed in, the more suffocated I felt. I cheated on him, I suppose as a way to escape—which is no excuse. After some unfortunate fights, he moved out, and Shaye and I got our own place. I felt bad for hurting him. He was a good man and he loved me in his way.

I worked in a lumber warehouse and made good money to pay our rent, while Shaye continued to excel in school. What I didn't see happening was that the breakup with Jake had left me vulnerable in a way I wasn't expecting. For a few weeks, I was fine; in fact I was high from the freedom, but then he refused to speak to me. Even though the strongest parts of me knew we were not good together, there were parts of me that he held together. Codependence 101. I begged for him to take me back. I was now fully exposed to the elements, raw and wind-burned, crawling bloody up the side of a cliff. This was the detonation that set off a series of internal implosions. Landslide. I was panicking. Panicking hard.

Each injury opened deeper injuries, like trap doors. Just when I thought I'd hit the bottom, another would appear and down I'd go. Searing pain wracked my body like lightning, tearing me to pieces. The fault lines cracked and swallowed me whole.

I couldn't breathe. I couldn't stop crying. I couldn't make sense of anything.

I quit my job and asked Danny if Shaye and I could move in with him so I could get my head together. He said yes, of course, but the next thing I knew, I had locked myself in my room at his house. Searching desperately for a safe place, I lay beside my guitar on the bed. The rain fell day after day, and I was disappearing, washing away. The emptiness was taking over. I had forgotten what I'd learned in London. I had lost my connection to everything. My reaction to the pain had made me small, frightened, delusional. I was falling into the abyss.

I could hear knocking on the door. I couldn't eat. I was dying. *Please just let me die.*

In the tunnels of aloneness, I tried to grasp the walls, but everything was slipping. I heard something up ahead, so I moved toward the sound, dissonant music boxes. All the demons from my life greeted me like old friends. I turned to run back, but the tunnel had sealed behind me. There was no return. I was trapped. All around me was fire and the groping hands of disgusting old men.

One of the demons opened a bottle of pills and poured me a glass of water so I could swallow them all. I was dizzy, sitting on the floor, back against the wall.

Caught on the floor now
This bottle in my hand
In the confusion
It seemed the safest place to land

The demons disappeared and the tunnels turned into the yellow walls of my dad's bathroom. I could see my hands, but they were blurry. I tried to stand but everything spun. *Oh no. What have I done?* I heard a song in the distance. A drum. A heartbeat. My heartbeat? "Shaye? SHAYE!" My hands reached for the light.

I woke in the hospital. My dad was sitting beside me in a chair, reading *Bury My Heart at Wounded Knee*. My throat felt raw. My nose hurt. I guess they had pumped my stomach, put charcoal into my body through a tube. I didn't really remember. My dad smiled at me and I smiled weakly back. A therapist popped her head in to see if I was awake, and she asked my dad to leave for a few minutes. Danny looked at me for reassurance and I nodded.

As the severity of the situation dawned on me, I knew I had to think fast or they would keep me in here or put me in some kind of institution. I couldn't go where Mum had gone.

The therapist was compassionate and gentle and asked me straight out if I still wanted to die. I lied and told her that I never really did, that it was a cry for help. I somehow reassured her that I wasn't a danger to myself, and she seemed to buy it. She had short hair and a round face, and she looked sharply into me. Maybe I wasn't fooling her at all. She told me I would be there for a few days to make sure my vital signs were stable and so that I could have some peace. She would check on me. They admitted me to the heart ward, which was perfect. Everyone on the floor had a broken heart of some kind.

The first night, Shaye came and crawled into the tiny bed with me. She said that she was the dark one in the family and was supposed to be the one locked up or dead. She hadn't realized that behind my smile was a lightning storm. We laughed and we sang. She cried and told me never to leave her again. She was the big spoon for hours.

The next day, my IV pole and I went for a walk through the halls, my bare feet on the polished floors, my little gown tied closed in the back. The walls were bright, and at the end of the hall was a TV room. It was empty except for a couch, a television and a desk and chair. The desk had a beige phone on it. I sat in the chair, stared at the phone and tried to think of someone to call. There was no one I wanted to speak to, no one I thought would understand. I was still climbing out of the hole. I went to the couch and looked at my blurred reflection on the blank TV screen. I felt numb. I was alive but completely empty.

I don't know how long I was there, but an old man was suddenly standing in front of me. Knocked from my haze, I observed that he had an IV pole and was dressed like me. He smiled gently and asked if it would be okay if he turned on the TV. Of course, I told him.

As he turned, his gown opened in the back. He leaned over to turn the TV on, and there before me was a wrinkly bum and a pair of the saggiest testicles I had ever seen. *Oh, dear God!*

I got up quickly and left, trying to suppress my laughter as I hurried down the hall to my room, hoping to get there before I started howling, the IV wheels impeding my speed. I didn't make it. I burst out laughing and it echoed through the halls of the heart ward. I got to my room and went to the window, to look out at the world. I couldn't stop laughing. A nurse came in after me to make sure everything was all right. I could hardly breathe, I was laughing so hard.

I guess she took this as a good sign. As I climbed back into bed, she said, "You're leaving tomorrow. I never want to see you in here again, okay?" She smiled sweetly. I was reminded of the women at the factory in London. It was a loving expulsion. I didn't belong in there.

Later that night, I made my way back to the TV room. It was empty. No balls this time. I turned on the news, and there was a story about the ancient temperate rainforests of BC being decimated by the government and logging companies. A mass arrest of over eight hundred protesters had happened already.

Then something inside me remembered. A light came on and the volume turned up. I heard the forest, the roots, the wind in the canopy of leaves, the birds. It was my natural habitat. I needed to go there. It would heal me, and maybe I could be of service. Everything made sense in that moment.

The beauty of everything falling away, falling apart, was the clarity.

It was the beginning of knowing the medicine from the poison.

I was standing in the middle of my own demolition, but at least I was standing. And as long as I had hands to serve, I would try to use them in service of justice. As long as I had a heartbeat, I had a voice.

14.

In the Darkness

Branching streams flow in the darkness.
—SEKITO KISEN, SANDOKAI

The night I got home from the hospital, it was raining.

I realized I could hear another voice inside myself that I hadn't heard for a long time, perhaps since I was small. It was gentle. I was tuned in to its frequency. It told me to go into the backyard, lie down on the grass and look up at the dark sky. I was just beginning to feel myself coming back into my body. The September rain was light and cool, and it mixed with my tears as they trickled down my temples, into my hair, and made their way into the earth. The ground and gravity held me in place as I wept until I found myself laughing a little at the state of myself. I was dirty, wet, raw, alone.

Nineteen years old. A seedling. It would have been pathetic had I not had some understanding that I was on the precipice of something else. I was burrowing deeper, chasing the darkness down.

Visions began to flash through my mind, of looming shadows, phantoms, and I felt a sharp bitterness come from my chest, into my throat and out of my mouth. My heart banged into my ribs like a prisoner screaming for water, running a cup along the bars. All I could do was be with it, let it go.

Then, peace.

I was just a girl lying on the ground, the sounds just of leaves rejoicing with the raindrops, a car driving through puddles, the ducks in the pond. It was just another moment of spinning around the sun on a little blue speck. A human in its natural habitat, learning how to get to the other side of suffering, coming alive.

I walked into the house, soaked, and went straight to my guitar in my room.

In about a half hour, the song was out of me. It had been just behind whatever had come out of my chest, stuck in the cold stone like the sword Excalibur. I needed only the courage and the pure, unhindered heart to extract it and hold it above my head.

I wrote a song called "Let Her Feel the Rain":

Captured in a photograph in black and white
Her hair brushes her shoulders as she leans
To turn out the light
She's warm and you can feel her
But she can't feel you
No, she's just too numb to move.

The next day, I moved.

I moved toward something. The calm voice called me to this threatened rainforest, where I could be a part of something bigger than my little, wounded self, where it felt like love was needed, love I had to give.

My dad Danny set me up with all the gear I needed to join the blockade at Clayoquot Sound. He and Shaye hugged me goodbye and watched me drive away in my brown 1978 Toyota Corolla, which had so much rust on the bottom you could see the ground through the floor.

I had five albums with me: *Acadie* by Daniel Lanois, *Passion* by Peter Gabriel, *The Mission* by Ennio Morricone, *Solace* by Sarah McLachlan and *Little Earthquakes* by Tori Amos. It was a four-hour drive, and this music accompanied me past the falls of Goldstream, over the Malahat and through some of the most beautiful land I had ever seen. Giant trees welcomed me through Cathedral Grove. Eight-hundred-year-old Douglas fir lined the highway, a scenic fringe, but just beyond the perimeter of the park was the clear-cut devastation. Deforestation. The wounded wreckage of the earth.

Whatever was calling me was pulling me forward with a force I had never experienced. The *World Scientists' Warning to Humanity* had just been released the year before, and it changed the level of urgency for many environmentalists. Seventeen hundred of the world's leading scientists said we had thirty years before things would start to go very badly. This call that I heard, it sounded like it came from the future.

When, finally, I climbed into my tent, it reminded me of when I was a child. I found myself wondering if our greatest moments of emptiness, delusion, aloneness are when the deepest connection takes place. That is when we stretch our understanding of our capacity to love, when our roots reach for each other underground, in the darkness.

It's known that trees talk to each other at a molecular level, warning of danger, sharing nourishment. It's a language that existed long before us. I wonder what their love song to each other sounds like. This world is a constant erotic dance.

At the time, the Clayoquot protests were the largest act of civil disobedience in Canadian history. With my respect for all things Gandhian, I thought I had a grasp on how to de-escalate a tense situation. I thought I understood the dynamics at play, but nothing could have prepared me for what I saw at Kennedy Lake Bridge that day.

As the sun rose and the mist cleared, a lone drum echoed through the waking forest. A heartbeat. The hair stood up on my arms and I began to weep silent tears. This was the sound from my childhood, the one that had lured me deep in the forest, the one that eluded me no matter how hard I looked for it. It was the sound that was missing from the symphony of the land. The song of the First Peoples. The drummer played us into our bodies, played our bodies into the trees, played the trees into the mountains and the mountains into the sky. He played a rhythm that kept our breath deep and feet rooted.

The sound that followed, of giant tires breaking through the dark morning, was terrifying. Everyone turned to look in the direction of the logging trucks as they pulled up to the bridge, police cars close behind. Immediately, a number of people stood on the road in front of the trucks, and they stopped moving. I joined the protesters. I knew this was right with every cell in my body. My body was the earth, and these logging trucks were moving in on me without my consent, tearing me apart, my pristine wilderness. I would say no this time.

A police officer, his gun in his holster, placed his hands on me. I was under arrest, not for protesting the clear-cut logging of sacred land, but for criminal contempt of court. I was being arrested as a criminal. I would be charged and tried as a criminal. Injustice, PhD level.

Still, I felt powerful. I had learned that voices raised in dissent had a resonance that could make real change. I learned that to defend a ravaged earth was to heal my own wounds, to honour my body, to recognize that I deeply loved life.

Even though we were just expressing our constitutional right to protest, we were sentenced in unconstitutional mass trials, each receiving different punishments depending on how we pleaded or who our judge was. I was sentenced to three weeks in the Nanaimo Correctional Centre, a men's prison, because the women's prison was full.

The population there was diverse but included an abundance of First Nations men. They shared stories with me about how their parents were taken away and forced into Canada's oppressive residential school system, made to give up their culture, language and spirituality. They were abused, beaten, assaulted and dehumanized. In many of these stories, the boys' parents had come home broken and turned to alcohol, which led to beatings, which was all they'd known. Often, the boys had to run away from home, sometimes just to look for shelter. The RCMP would find them, beat them and incarcerate them. It was a war, a spiral of pain, a continuation of colonization. The systemic silencing of their song.

After I got out of jail, I moved into a house in Victoria with a couple of friends I'd met in Clayoquot, Colleen and Sarci. Our big house on Quadra Street was filled with delicious, healthy food, music and like-minded, passionate activists engrossed in thrilling conversation. I began to learn how to nourish myself, how to see myself and my body differently. My friends had a library of feminist literature, and I would curl up in a sunbeam on a fluffy couch with tea and a book and delve into new understandings. Internal scaffolding was being built to hold new rooms. Expansion. Renovation.

Canadian singer Jann Arden's new album, *Living Under June*, was released, and I would listen to it on repeat. Every song was brilliant, and her voice was soothing and strong. There was something fearless in her vulnerability, in her softness. I was obsessed.

During that time, I fell in love with Sarci. She was unlike anyone I knew. Her long legs and exquisite face fascinated me, and I couldn't take my eyes off her. She had long, red hair and the softest lips. I loved how she moved, sounded, laughed. There was something about the way she looked at me with her ice-blue eyes, the way she understood me, the way she loved me that caused something deeper to heal in me.

I was invited to sing at an outdoor market on Salt Spring Island. Just off the coast of Vancouver Island, Salt Spring is a small and magical community of artists, hippies, farmers, activists and people just looking for a slower pace of life. The sun shone in Victoria that day as I raced for the ferry. I missed it, but it didn't matter. I had plenty of time. I felt free and light and unbothered by the inconvenience. The next ferry was hours away, but I was near the ocean, seagulls, waves, salt air. I was surrounded by friends who were coming for the weekend, and when we finally boarded the ferry, we went straight for the top deck and took out our guitars.

Birds sing because it is what they are. They sing because they are alive. I sang on that boat because it was a beautiful day. There was no other reason. I didn't know the ferry boat was about to sail through a gateway, leaving one part of my life behind and opening a new world to me.

There is a story about a man named Siddhartha who meets a ferryman. The teaching from the ferryman is to listen to the river if he wants to learn from it. If he listens carefully, he will learn that all life is a river, timelessly stretching eternally along, flowing in the darkness.

As I was being ferried across the water that day, songs flowing, two figures emerged from inside the boat and joined us in the sun. They were listening.

As we pulled into Fulford Harbour, I closed the guitar case, snapping the little silver buckles. As I picked it up, the two women approached me. One of them was shorter than I was and had piercingly beautiful dark eyes and a curious smile. The other was taller and had short brown hair, more elfin. We exchanged wide-open, warm smiles.

The little one, who introduced herself as Tonni Maruyama, said that she enjoyed my songs but didn't recognize them all. The other woman, Cathy Barrett, asked if the songs were mine. When I told them that I had written the songs, they looked at each other. Tonni asked if I had any more. I nodded enthusiastically, and out of one of their pockets was produced a little brown card with a logo on it. It was an *N* in a circle. I recognized it immediately: Nettwerk Records. I looked at them in astonishment and said, "This is Sarah McLachlan's label!" They laughed, delighted, and asked if I was playing anywhere. When I said that I'd be at the market, they said they'd see me tomorrow.

I walked off the boat in shock. What had just happened? The sun covered the harbour in diamonds, and the Salt Spring Island magic began to seep into my body. My friend Sally Sunshine was there to greet me, and we went to her house for one of her famous potlucks. She had a bathtub by a window that looked out onto the forest. When I climbed into it that evening, it was like years of pain washed away. I thought of the women I had met that day and how I wouldn't have crossed paths with them had I caught the earlier ferry. I had a Salt Spring sleep that night, deep and full of dreams.

The next day, fully rested and nourished, we headed off to the market. As I sat on the stool in my ripped jeans, holding my guitar, I noticed that Tonni and Cathy were there, standing with a beautiful blond woman. One of them had a camera and was filming. The crowd was listening closely as the sun beamed down. My voice floated across the park, like when I was a little girl at the country fair, but now I was singing my own songs.

After I finished, they approached me again with their huge smiles. We hugged and they introduced me to Suzanne Little. She lived on the island and was a singer-songwriter who was signed to Nettwerk. She and her husband, Tom Hooper, who was in the influential Canadian group The Grapes of Wrath, one of Nettwerk's very first bands, had recently moved to a little house in the woods. Suzanne was very kind and encouraging that day. She was pregnant with her first child. Everything about this trio glowed.

We spoke briefly about getting in touch when we all got home, and they disappeared into the market, swallowed by beeswax candles, pottery, flowers and farm-fresh veggies.

Head spinning, I returned to Victoria to make a plan. I desperately wanted to make music my life. It was only a few days later when I got a call from Terry McBride, president and co-founder of Nettwerk. He was Cathy's husband, and he told me how much he was looking forward to meeting me. He asked if I could come to Vancouver. He also asked if I could get some of my songs recorded somehow.

When I hung up the phone, I could feel my whole body buzzing with exhilaration. Was this really happening? Brimming with determination, I ran out of the house, hopped into my beater car and drove to the mall. I bought a blank cassette tape, drove home, ran upstairs into the room I shared with Sarci and shut the door. I unwrapped the plastic cassette tape, popped it into a player, took a deep breath and pressed record. My guitar and I poured out every song I had written so far: "If You Could See Me Now," "Let Her Feel the Rain," "Evidence," "That's Me" and others that will thankfully be lost forever, because they sucked. Not every oyster has a pearl.

Tonni offered to pick me up at the ferry in Vancouver. Before meeting with Nettwerk, Tonni wanted me to record "Let Her Feel the Rain" for a compilation album called *Lit from Within*, to raise money for rape crisis centres. I would share the honour of being a part of this with artists like Sarah McLachlan, Veda Hille, Kate and Anna McGarrigle, Suzanne Little, Mae Moore and many others. I was beside myself to be part of it.

Tonni brought me to Mushroom Studios, next to the Nettwerk offices, where we set up to record. The walls were lined with awards and gold records by Heart, Chilliwack and Sarah McLachlan. Greg Reely was to be the producer. He was cute, a little nerdy but profoundly cool, which is how I would describe absolutely everyone I was to meet in the Nettwerk camp.

I wore a long, flowing white sundress, black Doc Martens and a light-blue denim vest (very '90s) as I stood behind the microphone in the vocal booth for the first time. I could see everyone in the control room standing behind a huge recording console and a thick pane of glass. I was nervous, but Greg was encouraging and patient. It was a simple acoustic guitar and vocal recording, but it had magic. We were finished in a few hours and then they took me to the Nettwerk offices next door to meet everyone.

I had no idea what was about to happen, but it felt like I was on the river, in a little boat, and all I could do was let the current take me.

A giant poster of Sarah McLachlan greeted us as I was led into the offices of the owners of the company, Ric Arboit,

Mark Jowett and Terry McBride. Mark and Ric were warm and kind, and I immediately knew they were good, solid people. When I reached Terry's office, he smiled, hugged me and closed the glass door behind us.

"Well, you've caused quite a stir around here," he said. He sat back in his chair and took me in. I got the feeling that he saw everything around him happening at once and missed nothing from his window seat at the helm of this ship.

He was very handsome and sharp as he explained how managers work and what they do. Everything he said made perfect sense. He was brutally honest about the demos. He said that some songs did nothing for him, while others ripped his heart out. He said I was a raw talent that needed to be honed. He wanted to see me play live, and so he invited me to play the following month at the Vogue Theatre for the tenth anniversary of Nettwerk Records, with the other Nettwerk acts.

He explained that Nettwerk had two sides, a record label and management. Even though he was an owner of the label, he was the head of the management side and that was his main focus. I could have him as my manager, and if I chose Nettwerk as a label, that would be convenient, but he didn't want to push me to make any decisions.

How was this happening? It felt like everything was moving so fast. *Breathe.* He sensed my feelings, stopped talking, smiled warmly and asked if I had any questions. I have no idea what I said, but I recall feeling that I loved the place, loved that moment.

He finished giving me a tour of the different departments, where I met people who greeted me with genuine exuberance. Finally, Tonni pulled me away and out the door, because I had to catch the ferry back to Victoria.

As we left, Tonni explained to me that she was leaving Nettwerk after many years to go to Toronto to work with

Sony Music. She was happy that I'd met and loved everyone at Nettwerk, but she also wanted me to see the major label world. She gifted me two books: *Letters to a Young Poet* by Rainer Maria Rilke and *All You Need to Know about the Music Business* by Donald S. Passman. She wanted me to dive deeply artistically but to know exactly what pool I was getting into. Piranhas were everywhere.

Shortly after I got home, a team from Sony flew in to meet me with Tonni. They offered me a five-thousand-dollar demo deal to record five songs professionally.

I called Terry because though he wasn't officially my manager, I trusted his opinion and needed his understanding of the contract I was about to sign. Sure enough, he jumped right in to help me. He said I should definitely take the money and that I wouldn't be beholden to anyone by accepting the deal. This way, I could have an experience in the studio and see if I liked it. He then gave me two tickets to see Sarah McLachlan at the Royal Theatre in Victoria. This was a strategic move on his part. He was always weaving many things at once.

Sarci and I breathlessly entered the theatre and sat in the front row. I felt so proud walking in arm in arm with this magnificent, head-turning beauty, and she was giddy with excitement.

Sarah McLachlan's new album, *Fumbling Towards Ecstasy*, had been released, and it was a masterpiece. The concert was exquisite. The lights, the sound, the set, the vibe of the band, Sarah's down-to-earth demeanour and goddess-like beauty took my breath away. How could someone be so human and otherworldly at once? She'd have the Glamour Spell down, and then she would shape-shift back into a funny, East Coast girl. But her voice, her golden voice, was flawless. There was something else. She pulled the audience to her and let them into places I hadn't seen opened before onstage. Of course, I knew every word to every song, but she delivered them in a way that went straight into you, expanded you, broke you open. Everyone in that room was rapt. It was an experience of falling in love.

I floated out of there, a deeper devotee. The world looked different. Everything had changed. I saw what was possible at the height of it all. As a young, budding singer-songwriter, I had witnessed a woman in her full expression and power, and it gave me permission to dream. Terry was smart to have me go. He knew that nothing would be more powerful for me to experience in that moment.

Sarci and I walked slowly through the Victoria streets, feeling altered from the night. The street lights illuminated her wild, red hair and her eyes glistened. I remember warm hands, a wide-open heart and a feeling that anything was possible.

Everything was orienting toward healing and opening to a larger world where music and love and nature were carving me into something limitless.

I thought of Sappho, the Greek poet, who wrote in her "Ode to Aphrodite,"

> . . . I remember:
> Fleet and fair thy sparrows drew thee, beating
> Fast their wings above the dusky harvests,
> Down the pale heavens.

Such beautiful words. *Fair thy sparrows*. But then, before we know it, so unfair.

A few days later, I received a call from one of the men I had met in jail. He had been released and was hoping we could grab a drink. I'll call him D. He said he was staying at a hotel in town and that I should meet him there. He'd been so kind in jail that no alarms went off. I'd know a predator when I met one, wouldn't I? Besides, he owned a business. He had made a few mistakes that he had served his time for. He was ready for a new life. I could get behind that.

I entered the elegant hotel room and was introduced to his friend C. The two of them made a handsome pair, and they smiled at me sweetly. D wanted me to meet his best friend before we stepped out on the town. But first, champagne. Thank you, yes.

The walls of the hotel dissolve around me.

He reaches for me. Somehow, I move toward him. I'm on his lap.

Darkness.

I'm naked. *Did I shave my legs? Why am I naked?*

Darkness.

This hurts.

C shakes me hard by the shoulders and throws me down. He's upset. Frustrated.

I can't move. Someone is on top of me.

Darkness.

Sounds of smashing.

Morning light.

Everything hurts.

D is asleep beside me. I climb naked out of the bed. I find my clothes and get dressed. I'm nauseous, sore. In the living-room part of the suite, I find my shoes and another unconscious girl, with C asleep naked beside her. Where did she come from? When did she get here? Who is she? The room is trashed. *I have to get home.* My head is foggy. I feel nothing but a need to get out of there.

The gift of the Rohypnol tranquilizer is that it relieves the victim of the memory of the horror, and it gives the rapist all the time in the world to ensure evidence no longer exists, for if the survivor remembers, a year from then, five years from then, the rapist is long gone and there is no proving anything.

I began to shut down, pulling the shell around myself again.

For no reason that I could give, I distanced myself from Sarci, from everyone. I just packed my things. I didn't think of her heart. Some part of me was screaming to get away, to be alone, to hide in the woods, and I didn't know why. I left with no explanation and got on the ferry to Salt Spring Island. I stayed for a few nights with a friend, Dan Jason, who had a beautiful farm. I walked silently among the rows of flowers. Perhaps I could find a little place in the forest nearby. Something was pushing at me from the inside. A seed in the darkness was ready to break open. Whatever had climbed inside me needed to be released, and I couldn't do it with anyone around. I needed silence to find this song.

It was many years later that Sarci had the chance to tell me that I had broken her heart, and it's only now as I'm writing this that I realize why I did it. A rape, even one buried in the subconscious, makes an imprint on the amygdala in the brain, messaging subliminally that there is no safe place, even in the arms of Aphrodite.

15.

All That Glitters

All that glitters is not gold.
—SHAKESPEARE, *THE MERCHANT OF VENICE*

I found a little cabin in the woods, a short walk from the ocean. For three hundred dollars a month, I had a tiny bedroom with sliding doors that looked out into the giant forest, a bathtub and a kitchenette that was part of the living room. I parked my keyboard under the bay window, set up my guitar and cleaned every corner.

My cabin was my sanctuary, my altar in the trees. I got a cat, Solomon. He loved to sit on the piano in the sunbeam while I played. I liked to light candles on my windowsill, but his fluffy tail caught on fire once, so I stopped doing that.

I walked the shoreline of Beddis Beach during the day. At night, the gentle waves would glow green with phosphorescence in the moonlight. I would light a fire and play my guitar alone. Always, when the first star would appear, I would make a wish. I wished for music to ferry me across the water, to reach the whole wide world. I wished for my songs to be heard.

Eventually, when I felt steady, I began to travel to Vancouver to have meetings with Terry and record my songs. The deck of a BC ferry became my little office, and I would get a hot chocolate and look out at the ocean. Sometimes, I'd see orcas on my way to the city. My friend Colleen introduced me to her aunt and uncle, Kathleen and Tom, and they let me stay in their house while I did my work, which was such a gesture of generosity. In exchange for lodging, I would sing to them, and they would share their wisdom with me. They had a massive library, and I began to devour books by Carl Jung, Joseph Campbell, Dr. Gabor Maté and Thich Nhat Hanh.

Terry, as my acting manager, set me up with Greg Reely again to record five of my songs with the demo money from Sony. We went to his house, where he had a home studio set up. Stephen Nikleva, a local guitar player, was part of the deal and came every day.

We set up a bathroom as a vocal booth. The walls were painted toothpaste green. We invited Veda Hille to play piano, and once we were all set up, they put me in the bathroom with headphones and a fancy Neumann microphone. It was hysterical to me that my voice sounded better to me than ever through this gear, and I was sitting on the toilet seat.

Veda asked me to count in the first take of the song. *Hmmm*, I thought, *she wants a countdown. Okay.* "Four, three, two, one."

Silence. Was she going to play?

Then laughter. Everyone in the other room was howling. Once they calmed down, I asked what was going on. They explained that a count-in starts at one. I joined in the laughter, realizing that I was as green as those walls.

At the end of a long day of recording, Stephen played a moody electric guitar part. It was just two chords, but it struck me. I asked them to record it, and then to loop it over and over and let me take it home.

That night, I got a call from my mother. She was sobbing. Gene MacLellan had died. He had taken his own life.

I asked to take the next day off from recording and stayed in my room. I put on the loop that Stephen had played and wrote down some words. I had no melody, just the poem. The next morning, still raw from the news, I asked them to put the loop on and set me up to record. I had no smiles, no armour; I was just deep in the sadness.

The words blurred through the tears, my breath heavy and ragged, I sang the song in one go. I called it "Silence."

Nettwerk was making a tenth-anniversary box set of their artists, and they wanted to include "Silence" on it. I couldn't believe I was going to be on an album with all those great musicians. I thought that Gene would be proud of me.

Soon, the Nettwerk anniversary concert at the Vogue Theatre was upon us, and I was nervous. I was finally going to meet Sarah McLachlan in person. I was invited to sing two songs, and I asked Stephen to accompany me, as well as Sarah's drummer, Ash Sood. It was an introduction to the community. Even though I hadn't signed with Nettwerk, Terry wanted me to feel like I was part of that world.

Suzanne Little and I drove to the show in Vancouver in her baby-blue Volkswagen, and we laughed as we both applied makeup in the car before the ferry docked.

As I made my way through the hallway to my dressing room that night, I saw Sarah moving toward me. I stopped breathing. She was even more beautiful and radiant than I could have imagined. Surrounded by people as we met, she sweetly said, "Is this THE Tara MacLean?" I almost fucking fainted.

We all laughed and she gave me a hug. I think she told me she looked forward to hearing me sing. It was a bit of a blur. She was kind and welcoming, and I was pretty certain I was dreaming the whole thing. The memory is like Vaseline on film, since my body was clearly rushing with dopamine.

I had one good outfit that I could wear onstage and not look like a super hippie. It was black and flowy, and I felt elegant in it. My brown hair was long and straight, and I wore simple makeup. As I walked onstage, I felt confident that I could hold my own, but I noticed my hands shaking as I went to play the first chord of "Let Her Feel the Rain." The audience was respectfully silent as I sang, and they applauded when I was finished, so clearly, I didn't blow it. As I walked offstage, Suzanne gave me a tight hug. She was more excited for me than she was for her own performance, and that taught me so much about what it means for women to support each other.

When Sarah came on, she was phenomenal. It was different than the polished performance she had given at the Royal Theatre. She was funnier and freer. She swore, and I found her irreverence hilarious. Then she talked about her love of everyone at Nettwerk and gave a special shout-out to Mark Jowett, saying that she had no idea what the fuck she would have done in her life without him. The energy in the theatre was high, and she commanded that stage like nothing I'd ever seen. I loved her.

A few weeks later, Sony invited me to Toronto to meet with their team. I had finished the five demos, and they wanted to talk to me about them. Tonni had migrated east and was now in the Sony offices. The building was on the outskirts of Toronto, in a more industrial part of town. Like Nettwerk, Sony had two main parts to their business: the record label, which was responsible for recording and distributing the music; and the publishing side, which took care of the song-writers and collected the royalties. I would be staying at a hotel close to the offices and going to meetings, as well as attending a Sony Music dinner.

The morning I was leaving Vancouver, I looked at myself in the mirror. I had a look of determination that I'd never seen before. I was becoming something new. I put on *Passion* by Peter Gabriel, and as "A Different Drum" played, I danced around my bedroom as though I was doing some kind of cer-emonial preparation. My hands went in the air as his voice ascended, and I felt the power of the drums. I felt free and open.

When I walked into the lobby of the gleaming Sony build-ing, I noticed a beautiful grand piano, which had been pol-ished so perfectly there wasn't a fingerprint on it. I had a short fantasy of sitting down and playing it. A spotlight would cas-cade over me dressed in sequins, and the whole office would gather around and listen. I shook myself into the present reality as Tonni led me around, introducing me to dozens of lovely people, including the head of A&R (artists and repertoire).

He sat me down in his office and shared how much he loved the demos, especially a song called "Evidence." Then he said something I didn't understand. He said, "Can you write more songs like that one?"

I looked over at Tonni, who, I know, understood my con-fusion. I'd only written about fifteen songs at that point in my life, and they'd all come from inside me when I needed them. I didn't control what songs came out. I had never considered purposely writing a song for the sake of making it sound like another one, or even thought it was possible to write some-thing that someone asked me to write. That was the moment I learned there are two kinds of songwriting: Inside-out songwriting is when the song fills up inside you and then pours out. There is no thought of the listener, except perhaps to hope that it will connect, but that is an afterthought. The song is completely cathartic for the writer. Outside-in songwriting is when you are asked to write a song for a specific purpose, a jingle for a commercial, for example, or a song for another singer, or a formula that will sound good on the radio, for the ever-elusive search for a hit—well, not elusive to all.

I had no idea how to do what he was asking of me. Both modes of songwriting are equally important and valid, but I was in over my head and I knew it. Tonni smiled reassuringly and said that we should go and see the publishing division of the company.

In a smaller office sat a kind-looking man. He jumped out from behind his desk and hugged me. He introduced himself as Gary Furniss. He went back to sit behind his desk but kept his eyes closely on me. There was nothing false about him with his short grey hair and sparkling eyes. He had posters all over the wall, gold and platinum records, photos with celebrities, but not in a way that felt like he was showing off. This was the office of a successful publisher.

Tonni left us alone to talk. I had my guitar with me, and he asked me to play him a song. I pulled out "Let Her Feel the Rain." It was so strange to be sitting in an office playing across from someone at a desk, but Gary just leaned back in his chair, smiled and closed his eyes like it was the most normal thing ever. When I finished, he smiled at me, nodding his head.

"Beautiful," he said. "I'm curious, what music do you listen to?"

I told him about my deep love of Peter Gabriel, and his eyes lit up even more, which I didn't think was possible. He shared my love of Gabriel's work, especially with Daniel Lanois. We also shared a deep love of Daniel Lanois's solo work. I had this feeling, when Gary was with me, that he was really listening.

He told me that I could put my guitar in different tunings and suggested I get a capo. I was a baby songwriter and musician, and he didn't judge me at all for not knowing how to read music. He suggested I do some co-writing as well and wanted to introduce me that night to a group of songwriters on the Sony roster.

As I was leaving the building, a huge image of Celine Dion loomed over me. I stopped and looked at the magnitude of her face. Someone who worked there explained that she was one of the coolest women ever, and that when other female artists (they named them) were behaving less than graciously, they would be seated next to Celine at an event in order to learn public decorum.

That hit me hard. The message, of course, was that we had to always publicly maintain an air of composure and agreeability, no matter what was happening. The "quiet seat" prize. In other words, be a good little girl. I didn't think that would be a problem for me—I was so fucking sweet and just so grateful all the time. One sentence spoken at the altar of Celine indoctrinated me into the cult of compliance. It took me years to unlearn it. It took witnessing wilder women to help me untie the cords of cordiality.

As a Canadian, I have to say that it is also culturally ingrained to not say what you feel if it's not nice. We are supposed to always be polite. The result of this is that when someone is being horrible to you, you almost can't process it in the moment. You kindly excuse yourself and realize later how messed up that was. I could write a whole other book called *Things I Should Have Said*.

That night, I attended my first music industry dinner. In the mid-1990s, the business was thriving. There were waterfalls of money. The executives had expense accounts and car allowances. The meals eaten and the wine drunk were like nothing I had ever experienced before or since. It was epic. But this first dinner was magical. There must have been twenty of us around a huge table at a sushi restaurant. I was placed between two other artists who were signed to Sony, Melanie Doane on my left and Jon Levine from The Philosopher Kings on my right.

Melanie is also originally from the East Coast and plays the violin and sings. She is beautiful and real, and was about to release *Shakespearean Fish*, her major label debut. She was lovely and kind, and I was delighted to be next to her. Jon was a different cat. He was gorgeous in an introverted kind of way, hiding behind long hair. He intrigued me from his first words. He wanted to know what books I liked. When I told him that I loved Joseph Campbell, he said, "Isn't that like self-help stuff?" I laughed and said, "Maybe a little?"

He started talking about Jack Kerouac and suggested I read *Maggie Cassidy* and *On the Road*. He said it's good for songwriting to dig into those Beat poets. We decided to meet after dinner at the grand piano at the office. He would arrange for us to get in late at night when the building was completely empty. He was signed to both the label and the publishing company, and was one of their star artists. I know now that Gary sat him next to me on purpose, hoping we'd connect and create something together. You can't force a spark, but Gary had a feeling. I was completely enamoured of Jon already, and I couldn't wait to hear him play.

The sound of the piano echoing through the halls of the Sony office was magnificent. As he touched the keys, it was like he was touching me, my ivory bones. Jon and I talked about songs, and he shared some lyrics he was working on. He wrote them down and began to play as I sang his words over the chords. Out came a song called "Red." It was moody, rich, poetic. A scarlet painting.

I learned so much about songwriting from him that night. We were two scruffy kids in a fancy building making something beautiful.

On the plane back to BC, my head spun with all I had learned. I thought about how there were four aspects of the music business that I had to consider. The first was management. Terry was already doing that in an unofficial capacity. Managers are the captains of the career ship. They have an overview of everything. I had to also consider a booking agent, which takes care of booking tours. Terry said he had that sorted in Canada with the Feldman Agency, which he trusted implicitly. The next aspect to think about was the record label, which would work with me to choose songs, producers and artwork. The record label is in charge of press and promotion, as well as servicing the songs to radio. Lastly, I had to consider the publisher, which would, hopefully, give me an advance to live on while I wrote the songs for the album. They would then co-own my material and collect the royalties on my behalf. They would also help to get songs placed in films and on TV, and even find other artists to sing my material if that's what I wanted.

I landed in Vancouver and went right to the Nettwerk office to debrief with Terry. He wasn't surprised that Sony had asked me to replicate a song that had hit potential, and he smirked at that suggestion. When I told him that Sony Publishing wanted me to co-write, his body went more rigid than it already was. He leaned in and told me I had to be very careful with that, and he suggested I write the songs myself. He said that different situations have different songwriting etiquette. He suggested that if you write the lyrics or the melody, then you should have publishing. If you write a musical hook on an instrument or help with the arrangement, in his opinion that's not songwriting. Elsewhere, if you're in the room when a song is coming through, then you are part of its birth and you, regardless of what you contributed, get equal rights to the song. Neither is right or wrong; you just have to have a clear agreement and understanding before you go in. I noted his caution. I figured it wasn't time for me to tell him my theory that songs don't belong to anyone.

I had some decisions to make. Terry was patient and encouraged me to use my instincts. I decided to sign with Sony Music Publishing and Nettwerk Records as my label. Terry committed to being my manager. I was ecstatic. I was signed up to Feldman's as my booking agent, and Richard Mills was my guy. He was passionate and excited to get me on the road. Sony Publishing sent me $25,000 as an advance. I'd never had that kind of money. I sent some to my mom.

All systems were a go. Engage!

Nettwerk set up a photo shoot with Crystal Heald from the art department for some headshots. The plan was for her to pick me up and take me to a studio, but I had nothing to wear, really, and didn't know how to do makeup for camera. When she arrived at my door, Sarah McLachlan was there with her, with a big bag of clothes, her makeup and hair-styling tools, and a huge smile. Crystal and Sarah were best friends, and together, they were an enthusiastic, hilarious bundle of fun. They came in and immediately began going through my lame collection of clothes.

Sarah dumped her bag of beautiful clothes on my bed. She held up a little brown blouse and told me she had worn it in the "Hold On" video. It fit me perfectly. Crystal approved some outfits and off we went to the studio.

On the drive, I sat in the back seat. Sarah asked me how I learned to play guitar. I said that my dad taught me, that he went away a lot and so I'd practise what I'd learned from him so I could show him when he came home. She and Crystal exchanged a quiet look. I immediately wanted to take it back. It sounded so maudlin and sad. I felt like I had overshared with people I didn't know yet. I was deeply self-conscious. Then Sarah looked over her shoulder and smiled at me. Everything was fine.

As Crystal set up the camera, Sarah did my makeup. For sure, I was dreaming now. She told me she loved my eyebrows and hummed softly as she applied eyeshadow. I felt lifted and loved, like I had stumbled into the fairy-tale version of my life.

Sarah dressed me in beautiful clothes. They were elegant, earthy, a little bit sexy. At one point, she wanted to put me in a pair of pants, so she asked me to turn around.

"Yup, that's a good East Coast arse you got on ya," she said.

We all laughed. I fit in her pants perfectly.

As I looked at the lens, Crystal encouraged me to open and connect, to share the vulnerable, the innocent, the powerful, the flirty, the erotic parts of me. Sarah told me to look into the camera with a look that said I knew something they didn't, like I had a secret. Build a mystery, because, let's face it, I'm the least mysterious person in the world. It was the best first photo shoot I could have ever had.

The experience fostered in me a love of photo shoots from then on, because I saw myself as beautiful in a way I hadn't before. I was able to bring out something from inside myself and show it. I loved that part of the job, connecting with the photographer through the lens in an intimate way. Terry was happy that I was photogenic.

A few nights later, Crystal came over for tea. She immediately had a big-sister vibe. She said, "Tara, we know you can sing, but can you tell a story? Take us down into the bare places, and then when it's time, let it fly." I've never forgotten that.

Later that week, Sarah and I went for lunch. When I asked her for advice, she said she wasn't a big advice giver, but if she could pass on anything to prepare me for what was coming, it would be to not lose my centre.

I nodded like I understood, but truthfully, I didn't comprehend the profundity of those words at the time. I didn't know that I'd ever found my centre in the first place. Sarah had a solidity about her that made you want to orbit around her, a celestial body with its magnetic field intact. I felt more like an asteroid that was being flung randomly into space.

Sony mailed me a care package of music by Leonard Cohen, Neil Young, The Philosopher Kings and Pink Floyd—all artists on their roster. I immersed myself in the albums and kept writing new songs. I played with different tunings, and Gary sent me a capo. Sony had me do a few sessions of co-writing, which I loved. Terry wasn't thrilled with this, but he didn't stop me from doing anything I wanted to do.

It was around this time that I fell hard for a sweet boy, and when it didn't work out, I was heartbroken. I wrote song after song, but nothing could take away the ache. I decided to do a three-day silent retreat at Dan Jason's farm on Salt Spring Island. On the third day, after many long walks through the forest and flowers, I ventured off the farm and quietly moved through an outdoor market at The Salt Spring Centre of Yoga. I had a pen and paper with me if I needed to communicate. Everything felt amplified and kind of holy as I bathed in my own silence. The pain was beginning to subside.

I noticed a gathering on the lawn, and I made my way over to see what was happening. There sat an Indian man in a white robe. He was surrounded by devotees also in white.

Someone leaned in and whispered to me that he was Baba Hari Dass, the guru the yoga centre had been built for. At that time, he hadn't spoken in forty-two years. How funny that my silence had brought me to this silent monk.

The air was full of love. His presence was so tender and delightful at once. His followers asked him questions, to which he replied in writing. His words were read aloud so we could all experience the wisdom he was imparting. He was surprisingly funny. Then he looked at me. I smiled and wrote down a question: "I am a singer and I write songs. I have stepped into the world where the business meets the art. How do I stay true to my heart and to the music?"

He smiled knowingly as he read my note and wrote me one back. "Have no expectations. If you have no expectations, then you will have no fear, and your song will always come from the source."

No expectations.

I packed my things on Salt Spring Island and moved to Vancouver, to a little garden-level apartment on West 14th. I got a job as a cashier at Capers, a bougie organic food store in Kitsilano, a hip, gentrified beach community on the west side. I had to step into the world, without expectation, and begin to share my songs.

Terry gifted me with tickets to a concert at a little club in Gastown, a funky neighbourhood on the east side of Vancouver, to see a singer who was breaking into the music business in the United States. He wanted to know if I thought I was ready to do this, to perform a whole show.

Onto the stage walked this beautiful girl in a pink T-shirt and jeans. She plugged in her guitar slowly, like it was all part of her casual entrance. I'd never heard of her before, but I was riveted. She was confident and wide open. She was funny, she played the guitar brilliantly, and her songs blew me away. Her name was Jewel.

I was so inspired by that night that I went home and made a list of all the songs I thought were good enough to play. I called Terry the next day and asked him to set me up with a show. He booked me at the same venue a few weeks later, and Sarah McLachlan's drummer, Ash Sood, offered to accompany me along with a guitar player I had worked with on demos. I was on the bill to play after Holly McNarland, another local singer-songwriter with way more grit and edge than I had. She rocked the room, and I was a little jealous of her ability to channel her fury. Who gave her permission to be angry in public? She did, that's who. She didn't get the "be a good little girl" memo, or if she did, she tore it up and lit it on fire. But when she went to her tender place, she reeled us all in. It was like we had to get through her exterior and earn being let into the softness. Holly was truly great.

Sarah was in the audience, and I was wearing one of the outfits she had given me at the photo shoot: black pants and a white silky top. I sang my heart out and quickly learned what was happening with the microphone, how to lean in when I was singing softly and back off when I got loud. I told stories, and when people laughed, it gave me a rush unlike anything I'd ever felt. I sensed that if I could create a show where people could cry from the songs and laugh at the stories, it could be a balance that would work. I was beginning to glimpse what it was I had to offer onstage. This was my canvas. I was designing the experience.

I got paid $125—the first money I made from a show. The sound guy took it.

The owners of Nettwerk were all there, and they hugged me tightly when I got off the stage. Ric said to me, "It's like watching a butterfly emerge."

So, this is what came of the cocoon of silence. I went to the space where the songs were born, and I crawled around in the dark tunnels until I found the hand in the darkness, the song, the reason to keep moving forward, to break through, to fly.

Fly with no expectations.

I became ravenous to see live music. I had free tickets to most concerts in Vancouver now that I was with Nettwerk, Sony and Feldman's. I was on any guest list I asked for, and if it wasn't a show that was connected to those companies, Terry pulled strings so I could go. I saw U2, Peter Gabriel, Leonard Cohen, Tom Waits, Bonnie Raitt and all the cool, local indie bands. The seats were always great. Terry wanted me to absorb everything I could, to see the heights of what was possible production-wise, to get ideas, to be inspired. It was like being put through school.

One concert changed my life forever: when Dead Can Dance played at The Orpheum. When Lisa Gerrard took the stage, I knew I was in the presence of greatness. She was clad in robes, and everything about her was holy and sensual. She embodied what I loved but didn't know was possible to emit. As the music started, she dropped into a space right in front of my eyes that was between worlds, and she brought us all with her. This was not a performance; this was mystical, a trance, an opening in the fabric. Even though I never used the word, I felt God had entered me. I wept, because I now knew what was possible. I knew how raw and vulnerable I could be and still be safe. I knew that I would offer nothing less than all I had to give.

To sing is to bleed songs.

To sing is to open completely.

Then Ani DiFranco came to town. Veda Hille was opening for her, and she gave me tickets. Only if you've seen her live can you understand the force of Ani's power. A wordsmith of the highest order, she played that guitar and danced in a way I didn't know we were allowed to. Something was breaking free. Ani taught me that night to be fearless in what I had to say. Fuck, was she sexy. Her smile filled the theatre, and I was forever deeply in love with Ani.

Soon after, I saw Tori Amos live. As she straddled her piano bench and played like the wildest thing I'd ever seen, something else let go inside of me. I could be everything I was without apology. Between Lisa, Ani and Tori, I'd been set free. With Sarah as an example of kindness, sisterhood and success, I felt like nothing was impossible.

Terry decided to put me in an opening spot for the Dave Matthews Band at the Commodore Ballroom. Just me and my guitar, though, with no other support. I was terrified. The crowd was rambunctious and ready to party, not dive into a deep emotional ballad fest. There's no moshing during my set! This was my worst nightmare. They were going to hate me.

Before I went onstage, Terry came over to me. He said, "I'm throwing you to the wolves." He wasn't making me feel any better. "Find one person who is listening to you and focus on them. If you walk out of here tonight and you've connected with one person, you've succeeded." Oh, so it was a test. Fine. I'd show him.

As I walked onstage, I scanned the audience. It consisted mostly of young men, but there were some young women, and a variety of ages. Clearly Dave Matthews had a wide demographic, but the college boys were out in full force and the beer was flowing. I nervously plugged in my guitar and began to play. There was only a slight hush in the crowd noise, but mostly they kept talking through the song. I felt embarrassed and nervous and couldn't wait to finish this stupid test.

I remembered the Glamour Spell. I pulled a cloak of confidence over my head so that, from the outside, no one could tell I was shitting my pants. Then I scanned the crowd for someone listening and found a woman on the left who was leaning against the wall and watching me. I made eye contact with her as I sang. She started to move her body slowly to the rhythm. I grounded myself in her and then looked around the room. A few other listeners were with me. I did the same thing and smiled at them, making direct contact. I did this for my whole set, and little by little, the audience warmed to me. Though I was not what they had expected, and I knew they just wanted to see the Dave Matthews Band, I was able to win over a few people, and so I walked offstage with my head held high.

Terry smiled at me approvingly, but I just wanted to punch him in the face. He saw that and laughed at me. I would come to understand that he was never going to coddle me or make it easy. If I wanted this, I was going to have to work for it. I had no idea how hard he would push me, or how many times I'd want to punch him. But he also rescued me too. He was the teacher I needed.

It was time to make a record. I knew I was ready. Nettwerk thought I was ready. I had eleven good songs.

Mark Jowett and I hopped on a plane to San Francisco. Nettwerk had Suzanne Little make her record there and it had turned out great. I was to be there for a month. We arrived at Brilliant Studios, a huge warehouse space south of Mission Street. At the time, it was a pretty dangerous neighbourhood. Norm Kerner, who was going to produce my first album, met us at the door. He seemed excited to have us there, and proud of his studio. Truly, it was marvellous. Bright and spacious, it was filled with instruments and incredible recording gear. There was an office and stairs leading to a living space upstairs.

He told us we could do anything we wanted in this space. Nothing was off limits. We could bring in any vibe. We could set up a bed in the middle of the room and I could sing on that. We all laughed, and I began to envision how awkward it would be to lie down in a bed in front of strangers and sing. I was nervous, tight in my body. I liked Norm immediately, but something wasn't sitting still inside me.

We began to go through the songs the next day. Two musicians would be flying in from Vancouver soon, Veda Hille, who would play piano, and Ash Sood, who would be on drums. Other than them, we would be using local musicians from San Francisco.

We were scheduled to begin recording that afternoon, when the musicians arrived. Norm said, "We'll start bed tracks in a few hours; we just need to get the studio ready."

Bed tracks? I didn't agree to the bed thing. I had just laughed. That wasn't me agreeing to it. I wanted to throw up. I didn't know how to tell them I felt self-conscious about lying in a bed in the studio. I wanted to sing standing up. I was mortified.

Mark and I went upstairs to relax. I could talk to him. He was my friend. My heart was pounding.

"Mark? Um . . . I don't want to do bed tracks."

He looked at me calmly but with a spark of confusion. As understanding dawned across his sweet face, he laughed compassionately. He reached over and put his hand on mine.

"Bed tracks are when we record the fundamental parts of the song, the part that we build onto. Usually, it's the drums and bass. In your case, piano is a bed track on quite a few songs. We lay down bed tracks first always."

My cheeks must have been beet red from the misunderstanding, but Mark didn't let me feel stupid for one second.

"There is so much to learn here, and this is your first album. You can ask me anything, anytime." I relaxed and realized I was in good hands. I adored Mark. I'm pretty certain he is a real live angel.

As we began to lay down the bed tracks, most of it felt really good. Veda is a brilliant and sophisticated songwriter herself, and she had a way of wrapping like a ribbon around my simple songs. Ash is a genius drummer, and most of his takes happened in the first go. But something was happening that was making me feel uneasy again. I noticed that Norm was asking Mark what he thought, and not me. Mark would turn to me for my input, and when I would give it, Norm wouldn't really listen. After a few hours, I wasn't having any fun. I knew some of the tempos weren't right.

Norm held a baseball bat over his shoulder as he walked back and forth behind the console like a royal guard with a bayonet at Buckingham Palace. I didn't know if this was supposed to be intimidating or funny, but I pulled Mark aside. He recognized that I wasn't being heard and said he would call a meeting with Norm right away.

I asked Veda if she'd noticed what I'd noticed, and she nodded. She was a feminist and was hyper aware of what was happening. I'm lucky she was there, because her validation was all I needed to give me the power to speak.

Sitting in the office, Norm behind his desk and Mark and I beside each other, Mark began to tell him how I was feeling, but I interrupted. Though I felt a surge of fury move through my body, I grounded before the words came out.

"Norm, I don't feel like you're hearing me. If you aren't going to respect my input, I can't make this record with you."

Silence.

Mark looked at me like he had never seen me before. Norm raised his eyebrows and said, "Absolutely. I'm sorry you felt that way. I will absolutely defer to you from now on."

I looked at him closely. He was a sweet, strong man, but he had a sadness about him. As we left the office, Mark pulled me aside.

"I'm very impressed with you. You were professional and clear. I'm not worried about you one bit." He smiled proudly.

I felt strong and ready to go back into the studio and make the album I could hear. On occasion, Norm would ask me for my input on things I had no idea about. I didn't always know what I wanted, but I could hear and feel what I didn't want. I also had to learn to be patient, because sometimes Norm was building something sonically that I didn't understand, but then when it was all mixed together, it made sense. He was an amazing producer, and yet there were still moments when I felt uncomfortable. Mark wasn't around one day, and I had just finished a powerful vocal take where I gave it my all. Norm leaned into the mic in the control room and said, more to the engineer than to me, "That was great. I almost believed you, but you're a woman, so we know you're full of shit."

Norm and the engineer laughed because they were clearly sharing an inside joke, but it stung me deeply. He didn't mean to upset me, but I was so open and raw in that moment, and even though they were kidding, it left me deflated. It had such an impact on me, and from that moment on, I had armour when I sang, which is the enemy of openness.

One day, I was singing the backing vocals on "Evidence." After a take, the engineer informed me that I had an urgent phone call.

I took off my headphones with a sinking feeling in my stomach. It had something to do with my mother. I could feel it. Sure enough, it was Nana on the phone.

"Sweetheart, I'm sorry to tell you that your mother is in the hospital."

My heart sank. "What happened?"

"All I know is they think someone may have spiked her drink with something. She tried to break the windows in the waiting room, so they've taken her somewhere. Some hospital north of London."

I imagined her in a hospital gown, alone in a room, rocking back and forth, terrified.

I hung up the phone and looked up to see Norm standing in the doorway.

"I'm so sorry," he said. "What do you need? Do you want a break?"

"No. I want to sing."

We went back into the vocal booth and went to the end of the song. I put on my headphones, and we turned the lights down. I closed my eyes and started to sing, but it was more of a scream. I reached so deep into my belly to find the sounds I had to get out. Fury. I found it.

They kept recording, and then went back and had me layer it, scream upon scream. My nails dug into my palms, drawing blood. *MAMA!* Maybe she could hear me. Maybe in her locked-up room, she could hear me screaming for her. *I'm here, Mama. I'm here.*

I will always wonder if that moment created a bridge to her. We were so close and connected after we'd healed our relationship. We spoke often, and she had become the person who encouraged me to go into the world and give music my whole heart. Whatever someone had put into her drink that night had caused a break in her psyche. She'd been doing so well living in London these last years. She had met and married a wonderful man and had two great jobs. Though she was still drinking, it wasn't the centre of her life. She'd built something beautiful. Her father had died and so had Gene, so there was fragility in that moment, so whatever she'd been given broke something open.

Eventually, she, her husband and the doctor decided that this was an opportunity for her to heal. They transported her to a priory house in Buckinghamshire, where she began, step by step, to walk the long, courageous road to wellness. She was treated for trauma, depression and bereavement. She stopped drinking.

Her power to face her pain was evidence that I came from the strongest of women. There are few people in the world as indestructible as my mother, and for that, she is my hero. Most people would not have survived even a fraction of what she'd been through. If she could stare into the void, then I could scream into it. The echo that came back was love.

When I was finished singing, Norm's voice came into my headphones, bringing me back to the present.

"Thank you, Tara." He meant it.

The last week in San Francisco was for mixing, which is almost the last step once the recording is finished. It was late at night as we listened to all the songs. I felt there were moments that hit the depth of what I wanted, and others that only skimmed the surface. Something started rising in me: a fear and a doubt so powerful that I jumped up and ran out the door, into the foggy San Francisco night. I needed to get as far away from that studio as I could. I didn't know where I was going. I had failed. I'd had this chance to make something beautiful, and I was sure no one would hear it. So much was riding on this.

The pressure built and I ran faster. I ran past a homeless man, past the grimy street corners, past the over-stapled telephone poles and torn posters, past the lit stores that were open late, past the broken glass on the sidewalk glittering in the street light. Tears poured down my face. I finally ran out of breath and stopped. I sat on the cement stairs of a shop. Elbows on knees, head in hands, I cried. I cried because I was a phony. I cried because I was full of shit. They were right. My record wasn't great. It was too safe. I had let everyone down.

I felt a hand on my shoulder. It was Mark. He'd chased me through the streets. He sat next to me. I put my head on his shoulder and he pulled me close.

"It's not good." I sobbed. "I'm so sorry. I wanted to make you proud."

"Tara, look at me." Slowly, I raised my eyes to meet his. "You've made a beautiful record. Truly. I'm proud of you."

He held me for a while in the damp, misty night on that scary corner until my tears dried. We walked back silently, breathing deeply. Mark always knew what to say and what not to say. I loved his silence because, in that moment, it was all I needed.

We had one day left there, and Norm had bought us tickets for a concert. It was the Bridge School Benefit that Neil Young did every year with friends. The lineup was epic: Beck, Bruce Springsteen, The Pretenders, Hootie & the Blowfish and—*yes!*—Emmylou Harris and Daniel Lanois, who had just released *Wrecking Ball*, a masterpiece. I cried through the entire performance. It was perfection. Blind Melon was supposed to perform, but Shannon Hoon, the lead singer, had died of a drug overdose a few days before. At the end of the concert, all the performers came out together to sing "The Needle and the Damage Done" for Shannon. There wasn't a dry eye in the amphitheatre.

I was so grateful to Norm for bringing me to the show and for everything he had taught me—even when it was to stand up for myself. I looked over at him a few times during the last song, and he was a mess. I saw him. He was a sweet man who just loved music. His bat was his defence, because really, he was raw like me. He was hurting, like all of us. He just wanted to make beautiful records. He just wanted to teach me. He just wanted his work and life to mean something. Don't we all want that? Don't we all want, for just one moment in our lives, to be a prism of something true, to be a light unto the world, to glitter like phosphorescence under the moon or even like glass under the street light, to shine with no expectations?

16.

Reflection

The wild geese do not intend to cast their reflection;
The water has no mind to retain their image.
—ZEN POEM FROM *ZENRIN-KUSHU*

Who are we?

I once went for a walk on Chesterman Beach in Tofino, British Columbia, with my old friend Dr. Bruce Robertson. He was an activist and psychologist who had lived and worked at the Gandhi Ashram in India. Though he was in his eighties, he ran around the beach like a child. He came up to me, close, face to face, his wild eyebrows blowing in the misty wind. He said, "There is only one question. Who are you really?"

Fucked if I know.

Am I the consciousness behind my thoughts? The witness? Am I you and you are me? Am I the dreamer or am I the dream? Am I a virus on the earth? Am I damage control? Am I the damage? Am I just a temporary creature here to procreate and then compost? Am I eternal? Am I stardust? Am I a servant of humanity? Am I God? Am I an expression of nature? Am I the concoction of hormones in my brain? Do I even matter? Am I infinitely essential? A hologram? An experiment? Dust in the wind? Am I the universe experiencing itself as form? Am I love? Am I all of the above?

I didn't know how to get under this question, and I've never gotten over it. I'll never not see his eyes, burning that question into me, like fire on driftwood floating out to sea. I'll never not ask myself that question every time I step onto a stage, so that the songs can answer it for me, and I can give myself, whatever that means, whoever "me" is.

Back on the East Coast, in my hometown, the musical community was creating something to honour Gene MacLellan's life and work. The East Coast Music Awards show is the biggest event in music there, and that year, the tribute to Gene was going to be massive. He was the greatest songwriter to come out of the region, and his death had hit us all hard.

I wrote to the East Coast Music Association and asked if I could be part of the tribute. They didn't know who I was as a musician, but of course they knew Marty. They asked me to send them a recording, so I sent one of me singing "Snowbird." They loved it, and I was invited to perform on the show, and so was Marty.

I hadn't seen him or spoken to him since he drove away that day eight years ago, and now we were going to sing together on national television.

Terry gifted me with a flight home. There's a feeling I get when I'm flying into PEI that is like landing in a nest. There's a softness, a relief. I was nervous to see Marty, but happy to be home.

Since my grandfather had died, Nana's house felt safe. She was thrilled that I was going to be singing on the show, and she took me shopping for a classy black suit to wear. At the store, she stood behind me in the mirror as I did up the buttons. "Perfect," she said. "Now let me see your nails."

The next day, I went to the arena to meet the CBC producers and all the other musicians for a dress rehearsal. As I walked into my dressing room, there sat Marty on a bench against the wall, strumming his guitar. He looked the same as he always had, like a leathery old sea dog. He saw me and smiled. My heart was torn. Here was the man who had abandoned me, disposed of me like I was nothing, but also the man whose songs had built me from the inside out. The sound of his guitar and his sparkly blue eyes erased all my anger and confusion. All that was left was the love of a little girl running into her daddy's arms.

I sat on the floor and put my head on his lap and cried for a long time. Finally, I spoke.

"Why did you let her do that to me?"

It was the question that had been stuck in my throat since the bus station. He ran his hands through my hair.

"I'm so sorry, baby. I shoulda been stronger for you, for all of you."

Nothing mattered in that moment except that we were together. David and Shaye were both living with Danny in British Columbia now, and I think that affected Marty a great deal. I didn't know what life had been like for him over the last eight years as his marriage imploded and his children scattered to the four winds. But we were here now, and we had to get to the stage.

I can't imagine how Gene's suicide affected Marty, as Christian brothers, but he sat on a stool, eyes full of tears, and sang his heart out. Lennie Gallant, one of PEI's great singer-songwriters, joined us, and we did a medley for Gene. It was epic. Then a choir came onstage and sang "Put Your Hand in the Hand." This brought the house down.

What Gene gave the world as a songwriter was incomparable. What he had given me as a child—food for my family, a chance to sing on his album, the opportunity to witness up close the creation of new music, and now this reunion with my father—made me forever grateful to him. There would be one more precious, musical gift he would give me years later, but that was still a long way off.

With my album made, Mum sober and safe in England, Shaye and David safe with Danny, my little sister Bryde safe with her father, Izzy, and my relationship with Marty repaired, I had a base of solidity that allowed me to take the next step. It was time to hit the road. I had the frame of the puzzle built, and now it was time to fill it in, with any picture I chose.

Back in Vancouver, Terry brought me into Nettwerk for a meeting. In the office was a shiny new guitar for me. I squealed with delight. It was one I had mentioned that I loved, and he remembered. He said he had more surprises.

First, I was going on tour across Canada. I would be hopping on a tour bus with Tom Cochrane, who was doing an acoustic theatre tour. We would start in BC and finish in Toronto. That was the first time I realized people would define "across Canada" as going from the West Coast to the middle. There are five more provinces east of that, but I wasn't going to bring that up then. I was swooning with joy. As my booking agent, the Feldman Agency made all the plans for me on the road in Canada, and they had secured this tour.

Then Terry handed me a box. It was heavy. I opened it, and

there, in neat, shiny little rows, were the spines of the jewel cases of my CD. I pulled one out and looked at it. I gasped as I saw my face on the cover and the Nettwerk label on the back under the song titles. I don't know how long I held it, but I looked up at Terry and I will never, so long as I live, forget the look on his face. He knew what this moment meant to me. It was something he and I would always share, the moment I held my completed first offering. It was like holding my heart in my hands, to be given away a hundred thousand times, without expectation.

Terry said it was time to quit my job, and he would give me a monthly allowance of $1500 to live on so I could tour. This would come from the $25,000 advance from Sony, doled out over time so I wouldn't spend it in one go. He also recommended that I give up my apartment, because he planned to have me on the road from now on. I packed a few boxes of my favourite things to keep and gave away my furniture.

This was it. Untethered, guitar in hand, with a dream team behind me, I was flying.

As I reeled in that highway line toward my first show of the tour, I tuned into Z95 FM. A familiar sound was coming out of the radio—it was ME! I rolled down the windows as "Evidence" blasted from the speakers. I wondered how many other people in that moment were hearing the song. A song about confronting my grandfather. A song for my sister. A song about finding my voice.

> *Can you hear the child in tears*
> *Whose innocence was stolen from her hands*
> *Can you hold her in your arms*
> *And tell her that you'll try to understand*
> *When there's no way in hell you can*
> *Can you hear me, can you hear me now?*

Yes, they could all hear me now.

I walked into the Evergreen Theatre in Powell River, BC, chin up, shoulders back, holding my guitar and a small backpack that held my PJs, two performing outfits, a pair of heels, a pair of boots, tights, makeup, toothpaste and a toothbrush. I was wearing my third outfit, a casual one of denim overalls and a long-sleeved black shirt, which I could wear in interviews. I had also brought my Roland FP-8 keyboard. I was travelling light.

I also had my voice, my songs and a wide-open heart. These were the essential primary colours of me, to be mixed and matched to create anything I wanted. I aspired to make my life a masterpiece.

On the stage stood Tom Cochrane with his guitar, in the midst of a sound check. He saw me come in and waved. I waved back. My insides were churning with excitement—this was the "Life Is a Highway" guy! The song is one of the great Canadian anthems. I didn't know the rest of his catalogue well, but I was to learn what a truly iconic songwriter he is on this tour.

I made myself comfortable in a chair at the back of the theatre as his percussionist and guitar player came onstage and set up.

Oh shit. His guitar player, Bill Bell, was gorgeous. And I don't mean cute or handsome or anything like that. I mean drop-dead, Hugh Grant meets Paul Rudd meets Colin Firth meets Ryan Gosling gorgeous, but a rock star version. He was wearing a light-brown sweater that looked like a furry teddy bear and brown leather pants. He was tall and had dark hair and a huge smile, and then he sat down and played guitar, and from that moment on, I was a goner.

I opened the show that night with a half-hour set and did a pretty good job. I was nervous, but the theatre had great sound and lights, and my voice was in really good shape.

After my set, Tom asked if we could work out some songs that I could sing with him onstage. This was just getting better and better. Also, Bill was smiling at me, and I was melting. On the bus to the next show, we played dice games and worked on songs. These guys loved to drink, but I had brought them a gift from BC: a big bag of mushrooms. Though some of us didn't partake, the bus got really funny after that, and we rolled through the mountains toward Alberta.

Within three shows, I was singing on a bunch of Tom's songs, including "Life Is a Highway." Tom was generous and kind to me, but he was watching Bill closely. By the time we got to Banff, Bill and I were falling for each other. Tom talked to Bill about being careful with me, but the spell was already cast, and I was climbing into Bill's bunk on the bus when the lights would go out. I was falling in love, but Bill wasn't the fall-in-love type. I didn't know this, because he seemed crazy about me. He was thirty-two and I was twenty-three. He was a seasoned road dog, a killer musician and an insatiable lover. We were having an incredible time. I knew he partied a lot—his nickname was Rasputin because he could ingest incredible amounts of intoxicants and survive. Boy, was he fun. In fact, if you asked anyone about Bill, they'd say he was the most fun.

At the next stop, Bill insisted on taking me shopping. My outfits were fine, but he had incredible style. He also taught me the joys of sexy lingerie at that mall. We got my hair cut and coloured at one stop, so I looked less like I had just crawled out of the forest. I bought myself a white silk robe, and it became my uniform the moment I got offstage and onto the bus.

Word was getting back to Nettwerk that I was killing it and transforming along the way. Also, I was losing weight quickly. Sex is excellent cardio.

When we got to Toronto, we played our last show at Massey Hall. When the tour ended, the plan was for me to stay in

Toronto for a while. I had some solo shows lined up, including one at a café called C'est What? I also had an in-store performance at the iconic Sam the Record Man store on Yonge Street. I was staying at the majestic Quality Inn, but Bill and I spent most of our time at his tiny bachelor apartment in the magical kingdom of Parliament Street. When you're in love, everything sparkles.

Bill was clear with his words that he didn't want a serious relationship, but every day, he reached for me, and I knew something in him was melting too. I told him that I loved him, to which he replied, "Thanks. That means so much coming from you."

Ugh. The worst.

I went into the shower and cried, and decided I was not going to put up with that. I had just put my heart out there and I was not disposable. It was time for me to leave. I got out of the shower and was distant and cold.

Bill sat me down and apologized. It was the first time he recognized that I could bail. He asked me to move in. Funny how that works.

I was asked to cover a Bruce Cockburn song called "Pacing the Cage" for a documentary about Bret "The Hitman" Hart, called *Hitman Hart: Wrestling with Shadows*. Bruce contacted me to let me know he loved my version. I was elated. I was flown to Los Angeles to sing a song for a film called *Inventing the Abbotts*. I arrived at the sprawling estate of composer Michael Kamen and sang on a gorgeous song called "On Springfield Mountain." LA blew my mind. Things were rolling.

When I arrived back in Toronto, Bill had cleaned the apartment and was looking at me differently, a little more sparkly. A friend had gifted us some very pure MDMA, which I had never taken. In the late 1990s, before the fentanyl epidemic, MDMA was considered a safe and heart-opening experience. I went into the bedroom and put on a gold gown that I had purchased on the road, thinking I would wear it onstage. What better moment to pull it out? Bill put on "entrance music," and into the living room I walked. He had pushed the couch back to make a dance floor in the centre of the room.

Suddenly, I felt a wave crash over me, and I had to sit down. I guess the drug was kicking in and I was rolling. He sat with me and told me to breathe. Every breath felt like it was opening my body, opening my lungs, my eyes, my heart. I looked up at him and he was looking at me with more love than I'd ever seen in my life. I stood, shakily at first, on my gold heels, and he took me in his arms and we danced slowly. He was the DJ all night, and we danced to Al Green, Stevie Wonder, Aretha Franklin, Led Zeppelin, Rickie Lee Jones, Sheryl Crow, Ben Harper, Shawn Colvin and James Taylor. He made sure I had water, and we laughed until our cheeks hurt. It was like our wedding. We watched the sun come up.

A few weeks later, at our friends Allan Reid and Kim Stockwood's house, he asked me to marry him.

Of course, I said yes with all my heart.

Kim, a singer-songwriter, had just had a big hit with a song called "Jerk." Allan was a music executive at PolyGram and was the guy who signed Jann Arden to her deal. One day, Allan and I were walking down the street to go to a shop, and he said to me, "You know, you're the real deal. I love everything about you and your music. Sky's the limit for you." That meant everything.

I didn't think life could get better, but it did. Every day, more and more beauty presented itself. Who was I? I was pure delight, dancing in love through the slushy, grey streets of Toronto.

A new tour came down the pipe. I was asked to open for Ashley MacIsaac, an East Coast fiddler who'd been breaking into the United States. He had performed in a kilt on Conan O'Brien's show and did a dance move that exposed his twig and berries. Needless to say, his shows were sold out all over North America, and I was going with him. He had a song that included a Gaelic part, and so the original singer of the piece, Mary Jane Lamond, taught me how to pronounce the words phonetically over brunch. The song, "Sleepy Maggie," is an epic hybrid of music genres and was a blast to sing.

Some of us may have taken a bunch of mushrooms with the band in Cincinnati and been rescued by police from a dangerous neighbourhood, but I will neither confirm nor deny that story.

Since Bill had decided to come with me on tour, my stage show went next level. We started out in Seattle. It was the beginning of our deep, musical love story, and the start of a new phase of my life. It was like whitewater rafting through beautiful scenery, sometimes dangerous, always exhilarating. With my little CD in hand to sell at the shows, I started to learn what it took to be a touring artist. Every day, I did press and sang, sometimes two or three performances. We were on the move, and we were crazy about each other.

I got an agent in the US named Marty Diamond. I wondered if we were related in some way, as the name Diamond goes back through my maternal line and from what I understand is also Jewish. He had a company called Little Big Man, because of his diminutive stature and his giant heart. At least, I assume it was in reference to his heart. Due to his huge success in the US, I had a constant opening spot for almost anyone Canadian who was on the road in America. It started with Ashley MacIsaac and Ron Sexsmith and, eventually, the Barenaked Ladies. We followed their bus in a rental car and opened for them in fantastic venues. They were hitting huge, and it was wonderful to witness. They were unbelievably brilliant and hilarious, and made me feel like a little sister they were taking care of. I definitely had innocent crushes on all of them at one point. They were the ultimate nerdy, cool, sexy men. I felt so lucky. Sometimes, they'd play my songs in their sound check and make me laugh.

One time during a show, one of the drunk college boys yelled out, "Show me your tits!" I was shocked. When I came offstage, Steven Page saw how shaken I was. He joked that he got asked that all the time. He said that I needed to be ready the next time someone yelled out something offensive. "What's that? Play you my hits?" He came up with that, and I was able to use it multiple times in my career. Disarm them with humour. Don't let one asshole ruin the show.

Once, I did show my boobs from the stage on Vancouver Pride Day, but they were painted over with a rainbow. I'll never forget the show producer's face as I came offstage. She said, "Well, that was a great set!"

I had the opportunity to go home to PEI on tour to play at a little club called Myron's. Whenever I was in PEI, I'd always have a tweak of fear that the arsonist was going to show up. As I was making my way through the crowd to go onstage, I saw a familiar face in the audience. It took me a moment to place her. She was older, but the eyes were the same, beaming with love. It was Mrs. Morrison, my Grade 5 teacher. I stopped and gave her a huge hug. She looked me in the eyes and said, "I heard your song 'Evidence.' I remember. Just look at you now." Nothing could have prepared me for the feelings that went through me. My heart in my throat, I went onto the stage and sang like I never have.

After the show, on my way out, another woman stopped me. She was an old junior high school friend named Jeanna. She said, "Hi, Tara. I just wanted to let you know how proud we all are of you." She motioned behind her to a group of beautiful women standing at the bar, all smiling at me. Among them, one of the bullies who made my life a living hell in Grade 7. I smiled back and waved. I didn't go over, but it occurred to me that the best way to overcome something like that is to go on and have a wonderful life. In that moment, I was grateful to her, because without that experience, I wouldn't have had that time of solitude at home when I read and wrote and became who I am. She was part of me, part of my songs, part of my strength. She was, in fact, also my teacher.

I walked out into the cool evening air feeling a little in shock but changed forever. There was nothing to fear anymore in my hometown. There was as much love here as anything else, and from that moment on, I knew where I belonged. I knew that one day, I would come home to stay.

I loved life in hotels. I never had to cook, or make a bed, or clean a toilet. Every morning, the tour manager for whoever I was opening for would put a sheet of paper under my door with the schedule for that day. Appearing on morning television meant being at a studio at 5:00 a.m. Fortunately, they would do my hair and makeup. Then lunch radio, a meet-and-greet, the sound check at the venue, dinner, the show, bed or onto the bus to the next destination. It was constant.

My fan base was growing, and I would spend time with them after my performances, as they bought CDs from me. I signed thousands of them. I began to notice that some fans were travelling city to city to see Bill and me. The show was deepening, and our onstage banter was funny. He was a one-man orchestra with his guitar pedals. He gave my songs an atmosphere—emotive, ethereal, epic, industrial—that solidified my sound. I was finding my edge. It didn't come from fury; it came from all the ledges I'd stood on. It came from my scars.

In addition to singing songs from my album, we would play cover songs, like "Unloved" by Jann Arden and Jackson

Browne, "Dimming of the Day" by Richard Thompson, "The Maker" by Daniel Lanois and "Set the Prairie on Fire" by Shawn Colvin. We rarely had to do more than a half-hour set if we were opening, and seventy-five minutes if we were headlining.

Sometimes, if people couldn't afford my CD, I would just give it to them and say to find me the next time I was in town. They always did. It was more important that they had the music than for me to have the ten dollars.

Terry brought us back to Canada for a few shows, and sure enough, because we were having success in the United States, I was getting attention in Canada. It was called the "Alanis effect." I was scheduled to open for Jann Arden in Victoria, BC, at the Waterfront, and I was unbelievably nervous. No matter how many famous people I had met up to that point, when you're meeting someone who has had such a profound effect on you, it's different. After my set, she came up to me. When Jann Arden looked in my eyes, I thought I was going to die of bliss. She's gorgeous. She smiled at me and told me it was a great performance. I thanked her, and then she looked out over the harbour at the crowd and said, "They loved you. I don't usually feel jealous when I hear a singer, but you made me a little jealous."

I died.

It still kills me when I think of those words. She probably didn't realize it, but my knees were shaking as she stood with me. I loved her voice and songs more than I could ever express. What she let me know in that moment was that I'd made an impression, and I had an ally and a sister in song. She remains incredibly dear to me as she keeps breaking boundaries and paving the way for others like me. She's also the funniest person I've ever met, no contest.

When my dad Marty heard that a song I'd sung was in a movie, he walked through the Connecticut snow in his deck shoes and spent his last dollars to see the film. He called me and told me how proud he was.

The iconic Canadian band Blue Rodeo invited me to sing at an annual show they did with friends in Toronto. Bill and I went to a rehearsal and decided we would do "Dimming of the Day," a song I loved so much. I was pinching myself that I was getting to be part of this show. On the day of the performance, I was backstage with some of the heaviest musical cats in the country, watching the performances. They were electric!

When it was my turn, my heart started to pound. I was wearing a sparkly baby-blue top and long black skirt. I walked onto the stage, and they began to play the song, but it was so slow—a lot slower than Bill and I ever did it. I looked at Bill, who looked at me nervously because he wasn't in charge of setting the tempo. I could sing a ballad, but this? I started to panic but then realized the only choice I had was to lean into it and see what I could do inside the space. I had to trust them.

It took me milliseconds to realize that the sound of the band around me was the best I'd ever sung with. It was a truly transcendent experience. They knew exactly what the song needed and didn't rush a moment. Nothing was missing. I fell onto the magic carpet of music beneath me and let it take me somewhere I'd never been. When the song was over, I opened my eyes, and the band was looking at me with huge smiles. The audience leapt to their feet. As I walked off the stage, Molly Johnson, a singer I admire and respect greatly, put her arms tightly around me and said, "Wow. That was incredible." Behind us, I heard someone say, "I didn't know she could do that." I think that was the moment I gained the respect of the Canadian music community and, true to form, developed a crush on every member of Blue Rodeo.

We headed back down to the States and kept hitting certain cities, noticing that the radio stations were becoming more familiar with us and were playing the single from the album, "Evidence." We went to Chicago, Boston, Detroit, New York, San Diego, Atlanta, Austin, LA, around and around the country for a full year and a half without stopping. It was a carousel of stages, lights and faces.

Terry built a brilliant team around me, which included a meticulous day-to-day manager named Dave Holmes and a savvy New Yorker named Marc Alghini, who worked radio. Marc, Dave, Bill and I watched the sun come up over New York City from Marc's rooftop a few times, smoking cigars, drinking expensive red wine and listening to the best music ever made in the history of the world.

Bill always drove, I'd read the paper map, and we never missed a show. This was before GPS. We didn't have a cellphone yet. We were building something and having the time of our lives. We toured with Lisa Loeb, Paula Cole and Chantal Kreviazuk, Dar Williams and so many other artists, all over the United States. For the first time, internet fan groups were appearing and supporting artists on the US touring circuit.

Sometimes, we would stay in one town for three shows. Terry called this a residency tour, and the venues would seat anywhere from 50 to 150 people max. There would hardly be anyone at the first show, except maybe a local journalist and a few people who had accidentally shown up. The next day, we would do radio interviews, word would spread, and the venue would be full that night. On the third night, there would be a lineup outside the venue. It was the best strategy to get people to know us and fall in love with the music. It also gave us a few days off from driving and let us explore the towns.

We did a radio show in Boston during one of those tours, at a station called WBCN. A host named Oedipus had us on his program, and I sang in the studio. When I finished, he said in his caramel voice, "Well, it doesn't get better than that."

He came to the show that night and helped me carry my guitar to the car when we were done. Marc was flipping out and explained to me that Oedipus was a legend in radio in the States and didn't react like this to many acts. The next thing we knew, Oedipus was inviting us to play in massive shows that he was organizing in Boston, opening for bands like Garbage, Hole and The Cure.

Even though Terry thought these bands' audiences would tear me apart—especially The Cure's—we played our hearts out and won them over. Marc, Dave and Oedipus would be smiling in the wings.

The thing about music genres is that they are semantic divisions created to separate music into understandable boxes so people can sell it. They are quite necessary in the marketing of the work. Pairing my sweet folky songs with an alternative rock band shouldn't have worked, but a song that reaches into the core is destined to release something. Whether we are screaming it or singing it softly with a banjo or a fender or a cello, with a stack of amps or acoustic or with one little microphone, if a song opens you, touches you, moves you, then it belongs to you, and you belong to the song. All division is meaningless. This is the great medicine of music and why it is the universal language. This is also why Robert Plant and Alison Krauss can make one of the greatest-ever records together. Chocolate and peanut butter.

Robert Smith, the lead singer of The Cure, waited in the wings after I played to tell me that he loved my set, and then he told me some touring stories. My life was complete.

To increase my exposure, Terry and Dave would book me to play for the magazine or radio staff during their lunch hour or breaks. Some of those situations were painfully awkward, but it was all about making people aware that I existed. If a bigger act of Terry's was going to be on air, I would ride their coattails into the station. Terry would use his successful acts to pull favours for his new acts. The strategy was to win these people over so that the next time I came through town, they would put me on the air. He said I was my own best ambassador and had a way of making people want to support me. Sometimes, people would walk into the lunchroom, grab a slice of pizza and walk out while I was singing. Bill was beside me for every single one of those moments and made it possible to laugh about it later.

Then we hit gold.

I was singing in yet another magazine office, where the people seemed nice, though a little indifferent to the imposition of having a live performance in the middle of their workday. I was good with it because I was on my way to South by Southwest (SXSW), which is a very important and essential conference in Austin, Texas. Music industry folks attend and are genuinely looking for acts to sign. I had a record deal in Canada already, but from what I understood from Terry, we wanted a major label deal for my next record. Nettwerk had opened offices in LA and New York, and I would get their support to start, but Terry's dreams for me were global, and for that we needed huge money.

Hits magazine, whose lunchroom I had just sang in, wrote one sentence in their next issue that would change my life. It was something like, "Biggest Buzz at SXSW, Tara MacLean."

I had a fifteen-minute set in Austin, and you couldn't move in the room. A&R folks from all over the country squeezed in with their cellphones in the air, record-company presidents on the other end of the line. Terry and Dave had done everything right to position me as an up-and-coming star in the United States.

In Canada, my first single, "Evidence," won the Canadian Radio Music Award. The video was in regular rotation on MuchMusic. Terry was still using the "Alanis effect" in Canada. He would bring me home for specific shows and then send me right back to the States. I did dozens of photo shoots and had enough stage clothes to fill two giant suitcases that unfolded into a dresser. The strategy seemed to be working.

I absolutely adored all the American Nettwerk people who were working to help me build up to this moment. I became friends with many of them, and it felt like we were creating something magical. Offers poured in for record deals.

Then I fucked up. In life, there are things we can look back on that make us cringe, things we desperately wish we could undo but have to live with the rest of our lives. This was one of them, and I had no idea I did it.

In a TV interview at SXSW, I was asked a question: "Why would a signed artist like you need to perform at this conference?" I replied that I didn't have a deal in the US, and that I was hoping for a major label release for my next album.

To be fair to myself, that was my understanding of the situation. However, the US Nettwerk people didn't see it that way at all. I don't know if it was a miscommunication from management about my trajectory or if no one had told the US branch of the company that this was the strategy, but they all thought I was saying that they weren't my label in the United States.

After that, when I went to the US Nettwerk offices, I'd get the cold shoulder. I didn't understand how I had gone from being their darling to being treated like they couldn't care less if I was there. I didn't know what I had done. No one told me.

I still think about what I could have said in that interview that would have made it okay, that would have been true and honoured Nettwerk US while simultaneously letting the music world know that I needed a deal. I chalk it up to my own limited understanding of how it was all working. I was so busy driving to venues, singing and doing interviews that I didn't talk to Terry about what I should say, and that was irresponsible. I hurt people. For that, I will always be sorry.

That experience made me realize that as things were moving up, other things were falling apart. There was an imbalance happening. Some of my early fans would be angry if they couldn't get into a show because it was sold out. I was starting to become exhausted, overexposed. Before we made any decisions on the major deal, I asked Terry to bring me back to Canada for a break.

During this "break," Bill and I moved from Toronto to Vancouver (where Shaye was now living), into a sweet little apartment on West 4th Avenue. It had two levels and balconies that looked over the city and into the mountains. The sunsets were epic, and I felt like I could rest there. Terry booked me some low-key Vancouver shows, and it felt great to play around town. I went into the huge new Nettwerk office and saw a poster of myself on the wall. It made me so happy. The management company was at the back of the office, and the label was at the front, and it was always filled with exciting energy. Lilith Fair, the first female-only festival of its kind, was in the process of touring, and I learned that I was going to be part of it.

As I walked by the office of George Maniatis, vice-president of A&R at the time, he asked me to come in and sit down. He was a straight shooter from New York, and we'd become friends. He asked if I had said in an interview that I didn't have a US label. I wracked my brain and realized that yes, I had said it in Austin. I told him that it had been my understanding at the time, and he let me know that it hadn't gone over well and that everyone was mad at me.

Seriously? Fuck. I felt awful. No one asked me why I said it. No one except George had the guts to tell me I'd fucked up and why. When I told him where I was coming from, he totally got it. I didn't see Nettwerk US as my label because I was told we were looking for one. It was too late to repair my relationship with them, though I did try to contact the people I really loved there to explain, but they had moved on to supporting their other artists.

I've since learned that in every aspect of life, there will be people who have your back and people who will shoot you in it the moment you turn around. It's important to find the ones who've got you, and as for the others, don't take it personally. Back then, I didn't have the wisdom to understand this. I just figured that if I was kind, everyone would love me. I so badly wanted everyone to love me. What an impossible and exhausting mission that was.

After this incident, it occurred to me that Terry and I never had meetings. I was just obeying the schedule that was put underneath my door without question, week after week, month after month, year after year. I didn't have the time or energy to even wonder if what was happening was the right thing. I wasn't checking in with my gut. I'd lost my centre.

Then we got a call.

A TV show in LA was looking to cast a singer. The auditions were happening at the same time as I had a performance booked at the Troubadour in West Hollywood. The TV show was called Fame L.A. and was an effort to recreate the show Fame from the 1980s. I had watched every episode of that show when I was a kid, of course, and was a diehard Irene Cara (Coco) fan.

Jane Jenkins, one of Hollywood's most famous casting agents (The Outsiders, The Princess Bride, Home Alone), was casting the show. She had two assistants, Anya, who was working the camera, and Amy, who was reading lines with me. I sang "That's Me," and then read the script. When we were finished, Jane told me that I would be moving on to the next part of the audition. She asked if I was playing in town. I put them all on the guest list.

It was an epic night at the Troubadour, and seeing Jane, Amy and Anya in the crowd made my heart leap out of my chest. It was the beginning of Amy and Anya becoming two of my best friends in the world. Meeting the legendary Jane Jenkins and getting to sing for her remains one of the great moments of my career.

In the end, I didn't get the part. They went with a woman who was a stronger actor, which made sense. Jane had chosen me and had even put me in some acting classes to strengthen my chances, but the producers wanted someone else, and when I saw their pick, I thought they had chosen well. It was such a great Hollywood experience. They all made me feel special every step of the way, and I fell in love with California.

Meanwhile, Terry and Dave were busy working on the offers that had come in from SXSW. We'd had an early offer from Arista Austin, by one of Terry's good friends, Steve Schnur, but Terry was looking for something bigger. They wanted to set up two more showcases for me, one in LA and one in New York.

The first showcase was in LA, at Luna Park, in 1998. The higher the stakes, the worse my nerves were. I thought I might throw up. Many heavy hitters in the West Coast music scene were in the audience with offers ready to go.

From the beginning, Terry had trained me to be able to hold my own anywhere, any time. It had all been leading up to this—all the humiliatingly awkward performances where almost no one cared that I was there, all the conventions and corners of restaurants, all the sitting on desks and pouring my heart out under fluorescent lights, all the songs sung to me by my father in the cabin, all the courage I'd ever had to muster in my life, all the heartache. It was all for this. It felt like the most important night of my life—no presh.

The venue was dark and intimate, with great sound and a killer bar. It had two stages, one in the basement for a smaller audience, which I had already played a dozen times, and the bigger listening room upstairs, which had a more sophisticated vibe. I had graduated to the big space and was standing in my dressing room, trying not to panic. No amount of experience could have prepared me for the nerves I was experiencing in that moment. I had never had stage fright—what was happening? I was twenty-five years old and had been on the road for two years now. I had dreamed of and worked for this moment all my life. Was I going to blow it?

Terry was in the audience, calmly and confidently making sure everyone had a drink and telling them about my tours and the radio headway we were making. Amy was there too. She'd come to every LA performance since the Troubadour, and I could always spot her in the audience. I knew I would have someone to focus on who would ground me.

Dave burst into the dressing room with a huge, nervous smile. "Oh my God, you won't believe who's in the audience! There are PRESIDENTS of major labels out there . . ." Then he stopped when he saw my face.

How could he know I was freaking out? I never freaked out. He was freaking out too. He was as invested in this night as all of us. Bill gave him a look, and Dave came up to me, put his hands on my shoulders and looked me in the eyes. We took a deep breath together, and he said sweetly, "You look beautiful. They're going to love you . . . and this is your five-minute call." With a reassuring smile, he left the room.

I felt better but still nowhere near ready to go onstage. I put my trembling hands on the table in front of the mirror to steady myself, closed my eyes and suddenly remembered what Baba Hari Dass had written to me on that piece of paper: *No expectations.*

That's what was going wrong right now, I realized. My expectations. Not only mine, but my whole team's. I wanted to make them proud, but I had to drop those expectations and go back to the beginning. Why was I doing this?

I saw myself as a young girl at a country fair back home, singing for the farmers and fishermen on a plywood stage that sunny summer's day. I sing because that's what I am. A bird.

I came back to myself in the dressing room. I thought about how all of those powerful record executives in the audience were just people who wanted to be moved. I knew how to move them. I didn't need anything from anyone. If they didn't like me, I would still get to keep singing. I could do this.

Then I called on the Glamour Spell. I could tremble on the inside, but on the outside, I was something else. I embodied the knowledge that I had something to give them that no one else could: myself.

Centred, I stopped shaking and walked onto the stage. The lights hit me and everything I knew about opening came to me. I raised my hands to the light and lost myself in the music. I became the music and gave myself completely.

That night, after the show, after shaking hands and chatting with music executives, Dave, Terry, Bill and I got on the red-eye to New York. I had a photo shoot for *Vogue* magazine with Ellen von Unwerth. It was for a Levi's ad in support of Lilith Fair.

In New York, we got in a limo at the airport, dropped Bill at the hotel to sleep and went straight to the photo shoot. I was dead to the world in the makeup chair. I explained to the makeup artists that I'd been on an overnight flight and had gotten little sleep. They looked at each other and spoke like I wasn't there.

"What are we going to do with these cheeks?" one said matter-of-factly, like they weren't used to putting makeup on anyone who wasn't super skinny.

"I don't know. We have our work cut out this morning."

They laughed, not cruelly, but like it was normal to complain about people who didn't fit their beauty standard. I guess I wasn't human to them, not a person with feelings. Do models have to deal with this? I had just had one of the most successful nights of my life, but to be treated this way, and to be exhausted, gutted me. I held back tears and told myself I belonged there, that these people had a limited view of beauty. As they tried their best to contour the roundness from my tired face, I looked at myself in the mirror. The spectre of my grandmother stood behind me, telling me they were right, telling me I was failing her, failing everyone.

I put on a pair of black Levi's and a tank top and began the solo part of my shoot. The photographer looked at me and smiled. She said in an elegant German accent, "You remind me of a cat. I want that jacket on you." She pointed to a gorgeous animal print, and a stylist put it on me. I don't know if she really thought I had a feline quality to me or if it was her kinder way of covering up my body, which was clearly causing problems for their team.

From the photo shoot, the limo took Terry and me to the Sony Music Entertainment offices. We were meeting with Patrick, who had scouted me, and a cute A&R guy whose name I can't remember because I was so tired and distracted by his sexy smile. Terry, also tired, seemed nonplussed by the situation. As the Sony rep talked about the offer, he said he'd love to pair me with T Bone Burnett to produce my album. Well, that got my attention. I looked over at Terry, but he still seemed unimpressed. Sony praised Terry's success with his other bands and laid out how much they wanted to sign me. They weren't even going to give a number at the meeting because we could write our own deal.

As we left, Terry said, "Well, that was nice of them to offer, but I know who I want you to sign with. After your showcase tonight, you're going to meet him in Chicago. I want to know what you think. You met him in LA, Roy Lott. He's our guy, I know it."

So, he had already made up his mind before we went to Sony. No wonder he seemed inconvenienced by the meeting. I felt bad that Sony had gone to all the trouble, especially Patrick, who had flown around following my shows for months. I've often wondered how my life would have been different had I signed with them and moved to New York.

I went back to the hotel to try to get some sleep before the big New York showcase. It seemed like a waste of time if Terry had made up his mind, but I was excited to play in New York. We'd opened for people at The Mercury Room, Arlene's Grocery, the Bowery Ballroom and Irving Plaza.

That night, we played in the back room of a store that was set up and decorated beautifully. It's a bit of a blur because we were still so tired. Someone took our gear to the hotel after, and Bill and I decided to walk back. My feet hurt from the heels I was wearing, so Bill put me on his back and carried me home. We laughed the whole way, high from the crazy, fast-moving river we were on. The path shimmered in the New York night from lights that never go out. That's how I felt that night: inextinguishable.

The next day, we flew to Chicago to meet Roy Lott.

We went for dinner at my favourite restaurant, Nick's Fishmarket, and not one, but two bottles of our favourite wine, Opus One, hit the table. It was just Roy, Bill and me, and by the end of dinner, I understood why Terry loved him. He was a businessman for sure, but also a true music lover. He looked me right in the eyes when he spoke, which is my favourite thing. Roy was about to be president at Capitol Records, but he asked me if I was interested in signing with Virgin, which is under the umbrella of EMI. I remembered that Richard Branson was lovely and laughed to myself about his slightly meagre tip at the Queen's Club when I was a bartender. I drunkenly said, "No, let's go with Capitol."

Roy said, "We don't want to sign you for one album. You're a career artist. We want to keep making records with you." Then he regaled us with inside stories of Whitney Houston recording "I Will Always Love You." Well, that did it. By the end of the second bottle of wine, Bill was excited to move to LA, Roy was our new bestie, and I had shaken hands on a record deal with a major label.

Later that night, I sat looking out at the moon over the water from my beautiful hotel room. I could see my reflection in the window. My white silk robe was wrapped around me and the world was at my feet. My beautiful man lay in bed waiting for me. I was wide awake. I was rising, from a plywood stage to the top of the Capitol building.

What would I say to that young woman if I could go back and sit with her now? At first, nothing. I'd let her bask in it, just as she was, excited, naive, filled with dreams.

Then I'd tell her to remember to lean over the side of the life raft of songs and see herself reflected in the river, so she wouldn't forget who she really was—not the image looking back, but the depths of the water beneath.

Nothing can prepare you for the star-making machine.

17.

Shells

When the words come, they are merely empty shells
without the music. They live as they are sung,
for the words are the body and the music the spirit.
—HILDEGARD OF BINGEN

Bill and I moved into a very California apartment in Hollywood, near The Original Farmers Market. It was on Genesee Avenue, on the second floor. I loved that: Genesis. The beginning.

There were giant arched windows everywhere, a little balcony, and so much light pouring in all the time. I tried to grow things on the balcony, but they just dried up and died. Living in California was like nothing I'd ever experienced. Bill bloomed in the LA weather. He loved to be hot, but I preferred it when evening fell. We decorated our place in light desert colours—a white bedspread, a sage couch, white curtains, Dijon walls.

We gave ourselves a flower budget for fresh bouquets, and not a day went by when Stargazer or Casa Blanca lilies weren't the first things I saw when I opened my eyes in the morning. Fluffy peonies, tulips, daisies, ranunculus or sprigs of eucalyptus on the kitchen table made everything feel alive. I was reminded of when I'd gather wildflowers for the kitchen table at the cabin when I was little. Instead of being in the woods of Cardigan, I was in the wilds of Melrose Avenue.

Our group of friends was diverse and creative, and included a lot of actors and musicians. If they weren't people who performed onstage, they were producing, casting or writing. We had parties that are still legendary. We had a whole tickle trunk of costumes, a group of exquisite humans and some really great MDMA. We also had money because we were touring constantly, and Bill was getting paid. I still had my allowance. We were living the life.

We decided to get married. With fifty of our closest friends and family, Bill and I wed on Salt Spring Island. Mum couldn't come, but Shaye was there as my maid of honour to represent the family. She thanked me for being her voice when she needed me. We were all crying our eyes out. I felt loved and safe and like nothing could ever bring me down.

We went back to LA to prepare for the Lilith Fair tour. Nettwerk had given Shaye a job on the festival, and we were going to run into her all over the country. Lilith Fair was sold out everywhere, and included Tracy Chapman, Sinead O'Connor, Erykah Badu, Missy Elliott, the Indigo Girls, Sheryl Crow, Emmylou Harris, The Pretenders, Stevie Nicks, Beth Orton, the Dixie Chicks, Shawn Colvin. All these ladies were on the "A" stage. I was a "B" stage artist, so I played in the late afternoon. New artists were on the "C" stage in the Lilith Village earlier in the day. I met incredible musicians from all over the world. We shared dressing rooms, touring war stories, and our absolute awe of being a part of Lilith. Sarah McLachlan headlined every night, and during the day, she personally welcomed arriving artists with gifts and hugs. She was teaching us that there was room for all of us in this business. At the time, women were under-represented on radio and in festivals, so Sarah was making a massive and successful statement.

As I stood in the wings during one of Sarah's performances, I realized that Stevie Nicks was standing in front of me. This woman's voice and songs were part of the scaffolding of my own work and emotional landscape. I leaned in, as if by some strange instinct, to smell her hair, which in hindsight is super creepy. However, she must have felt me, because she turned around with a big smile on her face. Busted, I laughed. She put out her hand and shook mine, looking in my eyes as I gushingly thanked her. I don't remember what I said, but I recall that her hands were soft, that I was in the presence of greatness, and that she smelled really good.

At the end of every show was a big finale number. Sarah would invite all the artists from every stage to join in, and we would sing "What's Going On" by Marvin Gaye or "Rockin' in the Free World" by Neil Young. I got to share a mic with some of the greatest musicians in the world. The Indigo Girls, Sarah and Jewel did a version of "The Water Is Wide," an old folk song. It was pure magic. In different cities, Sarah and the Indigo Girls would ask different "A" stage artists to join them.

One day, Sarah knocked on my dressing room door. We were in San Diego, one of the cities where I had a strong following. She asked if I would be interested in singing "The Water Is Wide" with her and the Indigo Girls that night. I could have died right there from elation. I think I was cool about it on the outside. Sarah wrote the words down for me in her beautiful handwriting, and I practised all afternoon.

That night, I stood trembling in the wings. Shaye had come to be there with me. So had Terry, his wife, Cathy, and Bill. Shaye noticed my energy and pulled me aside, took both my hands and looked into my eyes. She said, "Ta, there is no past. There is no future. There is only this moment, and you are one of the great ones." I stopped shaking and walked onstage.

The sound of twenty thousand people screaming love at you is like no other sound. I thought I'd heard everything there was to hear in the world, but being onstage with that outpouring of love focused toward us blew my chest apart, and my heart was right there, wide open, like in pictures of the Sacred Heart of Jesus, or of Hanuman the monkey god.

The Indigo Girls' guitars started to play. I opened my mouth and harmonies came out. I had my own verse, and I gave it everything I had. Everyone applauded after I'd finished, and then Sarah had her verse. The audience screamed over her first words and then settled in to listen. At the end of the song, the sound was deafening. Sarah and the Indigo Girls looked over at me and smiled. As I walked offstage, my people wrapped their arms around me. Terry was beaming, and Shaye had tears streaming down her face. I looked at Cathy. Had she and Tonni not been on the ferry that day, none of this would have been happening. Sarah walked by and gave me a squeeze. That moment was the greatest musical moment of my life, and it has never been surpassed. It's always with me.

While on the road, Bill had begun learning how to record music using our laptop, and on rare days off, we would write songs together. We had collected some beautiful music over the years, and now it was time to make another record. Magically, Capitol Records had hired Steve Schnur, the A&R guy from Arista Austin. What a team I had! Even though Capitol was my label, I had the dream situation of still having Nett-werk involved at a creative level.

With our new collection of raw demos, we looked for different producers. I had access to anyone I wanted, though I was told Daniel Lanois was not available, and they didn't even want to ask him. I may have sulked a little about that. John Leventhal was up there for me, because he had produced *A Few Small Repairs* by Shawn Colvin, which was a Grammy-winning masterpiece. We went to New York and did two "demos" at The Hit Factory, but it wasn't the right fit—not because he wasn't a genius, but something wasn't gelling. What a sweetheart, though. We spent a ton of money on that experiment.

Then we went to Nashville to work with Jay Joyce, one of my favourite producers and people. He had produced a brilliant album with Patty Griffin, who is one of the great singer-songwriters of our time. I was feeling under pressure to make a great record, and I think I screwed up by being too picky. He was willing to do half the record, but I wanted to work with someone who would do the whole thing. I wish I could have just relaxed and realized at the time that Jay was the right guy, but I kept thinking, *This is my shot. This is my major label debut.*

At the time I'd made my first album, I could have counted my live performances on one hand. I was sensitive, inexperienced, naive, singing songs I'd written as a teenager. Now, I was a seasoned performer with hundreds of shows under my belt. I was confident I could make a strong record, and I loved the material we were working with. There was a maturity to the poetry, and it was less about my own heartbreak and more about the world around me. I had blossomed, but now there was more pressure. Expectation had crept back in like a pernicious weed.

Off we went to New Orleans to work with Malcolm Burn. I was a huge fan of his previous work, especially Chris Whitley's

Living with the Law—a very sexy record. Malcolm was a Daniel Lanois protegé and had a set-up in New Orleans like Daniel had, everyone recording together in one huge space. What I didn't know was that Malcolm had just quit drinking, and he was edgy as fuck. Between me feeling stressed about making a great record and his prickly demeanour, we were oil and water. Then his girlfriend flew in and they broke up in the middle of making my record. That just made everything a million times worse. Bill helped a lot, but we felt heavy. We drank a lot at the end of the long days, and I was hating every minute. I would get to the studio already armoured up and ready to fight him on everything.

He hired and fired engineers and brought in amazing musicians from all over the world, who played cool instruments. Sometimes, he didn't show up, so Bill would run a morning session. At the time, I was so focused on my need to create something beautiful that I didn't really understand what Malcolm was dealing with. I had my own demons and had found a way to dance with them. I was impatient with his process and began to see him as an impediment to me making the record of my dreams. It was all messed up. Bill and I were exhausted, depressed and hungover most of the time.

Mark Jowett came down to check on me. We went out for dinner, just the two of us. I asked him why it was so hard for me and so easy for Sarah to make great records. Was it because I sucked? Why was I failing?

Mark looked at me for a moment and said, "Oh, Tara. You can't imagine what other people go through making records. None of Sarah's albums were easy. She had different obstacles than you, but making something great often means you encounter adversity. Not always, but sometimes it's even necessary to make great art."

Here he was, assuring me again. At least he didn't have to

run after me down the streets. Maybe I was evolving a little, sitting there bawling into my jambalaya. Bless Mark Jowett.

We headed to Bearsville, New York, to record strings and piano at a stunning old church. It was a magical experience. I realized that, for all the challenges we'd had, the album was turning out beautifully. Veda Hille came down to add some piano, and we added bansuri flute to a song. Mark was there too. Bill and I were in better shape after a short and healing detour to a Florida beach. Malcolm seemed better too, removed from New Orleans and having had a break. There was a ladybug infestation in the studio, but it felt like a blessing. When all was recorded, we flew to LA to mix.

Steve Schnur had us mix the album at Ocean Way studio with the famous Jack Joseph Puig (U2, No Doubt). If you had three names in Los Angeles, you were extra cool and were often referred to by your initials. JJP and I got along great and the vibe was super fun. It cost ten thousand US dollars per song to mix.

One night, Paul McCartney was having a CD release party, and we were invited into the VIP balcony. Bill ended up chatting with Brian Wilson, while I hung out with Gwen Stefani and talked about No Doubt's new album. She is even more beautiful in person. Roy Lott came over and offered to introduce me to Paul. He grabbed my hand and led me through the crowd, but we just missed him. He'd left minutes before. Roy was apologetic, but I just laughed and said, "Are you kidding? I'm having the best life thanks to you."

Back in the studio, we hit a bit of a wall with one song, "If I Fall." We kept trying different ways to mix it, but it wasn't working. I wasn't worried; I knew we would have a breakthrough soon. Adversity is okay. We were expecting Steve Schnur to arrive soon with a giant feed of sushi, and my girlfriends Amy and Merrin would be joining us. Just then, Roy

Lott called to check in. I let him know that we were struggling a little but that I was happy with the record.

When I walked into the control room, Jack lashed out at me. "YOU NEVER TELL THEM YOU'RE HAVING A HARD TIME!" he yelled. "As far as they are concerned, everything is great."

I guess Jack had heard my call.

"But . . . but Roy is my friend," I said. "He knows about this process. I was just—"

"No! You never let them into this process!"

I was gobsmacked. All the stress of the month with Malcolm and the times I'd had to fight came crashing through. I ran into the bathroom and locked the door. I started to cry. I knew I just needed to let this all out, but something was wrong: it wasn't stopping this time. I could hardly breathe. Bill was knocking on the door. My phone rang, and it was my girlfriends telling me they'd arrived and were in the parking lot. I asked them to wait in the car, that I'd be right there.

I opened the bathroom door and ran by everyone and out the door. I got into the car with my friends. They sat quietly as I sobbed. I said, "I can't take the pressure. I can't take all these men telling me I'm doing it wrong. I can't handle this." They were so supportive and understanding, each holding one of my hands.

Then Steve came up to the car with sushi. We rolled down the window and he passed it in. He looked at me with so much love. I smiled through my tears. I don't know what I would have done without him then. There are so many different kinds of people in the world. There are those who will lift you, and those who want to use you to lift them. Steve is a lifter. Always has been and always will be.

Jack apologized and all was forgiven. I didn't understand the pressure on him. Everyone was watching this record. The expectations were through the roof—poisonous, choking, fear-inducing expectations.

Years later, Malcolm called to apologize and acknowledged the work Bill had done on the album. It was a healing I needed, and I'm grateful that Malcolm reached out. It's never too late to make things right. And truthfully, I love the record. It's full of tears, fury, fight, beauty and grit.

I also ran into Norm Kerner, my first producer from San Francisco, years down the road, and I was happy to see him so well. We had both grown and come so far. Creating something together is an intensely intimate experience that brings up a lot. Seeing him again, I felt a deep fondness for him.

On the last day of mixing *Passenger,* another Canadian band came through the doors to start mixing at Ocean Way: Great Big Sea, from Newfoundland. Alan Doyle looked perfectly East Coast Canadian with his friendly grin, and said, with a thick accent, "Well, look at us here in this fancy place! Loves it!" He gave me a bear hug. We were taking over.

Next, I needed photos for my album. I did a fancy photo shoot swimming naked in water, trying to capture some kind of image of me in my natural habitat. I floated, trusting the river, and lay in flower beds, trying to be earthy, elegant, open. At first, I was self-conscious about the scars on my breasts, but they had faded. It felt free to reveal myself in this way, like I was reclaiming my body. There are scars everywhere in this world, and they tell the stories of the past in their own secret language.

With the photos done, the album was quickly manufactured. I had asked what could be done to make the packaging more environmentally friendly. Could we use hemp paper, less plastic? I was told that there was nothing we could do. John Rummen from Nettwerk designed the booklet and it was truly beautiful, white and fresh. I loved his very first cover idea. He knew me so well by now. The artwork was nominated for a Juno award.

With more promotional money behind us for this record, we could add another musician to our little touring set-up. We brought Blake Manning with us, a Canadian drummer and a great backup singer. Laid-back and ready to roll, he added a sexy beat to the show and made the album come to life onstage. He totally got me when I said I wanted mostly hand drums and no cymbals. Very Peter Gabriel. He brought all his cool stuff and created a loop-like, hypnotic vibe to the show. It was perfect.

We were almost ready to head out on tour.

Roy Lott called me into his office at the top of the Capitol building. *Billboard* magazine had published a review of the album in its "New and Noteworthy" section. He was thrilled to show it to me himself. He asked me to do a little concert for the staff, downstairs in the famous Studio A.

Cool on the outside, freaking out on the inside, I walked down the hall with my guitar, passing huge pictures of Dean Martin, Frank Sinatra and Nat King Cole. A stage was set up and a buffet of beautiful food was being served.

Bill, Blake and I played our hearts out to the staff. Roy sat on the floor with my friends, eyes closed, listening deeply. I wanted to make Roy proud as his first signing. This was a big deal. I went into the sound booth to thank the sound engineers, and one of them said to me, "That was a great set. Good job. You should probably go have some food. You're paying for it."

The comment took me off guard as the other engineer laughed. I smiled and said, "Good idea." Something about the tone of it hit me in the gut. He was right, but I didn't want to think about that. I wanted to enjoy the high and bask in the history of the place. I had a piece of chicken and then realized I had no appetite.

We chose a single: "If I Fall." I was not happy about it, because I thought the song was bubble gum. I had written it as a potential theme song for the TV show *Felicity*, but they didn't choose it. I asked Terry if we could pick a more profound song, but he said that my record needed a door to the mainstream so people could walk through and be introduced to the less hit-like songs. Begrudgingly I agreed. We chose a video director and went out to the desert to film it. I had asked for a video along the lines of Natalie Imbruglia's "Torn," where things are falling away behind her. Deconstruction. I wanted it to mean something to me, like my first video for "Evidence" did. That video is about taking people into their own psyches and healing the child inside them.

I didn't know what this video was even about. I knew it was a two-day shoot with a stunt double and a police chase. I was sitting in a classic convertible, and the stylist was putting sunglasses on me that I hadn't seen in a mirror. Someone placed a giant yellow teddy bear in the back seat. *What the fuck?*

"Why is there a giant teddy bear in my car?"

Some random person said, "We were told they were going to push you hard in the Asian market, and this sells there. Makes you seem younger."

Younger? I was twenty-five. Did I have an expiry date? Was I old?

It was fifty degrees Celsius, and I was sweating. I was trying to use the Glamour Spell to pretend everything was breezy, but there was a toy in my car and everyone seemed to be really on board with it. I was too hot to protest. I was dying, and my fine hair was starting to look greasy. What in the world was I doing?

We were doing our final shoot, sitting on the convertible singing, when the skies opened and it started to rain. It was raining in the *desert*. It was an amazing moment and we kept rolling. After we wrapped, everyone was in a great mood, and we celebrated and danced in the rain.

I watched the dry, cracked earth darken where the drops were hitting. Parched, it soaked it all up, and everything seemed replenished for a moment. Had I made something beautiful? Had I given everything? Off the footage went to editing, and a video was put together that looked nothing like what I had envisioned. But it was colourful and fun—and young.

I was about to be catapulted into the stratosphere. I was assigned a publicist and something called a product manager. During a meeting, I asked him what products he managed. I assumed it was merchandise, T-shirts, all that. No, *I* was the product.

"Um. That won't do," I said. "Not to be a pain"—because that's the *last* thing you want to be—"but can we at least call him a 'project manager'? That makes me seem like I'm an animate thing." Everyone laughed and said, sure, anything to make us more artist-friendly. This was the first time I'd heard the term *artist-friendly*. I didn't understand how a record label couldn't be artist-friendly. I mean, weren't we what they were made of? Weren't we the foundation of the whole operation? Nettwerk was all about taking something raw and letting it grow naturally. They were all about the music and the artist. I was learning how deep I was in the machine. My project manager then suggested that we airbrush my wedding band out of my poster.

Once upon a time back in Canada, I was hanging out with some friends in the music business who had just gotten back from the United States and had been dealing with major labels there. My friends explained that there was something called an FQ, and that the amount of money a label would put into promoting a female artist was directly related to it. Her fuckability quotient.

After I listened to the Capitol guy explain why we needed to make me appear single, I said, "Have you seen Shania Twain's ring? Does it make her less of a superstar because she's married? I'm married and I'm not hiding it." Then I smiled sweetly, because, you know, I'm nice. My FQ would not be going up that day.

The tours were planned, the song was serviced to radio (it was the second-most-added song in the country—I guess Terry knew what he was doing after all), the press had started, and the rehearsals were completed. It was time to fly.

My first tour as a Capitol artist was with a British singer named Dido. Her album was taking off globally, but in the United States, it was about to go supernova. She had just done a song with Eminem that was a massive hit. She and I would each do a forty-five-minute set. I would open for her in the States, and she would open for me in Canada.

I sat in the theatre as she did a sound check with her incredible band, and I was floored. She was gorgeous in a natural way, smiled easily and was very stylish. Her blond hair pulled back in a ponytail, she was the picture of youth and freshness, and her music was phenomenal. I beamed at her. She saw me and waved. I knew we were going to be friends.

It was breathtaking to be with her as her audiences became more and more enthusiastic, and her single "Thank You" was topping the charts. We bonded deeply. She was a bright light and I loved just basking in the glow of her beauty, and she loved me back.

One way we were different is that Dido would never let anything go past her that she didn't approve. She didn't really care if people liked her or not. Her vision came first. I envied her for not needing to please. By seeing to her needs, she made everything better for everyone. She was an excellent leader. There was nothing wishy-washy about Dido. Even as she was becoming a superstar, she never changed.

On February 29, 2000, in San Francisco, she and I played at The Fillmore for my release party. Having a sister like her on the road with me was life-changing. Years later, I would show up on her doorstep in London, alone and a little broken, and she would remind me who I was. This is what sisters do.

It was right around then that we were starting to hear rumblings of Avril Lavigne signing to Nettwerk Management. I hadn't heard her music, but I heard she didn't give a shit what people thought of her "behaviour." She wasn't warm and fuzzy, and Terry, when asked about this publicly, said that she could be whoever she wanted to be. Wow, gone were the days of Music Business Finishing School. To be clear, Nettwerk never asked me to be anything other than what I was, either. It was the major labels. You were labelled a bitch if you didn't smile at every turn in the male-dominated music business. I was proud of Avril and what she represented. She was so young and feisty, so brilliant, and about to take the world by storm. I once saw her smashing wineglasses against a wall in a bar. Looked like fun. I made a mental note to do that someday.

Back in LA for some solo shows at a venue called The Mint, I was asked to sing at a private song circle at someone's home. He was a music manager and had some young songwriters to introduce to the music scene.

At Bill Silva's house, there were maybe six songwriters and ten music biz folks. Everyone was truly talented, but one young man in particular captured my heart. He was a brand-new writer and a great guitar player. He was nerdy in the cutest, sexiest way, with a voice that melted me, and I hung on every word. His songs were complex but totally memorable. There was an effortlessness to his voice and delivery that blew me away. The next day, I called Terry and asked if this kid could join me on my West Coast tour. If he could just do a short opening spot, then I could proudly introduce him to my fans. His name was Jason Mraz.

He slayed every show on that tour, and Bill ended up recording his first demos. Of course, Jason got a huge record deal and
became an artist who gifted the world with an incredible catalogue of brilliant music, as well as a clear message of love, unity
and sustainability. I love that I got to see him when he was a
sprouting seed, because watching him bloom was one of the
most powerful things I've ever witnessed. He dove headfirst
into the machine and managed to stay true to his vision—a
rare and powerful example.

Bill, Blake and I were scheduled to perform in Sacramento for
a Tower Records conference. Normally, conferences are set in a
vibeless conference space, but not this one. The stage was huge
and there were TV screens on either side, with pro-level production and lights. The sound was exceptional. It felt like we were at
Wembley Stadium. We only played three songs, but something
was happening by then with our chemistry, and we killed that
performance. The room was on its feet. After we played, we
took a seat to watch the next act. Roy Lott was sitting beside me.
He smiled and put a napkin in front of me that had writing on it.
The president of Tower Records had passed him a note that said,
"Whatever you want, whatever you need, we are behind this."

The next thing I knew, in every city we played, we would
have a Tower Records in-store performance in the afternoon.
We would always have a Capitol Records representative with
us in each territory, and after the show, they would let us shop.
Free music was one of the best perks. We would ship vinyl
back to LA, and our touring CD collection was massive.

Then we got a call from a TV station called VH1. They
wanted to do a shopping spree with me in New York. I was
booked at Bumble and Bumble to have my hair done, and then
Bill and I got to go to Armani and get a free wardrobe. They
filmed the whole thing. I was uncontainably happy. This had
to be the top of the world.

The schedule got crazier. We were doing no less than three performances a day, breakfast television, afternoon radio and a full show at night. A ton of my music was getting scooped up by Warner Bros. Television and big Hollywood films.

One day, we found ourselves in Seattle. Before the show, Terry booked us to play at a sketchy little office in an even sketchier part of town. The owner and staff sat in a makeshift conference room with low ceilings and carpet that had seen better days. They were some of the friendliest people ever, and they laughed at all my jokes. Bill and I played our hearts out and went to sound check feeling pretty good about ourselves and glad we went. Still, I couldn't help thinking that Terry was crazy to have us play at some little office called "Amazon" when we had so much other press and radio to do.

Sometimes, we had to drive through the night or be up at the crack of dawn to catch a flight. Sometimes, the people checking us in would look at our gear and tell us we couldn't get on the plane, so we'd have to hustle and rent a van and drive. Bill noticed that I was starting to get edgy and angry with people who weren't being helpful.

Where was that gracious Canadian who was nice to everyone? We needed everything to go smoothly in terms of our travel arrangements so we could give everything when we were onstage. We didn't have a tour manager, and so no protection, no advocate to fight for us when things went wrong. We were burning out. The music box was being wound too tightly.

Terry sent us back to our apartment in LA for a week to breathe. I only had one little thing to do while I was there. I was asked to audition for a Jerry Bruckheimer film called *Coyote Ugly*. They were looking for a singer/actor to play the lead, and they'd heard of me and asked me to drop in. I got off the plane, threw myself in the shower and ran to the audition looking not so much like a superstar, but more like a cat that had been left on the porch in a rainstorm.

When I arrived, a well-groomed young man with a clipboard looked me up and down disapprovingly and said, "I'm sorry, are you lost?"

"I'm here for the audition?"

He pursed his lips doubtfully and said, "Uh . . . okaaaay. Right this way."

I sat in a room filled with stunning women who looked like supermodels, with perfect makeup and professional hair. I wanted to disappear. When he called my name, I walked past him and said, "Just so you know, you guys called me to do this."

I had my guitar and played a song for Bonnie Timmermann, another legendary casting director. She let me know that I would not be reading for the lead. I packed up my guitar and walked out of there feeling like shit. How do actors do it day after day? It was degrading.

A few days later, I got a call saying that they wanted me to play a cameo in the film. That's how they treat you when they like you? What a weird place. Still, I was excited. I was going to be a singer on the stage at an open mic night when the lead comes in. I was going to get my own song in the soundtrack. I went to a recording studio to pre-record "That's Me." Through my headphones, I heard the producers in the control room on the phone with the film studio: "Oh, she's so pretty and the song is great. You're going to love her. Very Canadian."

I found that hysterical.

I was scheduled to go to wardrobe the day before filming to try on some options for my scene. When I arrived, I learned that there had been a last-minute change in the company that was doing the clothing. The stylists were beyond stressed. I introduced myself, and they looked at me exasperatedly.

"We don't have anything that will fit you. What are you, a

six? We only have size two and smaller." They looked at each other. "Well, maybe we can find something stretchy."

We walked through rows and rows of clothing. I saw a black lace top that looked like it might fit. When I asked if I could try it on, they said, "Sure, just take off your clothes. We'll pull some options. It says here you're an extra in the bar scene."

"Well, not exactly. I'm sing . . ." I stopped talking. They weren't listening to me.

I stood there in only my underwear, feeling like the fattest person in the world. They complained to each other about my arms. I wrapped them around myself like wings. In the end, we found a black outfit that would hide my figure.

Afterwards, I was supposed to go to the gym and get to bed early, to be on set at 6:00 a.m. Furious, I drove straight to Amy's. Amy, who had just started her own casting business, was livid. She knew people were treated that way on set, but she didn't expect it to happen to me. Instead of going to the gym, we hit the bar. We drank margaritas and I planned out what I was going to say to those stylists the next day. Or maybe I wouldn't even show up? Maybe I'd just fuck it up. No, I was going to go and give them a piece of my mind.

With only a few hours' sleep and still a little drunk, I was picked up by car and dropped at my trailer. The sign on the door said, "Tara McLean." Not the correct spelling, but close enough. I was too tired to care. I'd forgotten my guitar, so the crew had to hustle to find one for me. My clothing was laid out, and soon I was sitting in makeup. Piper Perabo, the star of the movie, was having her hair done, and she looked over at me and gave me a giant smile. Jesus, she was pretty. The makeup artist asked me what I liked, which surprised me. I said, "What would Cameron Diaz do? Flawless with a touch of danger, please." This cracked them up. Someone brought me a smoothie with a straw and I began to sober up.

My mood was lifting, and I was starting to feel capable of facing those stylists when they showed up.

I dressed myself and was brought to the set in a golf cart. I was going to pull a Dido on those stylists and tell them exactly what was so uncool about their behaviour. However, the director, David McNally, found me first.

Never in my life have I been so knocked over by surprise. He came up to me and began fawning over me like I was a huge star. "Tara!" He took my hands in his. "I'm so excited to work with you. I haven't been this excited since I worked with Madonna. You look fantastic. Your song is perfect and this scene is going to be great! Thank you for agreeing to do this. I know how busy you are. Now, I have a question for you. Walk with me. This scene is set at Arlene's Grocery in New York. You've played there, yes? Okay, so what would be happening here. Would someone have a clipboard?" David McNally was a sweetheart.

I did my best to advise him on what it might be like. I'd played there a bunch of times but never at an open mic night.

I looked up and, low and behold, the stylists were looking at me. The expressions on their faces were enough to make my fucking day. They ran over and began primping me like I was Sleeping Beauty and they were the fairies. I wished Amy was there to see this turnaround. They complimented me throughout the shoot, and it was one of the most fun days I'd ever had. They spelled my name wrong in the credits too, but that was just funny to me.

I was quite upset, though, when I found out that, for some reason, my song didn't make it onto the soundtrack album. I was told it had something to do with contracts and rights. The *Coyote Ugly* album was on the billboard charts forever and went five-times platinum. Talk about a miss. But still, to this day, I get about a hundred dollars a year in performance royalties.

It's not the same, but it has bought me a few cappuccinos and gave me an IMDb profile. You can't fight the moonlight, baby.

Off I went to another performance in Austin that was a showcase for something. I knew it was important because Terry and Dave flew in from Vancouver for it and Roy Lott was there from LA. I was just doing everything that was asked of me, and things were beginning to blur together. The carousel was moving faster.

We had lunch at the venue, did a sound check and went to a radio interview. In the car on the way back to the hotel, I started to sweat. My head was spinning. Bill carried me up to the room, where I began throwing up. But not just your regular throwing up. It was like *The Exorcist*.

I lay on the bathroom floor, the cold tile giving me some relief. I heard Bill on the phone and then felt him standing over me. He put the phone to my ear. It was Terry.

"Hey, love. I hear you may have a little food poisoning."

I laughed weakly.

He kept talking. "If you've ever needed to get up off the floor, it's now. I need you to get dressed and get in the cab and get to the venue. This is really important."

I felt like a badly injured boxer whose coach was getting them to stand up and fight one more round.

"Okay. I'm up."

Bill took the phone and I sat up. The room spun and I puked again. I lay back down on the cold tile. "Please, I just want to stay on the floor," I said weakly.

Bill sat me up again and wiped my face with a cold cloth. Then he pulled off my clothes, and I threw up again. He dressed me, propped me up and braided my hair. I threw up again before he carried me downstairs to the taxi. I had an ice bucket from the hotel room in case I threw up on the way to the venue, which I did, much to the dismay of the driver.

Once inside, they rushed me to the bathroom. Dave gave me Pepto Bismol, but that just made me throw up pink foam. I remembered the shrimp that had been in my lunch. I was pretty sure that's what had happened. Roy and Terry were very worried. The vomiting slowed down to about once every fifteen minutes. The two other acts went on, and I heard their muffled music from the bathroom, where my head was in my hands and the floor was the only thing keeping me from spinning.

The next time I threw up was twenty minutes later. I can perform four songs in twenty minutes. I gave the team a thumbs-up. Bill took my hand and led me to the stage. The lights and the sound of the audience applauding were like nails to my senses. *Glamour Spell. Now.*

I smiled. The music started and the songs came out. I made a joke about having food poisoning and how punk it would be if I threw up, and to please excuse me if I did. They laughed and the sound of that got me to the end of the set. I started to swoon and Bill helped me down the stairs at the side of the stage. The audience applauded hard, and Roy was waiting for me. He said, "That was the most professional thing I've ever seen. What do you want? I'll give you whatever you wish for in this moment."

I looked at him and said, "Can I please have a trip to Hawaii?"

"Yes. We'll send you and Bill to Hawaii."

I ran to the bathroom and threw up.

I was told this performance earned me the reputation as the hardest-working artist on the circuit.

The touring and press continued non-stop, and I was getting more and more rundown. I was becoming less able to handle stress. I was physically exhausted and easily agitated. The road seemed endless. I'd snap at people if they didn't have our rental car ready. Once, I lost my mind on the airline staff when they refused to put our gear on the plane. My nervous system was shot, and I was in no shape to handle the situation. Obstacles happen, and how we react to them is everything. Bill started to ban me from going to the check-in counter at airports. He'd handle the check-ins on his own until it was time for me to show my ID.

Bill, Blake and I flew into Little Rock, Arkansas, but our gear didn't make the flight for some reason. Maybe because I'd been an asshole to someone at the previous airport? We had no instruments. We figured we'd go to the venue, talk to the promoter and perhaps cancel. As we pulled up to the address of the venue, it wasn't there either. It had burned down.

Now, at this point, any sane person would go to the hotel, get in the bath and call it a day. We called the promoter and he explained that he'd booked the corner of a Mexican restaurant for us to play in, and they would borrow some instruments for us to play. The show must go on. I knew I wasn't okay, but I showered at the hotel and headed to the restaurant. If I could play with food poisoning, then I could play that night.

They had it set up nicely with rows of chairs, and when we entered, the crowd was excited. I stood in front of them and looked out at their smiling faces. Everything appeared distorted. My head swam in the swirling sounds and lights. I looked down at my hands and they were shaking. Bill was smiling nervously at me, waiting for me to say something.

I started to play the guitar, but I couldn't remember any words. I laughed nervously and looked back at the crowd. There was an awkward silence. Chairs creaked. It was every performance nightmare I'd ever had. I took off the guitar, handed it to Bill and walked right down the middle of the aisle and out the front door. Bill ran after me and opened the car door. I crawled into the back seat and went into a fetal position, shaking.

There is a point at which the winder on the music box can

be pushed too far. The spring in the mechanism breaks and the music stops playing.

At the hotel, Bill called Terry to explain that I'd been overwound.

We were scheduled to be back in Austin the next day and in Nashville in a few days. Everyone went into emergency mode. I had shows booked for the next nine months straight. Since Austin was Steve Schnur's old stompin' ground, he booked me at a spa for two days for massages, a facial, yoga, meditation. Two heavenly days of relaxation and care. I absorbed every moment I didn't have to move, talk or be *on*.

Terry flew in with a box of Mr. Bubble. I laughed when he gave it to me, but he smiled mischievously and said, "I have an even better present." And he did.

Enter Mark LeCorre. He'd been Dido's sound person on the road. Mark had also toured with The Tragically Hip and was probably one of the best sound people in the business. He was to be our tour manager, sound guru and all-around good-vibe guy. This was the moment Bill collapsed into tears. He'd been holding it all together and was finally getting help. Mark wasn't like a little dinghy sent to rescue us from sea; he was a yacht. Terry had given me the only thing in the world I needed to get to the next level.

Armed with a fresh team member, the tour kept rolling and it was fun again. The sound was guaranteed to be amazing every night, we always had good food, and he did all the airport, hotel and car rental check-ins. There wasn't anything I needed that he didn't figure out how to get. I was being taken care of by a pro.

It was decided that I would be part of something called The Girls Room tour with three other women who were signed to Capitol: Amy Correia, Shannon McNally and Kendall Payne. We had a tour bus and a multi-city tour of amazing venues in the United States. Each of the women brought a magic to the evening that was completely breathtaking. Each night, they blossomed as performers, and we supported each other through the tour. In New York, Chicago, LA, we crushed it. I became a massive fan of each of them.

Even though I was feeling better, I could tell that something was still off internally. I was getting nosebleeds and my voice was tired. I got a massage in a hotel in San Francisco, and the therapist told me that I had to stop touring. I laughed and said, "But I'm living the dream?" to which he answered, "This is not your body's dream. I can feel it. Your body needs you to stop."

I was irritable with Bill, and Blake was struggling, having been away from his family for too long. Management needed us to go to Canada to make another music video for a song called "Divided," which was to be my next single. This would give everyone but me a break.

Before landing in Toronto, I flew through Vancouver to sing a Christmas song at The Hudson's Bay Company during the annual unveiling of their holiday windows. This was an easy, high-profile opportunity, and it was an honour to be asked. I was brought into the building and assigned a security detail. The tall, familiar-looking bodyguard smiled at me. Jason?

Jason was the neighbour boy who had driven with me in the police car after the fire that night. He had accompanied me during one of the most terrifying moments of my life, and here he was, keeping me safe again. We laughed and hugged. He knew me, had cared for me and was right there beside me. A piece of home.

I shot my video for "Divided" and was happier with the result than I had been with "If I Fall." Before I left Toronto, I went to see an ENT (ear, nose and throat) specialist to check out my vocal cords. He said I was raw and gave me a hydrocortisone injection so I could keep on singing. Once again, a prize fighter was patched up and sent back into the ring.

After the next show, my voice gave out. I was knocked out cold. I was told that I couldn't sing or talk for three days. I was back on the bus with The Girls Room, but I missed a few shows. I enjoyed crawling into my bunk and shutting out the world. I started dreaming that maybe I would lose my voice forever, and then I could go work in a flower shop and sleep in my own bed every night.

Then I got the call.

Late Night with Conan O'Brien wanted me as the guest musician. This was the big break we'd been waiting for, and I had no voice. We asked if we could have a slot one week later, to give me time to recover. They agreed and it was all set. I would shoot the show in the afternoon in New York and then play a concert at the Bowery Ballroom. I had a week and a half to be at my very best.

Capitol Records gave Bill fifteen hundred dollars to get me a great outfit, and he came back to the hotel with a colourful Dolce & Gabbana top and a pair of sexy black pants. I was going to look amazing. Every day, I reached a little deeper and worked with my voice to get it back in shape. When I'd feel my nervous system beginning to get overwhelmed, I would lie down in the hotel and bring myself back to the cabin in the woods. *I am a bird. A sparrow on a branch. Singing with the wind in the leaves. My voice is always with me. Calm. Breathe. I am a bird.*

Day by day, I found my way back to having a voice. It was not at its best, but it was good enough to get through the song. We were going to play the new single, "Divided," which felt so much better to me than "If I Fall." It had a great beat and was one of my favourites to perform live. I was able to embody it and move a little. The song felt closer to how I wanted to introduce myself to the world as a writer. I was excited. I had the outfit, but there was a problem: the top exposed my bare belly. I decided I didn't care; I was just going to be myself. I was beginning to make peace with my body. Also, I didn't have time to stress about it too much. It felt brave.

When we arrived at the studio, it was cold in there, but it didn't matter because I was just pacing the halls. I had so much pent-up energy and my nerves were through the roof. We did a sound check and everything sounded amazing. I asked Blake to use his metronome in his ear so that the tempo would be perfect. Sometimes, nerves can make you speed up.

Conan came up to us after sound check and introduced himself. He was incredibly tall and kind—the friendly giant. He loved the song and said he was excited for the show. He told me that something interesting happened when the musicians started to play when the show was being taped. Nine times out of ten, they would start the song and then stop, and then start again. He said it would be totally fine if that happened, that I could stop if I had to, and they would edit, because there was a delay before it went to air.

Well, my über-professional live-performer self made a silent note that under no circumstance was I going to let that happen. I wanted the live audience in the room to experience a seamless show. I would impress Conan by not having a false start.

If Bill and Blake were nervous, they didn't show it. They sat calmly in the green room, letting me be the nervous one. It turns out they were crapping their pants too. I checked the mirror a hundred times and kept telling myself that my belly was beautiful, my hair was good and my outfit was perfect. I also told myself that my voice would hold out and to trust it. It wouldn't let me down, not then, not there.

The other guests that day were Bernie Mac and Siskel and Ebert. I would sing at the end of the show. I watched the interviews and felt excitement taking over my terror. I ran to pee about three times.

When it was almost time to go on, we were brought to the side of the sound stage. Someone with a headset showed us to our places as The Max Weinberg 7, who were not there during sound check, started to play. The horns blasted in the little room so loudly that it startled me.

As Conan announced my name, Bill and Blake were given the signal to play. Something was wrong. I realized that my monitors must be off. The sound was so quiet. But I wasn't going to stop. Blake was playing too slow. I wasn't going to stop. I rushed my first line—I could have done that a million times better—but I wasn't going to stop.

After the first few lines, I settled into the rhythm and let it all go. I connected with the audience and gave my voice all the gas I could without blowing it out. I knew it was still fragile, but this was the moment. I needed to use every skill I'd learned in every show to make this performance the best I could.

When the song ended, Conan came over and congratulated me as we went to commercial. He invited me to sit with him at the end of the show, with the other guests on the couch, and we chatted a little. He commented that he was so surprised we didn't stop playing. Boom! Bernie Mac leaned toward me and whispered that my performance was awesome. I told him how nervous I was, and he looked at me with his great big eyes and said, "You never need to be nervous. You're great." Swoon.

After the show, Conan showed Bill his guitar collection in his office, and I got ready to hop in the limo and go to the Bowery Ballroom for a full show. I was on top of the world.

On the way there, weaving through Manhattan traffic, it occurred to me why musicians had to stop and restart playing on Conan's show. They stopped because The Max Weinberg 7 were playing so loud that it changed your sense of the deci-bel level in the room. In relation to them, your band seemed extremely quiet, which threw you when you started to play.

Also, Blake was hitting exactly the right tempo, but my nerves had been trying to rush us. I understood now what had happened, and I was proud of myself for playing through. That mattered more to me than having a perfect performance. Terry didn't agree.

He called me. "Your performance was okay, but you looked fantastic." Could the man just lie to me once? Just today? Could he just tell me I was spectacular? And brave? Terry never said anything he didn't mean. The wind went out of my sails a little. When I watched the performance, I realized he was right. My voice was about a seven out of ten of its usual power and control, and my entry was shaky. If I was to play in the big leagues, I had to be a champion. I had to knock it out of the park. I'd chosen to sacrifice the TV experience for the live experience. I wanted to impress Conan, the production team and the live audience rather than get it exactly perfect for the five million viewers. I had so much to learn.

However, the show in New York City that night was epic. I was headlining in a famous venue and was introduced as having just come from *Late Night with Conan O'Brien*. I was unprecedentedly relaxed. All my nerves had been used up and the crowd was with me. I felt like I would never come down.

But down we must always come. There's no peak without a valley.

The music business collapsed.

Something began to happen that the record companies were not expecting: downloading. A website called Napster was allowing people to take music for free. Entire albums were being "ripped and burned." The industry went into an uproar. Until then, music could be obtained through four main portals: live shows, album sales, radio and bootlegged tapes. The labels controlled the first three, and the bootlegged tapes were a cool, underground promotional vehicle that were overlooked because of the cachet in trading obscure performance record-ings. They didn't hinder album sales. On the contrary, they boosted them. But downloading? That's the torpedo that sank the ship.

As more people began stealing music, the record companies scrambled to find ways to punish downloaders and to adapt to the new way that people wanted to access music: online.

I've heard it said that the record executives went from kings to beggars in one fell swoop. With the music business in the toilet, the pressure for hits was greater than ever. I feel lucky that I was able to witness the music business before "the Fall." Technically, I was still in the pre-celebrity developmental stage of my career, about to lift off. Did Capitol Records have enough runway space left for me?

So much money had been spent, and I was spending all my money and management money trying to keep up. I tried not to think about the mounting debt, and focused on showing up and singing, and obeying the paper that appeared under my hotel room door.

People were scared, I was scared, and the pressure for a hit song was growing.

A new management point person had been assigned to me, since Dave had moved to working with Coldplay. Her name was Aziyn and she was a sassy beauty who was up for anything. I'd worn Dave out, honestly. He was constantly dealing with an edgy, stressed-out version of me and wasn't into it. Who would be? The time came for him to go to the next level. We had come as far as we could together professionally, and I will be eternally grateful for everything he gave me during those years. He always held himself with integrity.

Mark LeCorre, our fearless leader, ended up back on tour with a bigger act, and so we were assigned a new tour manager/ sound person named Al Vermue, who was excellent at his job.

"Divided" was climbing the charts all over Asia, and plane tickets were purchased for us to go there. I began to do phone interviews with press in Japan, Korea, Taiwan and Thailand. I was told that one Japanese interview in particular was of utmost importance and to be ready to make it great. Her first question to me was "Why doesn't your music video for 'If I Fall' tell me anything about you or come close to representing the beautiful record you made?"

Fuuuuu . . .

I told it to her straight. I told her it had gotten away from me. With all the cooks in the kitchen and the pressure to make something commercially good, the story I'd wanted to tell fell away, and what was left was an expensive ad that made me cringe. She laughed and I felt we had gotten off to a good start. It was an honest interview.

Having begun my life in an off-grid cabin with an outhouse, perhaps my reaction to stepping into first class on an intercontinental flight could be understood. My jaw hit the floor. For all the red-eyes and early-morning, squishy, hot, smelly flights I'd taken the past years on the daily, this flight was my reward. Blake, Bill, Al, Aziyn and I settled into luxurious little cocoons and enjoyed every second of that ride. We were spoiled from head to toe with hot towels, movies, wine, chocolate. It was heaven.

When we got off the plane, a little dazed but well rested, we were shocked that there were crowds of people in the airport, screaming. Someone famous must have been on the plane. I looked around to see who it was, and Bill started laughing.

"They're here for you."

The signs they were holding came into focus and I realized these were fans of mine. This had never happened to me, not even in my own country. Smiling, bowing EMI Asia representatives met us and drove us to the hotel. There, we were greeted like royalty. Bill and I were shown to our room, which was the presidential suite. It had a twelve-seat marble table that was covered in food and gifts. We also had a butler at our service.

We were given our press schedule and told that hair and makeup people and a translator would be arriving. I'd have a glam squad following me around so I would always look amazing. The schedule was tight. It had notes like "7:40 a.m. Meet in lobby of hotel. Travel 7 minutes to TV station." It was precise. Some days, we'd have press come to the hotel room before we went out.

That was the case on the second day. A reporter asked me a question that took me off guard. He said, "Why do you look one way in your videos, and another way in person?" I asked for clarification, wondering if my translator had gotten it right. I was all done up and glamorous, so I was confused. Then it was made clear to me what he meant.

"You look like a housewife." He was referring to my weight. I was still a size six, and I guess they expect their pop stars to be tiny. I knew I was bigger than other North American acts that had been through, but I didn't think I was THAT big. But it became a problem. My weight was remarked upon in many of the press situations, and I would just laugh it off and say things like, "Well, I guess you have pretty glamorous house-wives here?" But it stung.

In one press session, the translator refused to tell me what the press was saying. He looked at me regretfully, and the EMI rep excused him and ended the interviews. I was assigned a new translator.

That said, when I sang, I won them over, despite my gargantuan physique. The press also began to focus on me and Bill as a love story, which distracted them from their obsession with my being "fat." We worked hard all through that tour and played up our affection onstage to the delight of the press.

I ran into Stephen Hawking, the famous theoretical physicist, in the lobby of our hotel in Seoul. I got to say hello and tell him how much I loved him, and he answered me sweetly through his voice generator that he was so happy to meet me. That was a life highlight.

I ate my way through the best Korean barbecue. I'd decided that if they thought I was fat, I might as well enjoy being spoiled by the record company. At one point, we ended up in a bar in Thailand with naked dancers trying to seduce Bill, but we got out of there before it got crazy.

I was moved by the temples and images of the Buddha and brought one home with me. I didn't know it then, but that was the beginning of something that would change me forever.

We flew back in the same first-class pods we'd come in and went to our apartment in LA to rest up. It wasn't long before Terry told me he needed me to write another record, fast.

But what in the world could I write about? I'd been in a high-speed chase for years and had nothing to say. I was empty. I could barely form a sentence, let alone write a song.

LA was doing my head in. With no instructions arriving under my door every day, telling me what to do, I found myself drinking and partying like there was no tomorrow. Since I didn't have to sing, I could dance all night until the sun came up, and then do it all again. One day, I woke up to strangers sleeping on my floor, and I knew the parties had gone a little too far.

I told Bill we needed to get out of LA. That was the moment I broke his heart. Mine wasn't the only music he wanted to be a part of. LA held the best chance for him to live out his dream of being a music producer, but I pulled it out from under him because it was all about me and my needs.

If I was going to stop moving, I needed to get to the forest. I needed the trees to catch me. I wanted to go back to BC and heal. We packed up the apartment and headed for the border. As soon as we crossed into Canada, I felt like I could breathe.

Our old landlord in Vancouver set us up with a little one-bedroom. Bill had to put his studio in the living room. We had floor-to-ceiling windows that looked out over the mountains to the north, and I would sit and stare at them for hours as the light changed. This pace was exactly the opposite of what Bill needed. We tried to do some writing and recording, but everything seemed trite and boring. Nothing great was emerging. Maybe I was broken, my mechanism in pieces. We were running out of money too. The apartment began to feel smaller and smaller until, one day, Bill told me he was going back to LA.

"You stay here. Walk in the forest, find your songs. I have to go find mine," he said, and with that he was gone. In LA, he slept on couches and set up his studio in a friend's storage space. He did whatever he could to stay there. Bill wasn't a sit-still kind of guy. He had a constant energy flowing through him and was always in motion. His fingers moved on their own when he wasn't playing guitar. He needed release, and the only thing that quenched his restlessness was to be on the move, to fill every waking moment with music.

I, on the other hand, needed silence and stillness. Something else was stirring within me. As I walked the paths through the trees and the mountains, listening to the wind and the birds, wondering where my songs were, I heard the voice. It was the one that came from the centre of me, the one I had lost touch with somewhere along the yellow highway line.

Deep and calm, she whispered to me, and it echoed through my bones, through the branches in my lungs and deep into the spiralling roots of the double helix of my DNA.

"It's time. Time to become a mother."

18.

Listen

The river taught me how to listen;
from the river you too will learn how.
—HERMANN HESSE, *SIDDHARTHA*

You want a what?"
    "A baby."
    "No!"
"Please?"
"No!"
"Just one?"
"No!"
"Just a little one?"
"No!"
"They're portable."

Bill and I burst out laughing over this phone call. I was twenty-eight and the only thing I could think about was having a child. I'd bought *Spiritual Midwifery* by Ina May Gaskin and had read it cover to cover. It filled me up with a new sense of purpose and wonder. Learning everything I could about pregnancy became my obsession.

If I couldn't birth songs, then maybe a baby?

Bill asked me to fly down to LA to talk about it, and Nettwerk put us up in their apartment in Beverly Hills, where Bill couldn't say no to me. When exhausted, he'd laughingly complain of feeling used, while I did headstands naked against a wall to make sure the sperm found the egg as quickly as possible. There is no proof that this helps, but it felt proactive.

Terry was shocked when I told him my plan, but far be it from him to stop me from going after a dream. I got pregnant on the first try.

We handed in some new demos to the label, but I wasn't sure there was anything great happening yet. My focus wasn't on the music at all. However, I figured that once I stopped throwing up, I'd feel amazing and get to work writing killer songs for the next album. To celebrate reaching three months pregnant, Bill and I took a ferry to Catalina. Sitting on the beach together, I noticed I was feeling better. The ocean and the sun were exactly what we needed. We couldn't believe our life. Here we were, in love, having a baby, with a record deal, sitting on the beach in paradise.

The cellphone rang.

It was an A&R guy from Capitol who I didn't know well. He told me that my demos weren't what they were looking for and that my record deal was being terminated.

"Maybe you should just go be a mom," he said, before he hung up.

I sat there in shock. Roy Lott didn't call me. Steve Schnur

didn't call me. Terry didn't call me. Why did this guy call me to break the news? What was up? I called Terry immediately, crying my eyes out the way only a pregnant woman can, my bare toes digging into the sand.

He explained that Capitol was going through a shift, as everything was in the music business. Roy would no longer be president, and so I was a passion project that, on the books, didn't look lucrative. The new president wasn't interested in me. They'd spent hundreds of thousands of dollars on me, and I hadn't made money yet. It was over with Capitol. I suppose my FQ had gone way down. Had I not been pregnant and if I'd handed in some hit songs on my demos, maybe I would have had a small chance of staying on. Terry reminded me that I still had my record deal with Nettwerk and that I could keep making music with them as long as I wanted. That made me feel so loved in a moment when I felt rejected.

Bill put his arm around me and said, "Look at the bright side: you're off the hook for a little while. Let's grow this baby."

We rented a temporary furnished apartment in Hollywood while we figured out where we were going to live. This way, Bill could hustle for work there and I could hang with friends and enjoy the stillness. LA could buzz with desperation, creativity and ambition, and I could walk in Topanga Canyon, sit in a café on Hermosa Beach or stroll slowly through the farmers market for flowers.

We were brought up to Canada to do some shows, but singing while pregnant wasn't my favourite thing. I didn't have the air. I got *huge*. That part I loved. From the moment the baby was in me, I let myself be nourished. Surprisingly, Bill loved my belly and my growing body in every way. We'd had some space in our relationship because he was working on music with Jason Mraz, and I had shaken myself free of the thing that was causing me damage. The bigger my belly grew, the further

I felt from the pop princess on the posters, the girl for sale. FQ be damned. I felt so sexy. I'd taken myself back in order to belong to this baby. Nothing else mattered to me.

When I was seven months pregnant, Bill and I agreed that we wanted the baby to be born in Canada, so we got in our car, drove to Toronto and rented a townhouse in the Beaches.

Tom and Kathy Cochrane offered to host us in their beautiful home so I could have the baby there, in their huge bathtub with midwives and friends and family around. I couldn't do something that awesome without an audience, could I?

I stopped performing or doing any public appearances as the due date got closer, except for one photo shoot for the cover of *Flare Pregnancy* magazine. This was the opposite of spreading myself thin. I felt myself solidifying. I was gathering all my energy and power. I was sure I was ready for motherhood. How hard could it be? People did it all the time.

The birth was not the peaceful water birth I'd seen on You-Tube. There were no dolphins swimming around me in the sea. The baby was in a position that didn't birth easily, and it wasn't turning around. Stubborn kid. Friends had flown in from LA and BC, and Nana, Mum, Shaye and Bryde had come to be there when the baby was born. Kim and Allan were there. The Cochranes created a beautiful, loving cocoon for everyone, and gave me their bedroom and tub to birth in. Amy held my hand for hours as the contractions came sporadically. Shaye timed them and wrote them down.

Fifteen hours later, I was throwing up from the pain of back labour. The position of the baby, "posterior," meant its spine was against my spine. Imagine someone playing the xylophone with white-hot pokers on your vertebrae. The midwife agreed to transfer me to the hospital. I had been adamant that there was no way I was going to use drugs; I was going to do this naturally. But after experiencing this level of pain, I was going to do anything to get the baby out and have it over with. They gave me something called a walking epidural, which meant I could still move around and feel everything, except for the pain in my spine. I slept. Then the epidural wore off.

The doctor at the hospital told the midwife that there was no way I could birth the baby without doctors. The midwife came into the room and told me what the doctor had said.

For me, there is no better incentive than someone telling me I can't do something. Shaye took over from Bill and held my hand. Hers was the most familiar hand in the world to me. When things began to get really intense, she leaned in and whispered to me, "Remember who you are. You are a warrior goddess, and I have seen you use your power in ways that have changed the world. Call on that. You can do this."

She took my hand in both of hers, and I reached down as far as I could. Hand over hand, I pulled myself underground by the roots. I dove far beneath the trees and mushrooms and tunnels of ants. They stopped and let me pass, like cars on the side of the road during a funeral procession. My hair filled with moss, my ears filled with dirt and my mouth with mud. I pulled myself through the layers of earth, through the bones of my ancestors that lay, in rows, white like shells. Further I went, through the lava, where I burned off everything I knew to be true. All my flesh was gone as I broke into the centre of it all. Silence. There was no pain here, just stars. Just space. Voices around me began to echo. Sounds came from somewhere deeper. I listened to the bass, the far-off drum on the moors, the pipes, the low drone, the dungeon in the castle. The stones.

Little bare feet running on red dirt. *Don't run away. Run toward.*

My mother was holding me in the water, telling me to trust the river. *You will float.* The cold water surrounded me, swallowed me. I was sinking. *No! Trust. Trust.* I surrendered.

I lay with all the other stones at the bottom, looking up at the moon.

PUSH.

Surfacing, gasping for air, the scream.

Then the crescendo of every sound that had ever been.

I saw the sound of the bright sun of eternity. A synesthetic union. A burning threshold. I stepped through, breaking open. Only I wasn't me anymore. I had divided.

We named her Sophia, goddess of wisdom.

To give birth is to become everything and nothing at once. It's to be part of the cycle. I'd had no idea that emptiness would follow. No one told me that I'd have to grieve the girl I'd been. I'd thought it was all about celebration, rejoicing at the successful creation of life. Something in me was still underneath, gasping for air. I had surrendered, but not completely. I was on the other side with a perfect baby, and I was sad. Buried alive.

She never slept. My nipples cracked and bled. Bill held her and soothed her and wiped my tears, but he wasn't looking at me the same way. We were both exhausted. When she did sleep, I would reach for my husband, but he wasn't really there. Where did he go? He was there before the birth, during the birth. But after the birth? I didn't understand. What happened to my life? What happened to my body? My empty belly lay beside me on the bed, deflated. No one had warned me about this. No one had warned him about this.

When I could climb into the tub with Sophia, that is when she would relax with me, and my love for her would almost overwhelm me. She would rest and nurse if we were in the water, and Bill would light candles and play guitar for us. It was like a normal life.

Some friends volunteered to watch the baby while Bill and I went on a date. I was so relieved to be able to dress up and have a beer and oysters with my husband. Rodney's Oyster House was the cure for everything. Bill held my hand as we crossed the street to the restaurant. My hair was in two low pony-tails, and I was wearing lip gloss and a long, black wrap dress. We looked at each other across the table and smiled. There he was—or was he? He looked nervous. I asked him about it.

Bill's most wonderful and worst quality is his honesty. He looked at me and said, "I love you. But I don't know why, I'm just not attracted to you anymore."

I felt the blood drain from my face. I'd never felt more alone or rejected in my life.

There is something that sometimes happens psychologically to men when they see their partners give birth. They no longer see us as lovers; they see us only as mothers. It's the reductive Madonna-whore complex, to be sure. But still, neither of us understood why the light had turned off for Bill. I was sure it was about my body. I thought he couldn't be a father and husband at the same time, that he didn't have the capacity. I was so embarrassed and devastated that I didn't realize he was grieving too. He didn't know what had happened inside of him that made him unable to touch me or see the woman that was still there, needing intimacy. We left the restaurant a little tipsy, thanked our friends for babysitting, and Bill went to bed. I stayed up with the baby, completely numb from Bill's revelation.

I wasn't a star anymore. I had imploded, and now there was a black hole where I'd once shone. I went through the motions. I showered, fed the baby, changed the baby, slept when I could. Bill looked at me less and less, and drank more and more. He cooked food, did laundry, played with Sophia, but he didn't touch me and could hardly look at me. On top of that, without touring, our money was running out. The gravity of the black hole was sucking all the light particles down with it.

After a month, I decided to do something bold. I was going to walk to the grocery store by myself.

I walked outside and closed the door behind me. My grey sweatpants and hoodie didn't help me to feel any more like myself, but Bill had encouraged me to just get outside. My red-rimmed eyes squinted from the light. I walked around the corner, out of sight of my doorway, and thought, *What if I just take off? I should have brought my passport. I could just make a run for it.* That lasted all of thirty glorious seconds before it occurred to me that this was one situation I had to face. No take-backsies on this.

I pushed my shopping cart through the aisles, pretending to be normal. I watched all the other people shopping and wondered if they had ever been catapulted from their lives into some strange land they didn't recognize. People looked at me and looked away—I may have been staring too long. I had no glow. I looked at all the different kinds of cereal and wanted to cry. All these choices and yet I was trapped.

I stood there thinking about how I'd married a man who didn't love me anymore, how I was failing my baby by not being able to figure out how to make her sleep, how I'd wanted something so badly that everything else had fallen away. Just then, Dido's song "Thank You" came floating through the store, and I was at the side of the stage, watching her win over the audience. She looked over and winked at me . . .

I came back to reality standing there in the aisle, still wearing a giant pad, looking into the crazy eyes of Cap'n Crunch. I bought my groceries and walked home, tears rolling down my cheeks. What the fuck was wrong with me? I'd had it all. Where did it go?

Sophia was crying when I got in. She wouldn't take a bottle yet, so if she got hungry, there was only me to fix that.

I traded the groceries for the baby, and sat on the couch and nursed her. Bill quietly put everything away and then went to his studio in the basement and closed the door. I wanted a door I could close. I wanted a time machine. What I needed was help.

I looked in the kitchen from where I was sitting and could see that he had left a cupboard door open. I couldn't move because Sophia had fallen asleep in my arms, and putting her down was impossible. I looked at that open cupboard and wanted to scream. I let myself scream inside so Sophia could keep sleeping. I was crumbling. How could I hold a baby when I was disappearing?

Bill said to me one day, "I can even hear your silent screams." He had good ears.

Just in time, music came along to save me.

Two friends, Kim Stockwood and Damhnait Doyle, decided they wanted to do a trio project. It would be one album, and there was a record deal already in place with EMI Music Canada if we wanted it, as well as a built-in manager for the project, Sheri Jones, and her partner, Wayne O'Connor, on sound. They asked if they could come over and talk to me. They had just been sitting in a café, talking about who the third person could be, and my song "If I Fall" had come over the radio. They saw it as a sign that I should be the third person.

The fact that I looked like hell, was a nervous wreck, was bloated and miserable didn't seem to deter them. Even the fact that I had a new baby was no big deal. We could tour on a bus and stay mostly in Canada. But for the next six months, we could work on demos and learn what we wanted our sound to be. The best part was that Bill could get some work helping us record in our home studio. I could stay still.

I called Terry, and he said that it sounded like a good project for me to do while the baby was small. It would keep me singing, and when I was ready, I would hit the road again with Nettwerk. He wouldn't be involved with the trio, but he was supportive. He was friends with the EMI folks, and he knew they'd look after us.

I loved this plan because it filled the house with new music. The girls came over three or four days a week. Bill was lighter and laughed more, and I had two more pairs of hands to hold the baby while I showered. Also, the pressure was off to be the front person. We had to come up with a name for the group. Tidal? No. Salt Water Trio? No. The Lilacs? No. Atlantic Pussy? Mmm . . . no.

We demoed song after song, all covers, but it seemed silly that we wouldn't try to write. Our friend Gordie Sampson came over one day, and we wrote a beautiful song called "How the West Was Won." It was magical. Suddenly, something was happening. Like all the cover songs we'd sung together were part of the process for us to share the music we each loved, so something new could be born that was a perfect combination of us. EMI hired a vocal arranger to teach us to optimize our harmonies.

As we got more seriously into writing, I needed more help at home. I asked Shaye if she would come to Toronto and help for a few weeks with Sophia. Shaye jumped at the chance and was on a plane the next day.

The next weeks were a blur of creativity. I felt alive again. Sophia had taken a bottle from Shaye, and so I was more rested. She was selflessly present and did everything she could to make sure I had the space to dive into the music.

One night, Bill decided to go out for drinks since Shaye was there with me. She managed to get Sophia to sleep, opened a couple of beers and sat on the couch with me. She looked at me in such a way that I knew she needed to say something. At first, we laughed as we usually did, our sisterly ease overcoming everything.

We talked about what it meant to raise a girl in this world. We would teach her to scream if anyone ever touched her. She would have a voice. She would be fierce. Shaye was going to help me. She would be there all the time and would be the safe place for Sophia when I couldn't understand her, when she needed somewhere else to go. Shaye would be her sanctuary.

Then she got quiet and looked at me. I knew something was coming.

"Your voices are different. You and Bill. When he talks to you, his voice . . . it's not the same. And when you talk to him, I don't know. When you guys talk to Sophia, it's there, but . . . I don't know. I can't hear the love."

I knew she was right. He had become a stranger to me the moment the baby came. All his light went into Sophia. What little light I had went to her and now to the music. I had tried so hard to do everything to show Bill I was still here, but I was still silently screaming. Shaye could hear my scream now too. Sisters know.

Two nights before Shaye left, she and Bill had an argument. She'd been drinking white wine, which made her mean and honest. Between her drunk honesty and Bill's, the argument exploded. They'd never fought before, not once in the seven years Bill and I had been together. Bill left the house the next morning, since he had to be away for a night doing something music related. Shaye and I were quiet as she nursed her hangover. She had to leave the next day, so she spent the rest of her time silently cleaning, playing with Sophia and being distant. I didn't know how to bridge it. She'd been clear, while drinking, that she thought we were living some kind of fake life. I felt judged and confused, like I was failing in front of her eyes. I was so tired, just trying to survive.

That night, she slept on a mattress on the floor of Sophia's room. I wanted to ask her to come in and snuggle with me. I wanted to spoon like when we were kids, but she had shut down. I lay awake, aching.

If I could go back to one moment in my life and change it, it would be that one. I would have insisted she come sleep with me that night, so we could have talked and laughed and looked at the moon out the window, so we could have figured it all out like we always did, so we could have sung and held hands and risen above everything. We'd survived our grandfather, the fire, the years apart. We could get through this. But I didn't insist. Instead, I fell asleep.

In the morning, Bill returned. We drove Shaye to the airport together in an uncomfortable silence. When she got out of the car, I got out and hugged her without meeting her eyes. She took her bag and stood watching me get in the car. I looked out the window at her and saw the pain on her face. Everything in me softened and I held her eyes from behind the glass as we drove away. I wanted to stop the car. I wanted to let her know I loved her. She smiled sadly at me. I kept looking until I couldn't see her anymore. When I turned around, I saw that Bill was irritated. His jaw was set, his brow furrowed. He said nothing all the way home.

That was the last time I saw my sister.

"I can't go another minute without kissing you."

Her last words.

She was driving from PEI to Montreal with her boyfriend, Dean. She pulled over onto the shoulder of the highway in New Brunswick and took off her seat belt. As she leaned in to kiss him, a car hit them from behind. It was a distracted driver, playing with the car radio, trying to set the clock.

Shaye's time was up.

She knew no fear, felt no pain. She left in a moment of perfect love.

She was brain dead on impact, her neck broken as her head hit the windshield, but Dean was physically unharmed. Her love wrapped around him and kept him safe.

The Tibetans call death "the Great Liberation." I once heard a monk say that the first sound that is heard at the moment of death is a rushing river.

Come on now, little sister. This way through the woods. Come and meet my friends the flowers. Come and hear the trickling stream. Come and sing with the birds with me. Come on. No . . . no, don't go that way. The water is too deep and fast. Trust me, I know. Don't go without me.

My little sister.

I couldn't seem to get past that sentence. I wrote it over and over. It is not a sentence, actually. It has no verb.

The first verb we learn in school is *être*, "to be." My little sister is. She exists. Her form may have changed, but her energy is. This is a law of physics.

Then, *avoir*, "to have." I have my little sister. She is mine. That cannot be changed either.

Then, the third fundamental verb, *aller*, "to go." In some ways, she is gone. Gone from the physical realm. Gone from the detection of my five meagre senses. Gone from this dimension.

My little sister is gone, and I have to go on without her. That is my sentence.

I'd gotten to earth first. I'd taken her hand and shown her around. Now, she'd gone ahead of me. She will be the know-it-all next time. She will know the lay of the land. She will already have made friends with all the creatures, like I taught her to. I had a feeling I couldn't shake, like she was all right. I could almost hear her telling me so. Even though I'd seen her broken body. Even though I was ravaged by grief. Every now and then, there was a glimmer that this wasn't tragic, that it was perfect. But that would disappear in the fury and the falling and the screaming out loud.

I composed myself for her, to take care of the arrangements the way I would have, had it been her wedding. That would have been my job.

Mum flew in from London. David, now the captain of a sailing yacht, flew in from New York. Bryde was on PEI, days away from graduating high school. Marty had to come from Connecticut, where he'd been living. Kim and Donna, Marty's older daughters, came. My best friend, Jenny, and her family were there. Our dear friend Chad from BC showed up to watch over me. Kim Stockwood and Damhnait Doyle stayed close to me. Amy flew in from Los Angeles and wouldn't leave my side. Kathy Cochrane flew to be with us. Colleen from Salt Spring was there, grieving with our family. Nana sat still and quiet, weeping as we all sat at her feet and, one by one, held her hand, letting her know we felt her. No one batted an eyelash when Mum started drinking. After ten years of sobriety, there was no judgment. In fact, we all joined her. The impossible had just happened.

When Marty arrived at the door, he took Mum into his arms. Collapsing in grief onto the floor, they made sounds like I'd never heard. I thought I knew all the realms of emotional sonics. Never had I witnessed an expression of love so primal as the moment I saw Mum and Marty, who both knew that only the other could touch the understanding of this loss. We all loved Shaye in our own sacred way, but there is nothing that can rip a heart from this world like losing a child. No comparable pain exists.

The banshee. There she was, writhing and screaming on the floor.

The sound of love for a dead child. A song no one should ever have to sing.

The celebration of Shaye's life was beautiful. They let us take her to the ocean. *Come to the water, stand by my side.* She was in a plain pine box that we could write messages and poems on or colour on. Children traced their hands. The piper played as the hearse finally drove away and took her to the fire. She had escaped it once before, but this time, I couldn't wake her. This time, her ashes too would be scattered on the Atlantic winds.

We played music all night as Sophia bounced in everyone's arms so I could sing my heart out. I watched as David and Marty poured rum into the sea, a sailor's farewell. We were all high from the pain, from the exquisite sharpness of life. I tried to find Bill, but he was numb, his reaction to being distraught. He couldn't meet my eyes. He had loved her dearly. He wished he'd said sorry. He began to close down completely.

Bill and I returned to Toronto a few weeks later. We went for a walk to the beach with Sophia in the stroller. It was a warm day, and I was beginning to emerge from the shock and move into a new place. I found myself talking to Shaye a lot in my mind. I'd written a song for her called "Last Kiss." The pain was moving and morphing into something else. I'd never been so sad in my life, but Shaye was all around me, closer than ever somehow, dancing like the sunlight on the water. This sorrow made me hyper-awake. Like I couldn't miss anything. Like I had to report it all to her when I got to where she was—a full debriefing. I was living for her now.

Bill stopped me on the walk and looked at me for what seemed like the first time since Sophia had been born. His eyes were warm, his voice soft.

"I'm so sorry. I can't do this anymore. I have to go. This is all too sad."

I felt my legs try to give out beneath me, but I held on to some invisible frame of this doorway I was about to pass through.

"You don't want to do that," I replied. "Everyone will think you're an asshole for leaving me right now. We'll get past this."

"I'm so sorry. I'm moving into another place."

That is all I can remember about that conversation. I remember I was wearing white pants. I remember the little dress on Sophia. I remember thinking that Shaye had been right, the love was gone. I remember he started to walk back to the house as I stood still, watching him go. He'd given up on me. A broken vow. Nothing was left of my heart except what was sleeping in that carriage. I pushed her back to our little house and watched silently as Bill packed. I could feel his desperation to escape. I know it was exhausting and sad and hard, but we were invincible. Unbreakable. No, he was done. It was the last curtain call.

He left the house, and I sat holding the baby on the couch we had bought and moved to Vancouver, to LA and back to Toronto to start our dream of a family. I looked around at the curtains he had hung and the walls we'd painted. I looked at the closed cupboards in the kitchen.

Everything stood still
Like the clock in the car
Before it was set,
Before my sister
Hit her head.
Everything frozen
In time.
Once again,
I'd been left behind.

It turns out that rock bottom isn't always the bottom. There are trap doors that lead to tunnels that have ladders that go down into cellars. It's a bottomless bottom. You can fall until it gets so dark that you're extinguished altogether, or you can learn to fly.

Bill eventually found his way to work on the road as musical director for Jason Mraz. Even though he tried to travel lighter, he carried a massive emptiness that he continued to fill with vices. He eventually had one more short marriage and a string of relationships. We stayed close through it all, but it took him almost twenty years to understand what happened to him, to us. Though it is his story to tell, he did eventually see the root of his suffering. When he found the courage to get sober, he apologized for leaving me when I needed him most, and it meant everything. He is one of the truly great men in this world, and I'm so lucky to have received incredible teachings from him. The hardest lessons are by far the most valuable. I learned what I was made of and so I am grateful, even though it almost broke me.

Maybe it just looked like I was being left over and over. Maybe the truth was that I was hurtling through an amplified evolution, leaving everyone else behind. Pain is precious. It's the diamond that cuts through it all.

When everything crumbles, look for signs of life among the ruins.

Life showed itself in the eyes of my baby girl and the endless details of caring for her. Life showed itself when I found a note from Shaye in my journal telling me how proud she was of me. Life showed itself in the new music that was coming through. I was listening.

There is no opposite of life. There is birth and death, the intro and the outro, but life goes on, carries through, with or without us. It is the eternal song.

Find the song, and we find the glorious, constant regeneration of existence.

This is the resurrection.

This is the key.

19.

Dreams

Row, row, row your boat
Gently down the stream
Merrily, merrily, merrily, merrily
Life is but a dream
—TRADITIONAL FOLK SONG

Dreams are different than expectations. Life owes us nothing, so expect nothing. But do dream. Wish with all your might on that first star. Dreams are transient; they are honest. Start with a dream and then work toward it. If it falls apart, dream again, something new. Dreams dissolve; they reform. They are a renewable resource.

All the dreams I'd had for Bill and me, for Shaye, for myself were over. The detonation of who I'd been was complete. My family had blown apart. I was starting over. For a time, I had to sit in the dreamless place and let it all die. There is nowhere darker to be.

Then slowly, I stood on shaky legs and began to pick little bits of me off the ground, pieces of sea glass in the sand. I held them up to the light. The edges were worn off. They were like gemstones. This is the gift of being tumbled by tides.

Kim and Damhnait stood like sentinels on either side of me until I could fully stand on my own. We called the band "Shaye." It became a living, healing, moving musical tribute. We invited producer Jay Joyce to come to Toronto, and we made a fabulous album, *The Bridge*. We had a hit song called "Happy Baby" that won awards, and we toured on that bus like they promised, back and forth across Canada. We were invited to Japan to represent Canada at World Expo. We were sensational, classy and real. I loved Kim and Damhnait with all my heart. They reminded me who I was, my worth. They helped me create a new vision. Who we were together was completely different than who we each were solo. It was a perfect combination, elemental in design.

Breath by breath, song by song, city by city—that's how I remembered myself. The feeling like I'd been shot in the stomach didn't go away for a long time—or maybe it never did. Perhaps I just got used to it. When a person central to one's existence dies, there is no going back. You learn to live with the missing pieces of yourself.

I dyed my hair blond and kissed boys and took care of my baby girl. We shot a gorgeous music video. I fell for the video director, but he turned out to be a player. Then a couple of beautiful musicians caught me in the net of their poetry, but in the end, neither wanted a package deal with a baby. I flew to Ireland to write some songs—where the boys say my name perfectly—and I kissed a real cutie there. Sambuca was involved. He was another sexy poet, but it turned out he was spoken for.

I flew to London to visit Dido and catch up on each other's hearts, and was able to admit how exhausted and sad I was. She let me sleep and sleep. She gave me an incredible, brand-new contraption for songwriting, something called an iPod. I stayed with her in her gorgeous house in Islington. She was in good shape in every way, working on a new album, designing her life inside and out. One afternoon, I got to watch her rehearse and saw that she was more open than ever, moving, singing, shining. Watching her that day reminded me of what we'd accomplished together, and how we can't make it in this world without our sisters to mirror our light.

Back in Canada, Shaye was nominated for a Juno award, which is the highest musical honour in the country. We got dressed up and had the time of our lives at the event. We didn't win, because Nelly Furtado was also nominated and we couldn't compete with her, but then she took us on the road with her as an opening act, so that worked out well. Also, when Dido came to Canada for a show, she had us open for her.

Soon we were invited to open for the legendary Bryan Adams at the Salmon Festival in Newfoundland. Bryan and I ran into each other backstage and had an immediate connection. We hung out in his trailer talking, and it was as though I'd always known him, which in some ways I had, through his music. Bryan is hilarious, super smart and sophisticated but edgy, which is a fascinating and rare combination. He is generous, kind and an excellent listener, true rock'n'roll, but in a healthy, sustainable package. We became fast and dear friends.

Damhnait taught me to stand up for myself and be more badass. She had zero tolerance for bullshit. She was also one of the most powerful singers I'd ever heard and a poet of the highest order. She could match my humour, and it became a game to see who could crack the other up the most onstage. She was also breathtakingly beautiful.

Kim taught me the value of an obvious musical hook, which I'd so far been avoiding for some reason. She was also an amazing mediator and could see all sides of every situation. She didn't get stuck in her opinions. She was humble and talented and had a giant heart.

Damhnait and Kim were both salt of the earth Newfoundland girls, who are probably the only people in the world who are as kind and funny as Prince Edward Islanders.

We were asked to sing "When You and I Were Young, Maggie," written in 1864 by George Washington Johnson, at the Canadian Songwriters Hall of Fame. Backstage, we searched for our dressing room and were told to look for the door that had a piece of paper taped to it with "Miscellaneous Female" scrawled in black Sharpie. When we walked in, sitting there in the glow of the mirror lights were Buffy Sainte-Marie and Loreena McKennitt.

We talked with them about life and laughed at the sign on the door. Here were two of the greatest musicians in the world, and still they had to put up with that crap. For the record, there was no "Miscellaneous Male" cave.

The night before we were scheduled to shoot a music video for a song called "Beauty," I got a phone call. It was around six in the evening, and I was in PJs because I had planned to go to bed early to get my beauty sleep. We had to be in hair and makeup at dawn.

I answered the unknown number and the voice said, "Hi, Tara? This is Dan. We have a mutual friend and she told me that when I'm in Toronto, we should meet. She says you're a great hang."

"Oh, hi. Dan?"

"Sorry, yes. Dan Lanois."

I'd like to take a moment here to pause.

On this great green earth, there was no one who had inspired me more, whose music had become more a part of my very being, whose songwriting and production had influenced me more profoundly. I was a hard-core Lanois devotee. WWLD— What would Lanois do?—was a thing in the recording studio. And here he was, calling me on my cellphone, asking if I wanted to come over. I almost dropped my phone.

Falling over myself to get dressed, I grabbed a pair of tight jeans, a blouse and a black blazer. I left my hair down.

He wasn't far from my apartment in Kensington Market, so I walked (trying not to freak out) to the loft where he was staying. Our mutual friend had set this up. I wasn't going to embarrass her by acting like a fangirl. I took an elevator up, breathing deeply. *He's just a human. Right?*

When the door opened onto his floor, he greeted me with a sweet smile. He looked exactly like I'd imagined. We hugged and I hoped I wasn't shaking. In no time, it felt like I was with an old friend. We talked about his work with Peter Gabriel, and he had me in stitches. I asked about *Wrecking Ball* with Emmylou Harris, and he shared beautiful stories about working with her and choosing the songs. This was my candy store. I got to tell him that I sang "The Maker" at my sister's funeral. I wasn't going to ask him to sing it with me, but I wanted to so badly.

We drank red wine, and he asked if he could play me something he'd been working on. Was I dreaming this? Had I fallen asleep and dreamed the phone call and this meeting? The whole thing was so surreal. He said he'd laid down a vocal so I could hear it. It was beyond incredible, a song about an angel. Then we sat down at the pedal steel beside each other, and he began to play.

If veins were strings and the heart was the body of an instrument, that's what he played. I was in the presence of a master.

It was transcendent. As the music circled me, like Jericho all my walls came down. I was immersed in something beyond understanding. I wanted to cry with the absolute perfection of the moment, but I held it and let it fill up inside me instead.

If this was a move, then it was the greatest move in the history of moves. I would have made love to that man there and then, but he was treating me with such sweet respect, like a sister—sigh. We played pool, listened to music, and he commented on some of my demos. I was shy to play them for him, but he was encouraging, generous and kind. We went out for seafood nearby and then headed back to the loft. It was getting late, and I had to go to sleep to prepare for the morning.

As I was leaving, the elevator door opened and I stepped inside. He came right up to me, holding the door from closing, and looked me in the eyes very seriously.

"The key for you, Tara, is to keep it simple."

Simple.

I walked home in a daze. Nothing would ever be the same.

Simple.

This instruction permeated every aspect of my life. I needed to get back to the woods, to peace, to my bare feet on the earth. Just me, my guitar and my baby girl.

He gave me a key.

Since I could feel my own music starting to emerge, and since we had only committed to one album, I felt like soon it would be the right time to end the Shaye project.

I'd learned and grown and healed in this process, and I was eager to find my own voice again. I was on my own with my baby, though Bill came back as often as he could to be with her. He called her every day on the phone so she could hear his voice. He was as devoted as he could be while he was away. He was still the musical director for Jason Mraz, and his tours were selling out all over the world. It was a far cry from the little cafés and theatres we did together.

I made a silent vow to myself that I would always treat Bill with love and respect and that I would be good to anyone he chose to love. We promised that Sophia would never hear us speak badly of the other. We promised to support each other always to play music. These new vows made up the foundation of how we recreated our family. We had a mantra: marriages end; families don't.

I started from scratch again.

With simplicity as my guide, I gave away almost everything I owned—all my clothes except one suitcase, all my furniture and belongings except my record player, vinyl collection, and a few boxes of keepsakes. Every time someone came to pick something up, I felt myself able to breathe easier, felt myself lifting. It was like dropping stones into the water. I was going back to the forest. I'd found a cabin on a friend's property on Salt Spring Island.

I had my guitar and my baby and was travelling light again. I was thirty years old, and I still had a record deal with Nettwerk, a publishing deal with Sony, and more to give the world, I was sure of it.

Two weeks before I left Toronto, I was staying at Kim and Allan's house and remembered that I was supposed to connect with someone before I left, a yoga teacher named Ted Grand, who was close friends with my friends out west. I put in the call, and he was excited to meet Sophia and me.

Legend has it that when I opened the door, we were both hit by lightning. This is the story we tell our children.

Shit, no. I'm leaving for the West Coast. I'm not staying here for anyone. This is no longer simple.

We spent the next two weeks together, falling deeply in love. Unlike the other men I'd met, he'd get down on the floor with Sophia and play marbles with her, or skip stones on the lake with her, or understand things she needed that I didn't know how to give. He came from old, wealthy Toronto society, but you'd never know it. He didn't care about any of that. He cared about the earth, about social justice, about teaching people to find peace. He was handsome and fit, kind and smart.

I told him I was running back to the forest to find my songs and to raise my baby amongst the trees. He understood and even drove me to the airport. We wrote each other every day and talked for hours on the phone. He asked me to fly back to meet him at his cottage in Muskoka, outside Toronto. Bill had flown in to take Sophia to California for a few weeks, so I had the space.

As I drove into the driveway at his cottage, he was standing at the doorway, waiting for me. He came out to the car and kissed me, then laid me down and made love to me right there, on the ground, in front of all the birds and squirrels. That weekend, we swam in the lake, made fires, ate beautiful food. He told me he wanted to be with me, have more babies, give Sophia and me a real home. How could I refuse?

We moved into his house in Riverdale, a Toronto neighbourhood. It was a cute little semi-detached home with a big yard and two bedrooms. I felt safe and loved and home—finally. Ted was the most grounded person I'd ever met, and he was everything I needed. Soon, I was pregnant, and he took me back to the cottage with Sophia for a weekend with his family.

We slept above the boathouse and were rocked to sleep by the soft Muskoka waves. Early one morning, Ted asked me to get dressed and have Sophia join us for a tour in the old green canoe. There is nothing like a morning paddle in a canoe. My favourite place was a little lagoon where we'd paddle through water lilies, ducks, frogs and dragonflies. The loons were always calling and a blue heron stood regally in the distance. It was like the rowboat scene from *The Notebook*.

As the canoe cut through the dark water, I saw something floating. A bottle? I asked Ted to move toward it. He mumbled something about garbage in the lake. When I picked it up, I saw there was a roll of paper inside. I pulled out a piece of parchment that had singed edges to make it look old. It was a letter from a pirate, a treasure map. Ted must have created an elaborate game for Sophia. The map had us paddling to a little island.

Sophia scrambled up the little bank and found the treasure under a picnic table. It was a small treasure chest filled with toys and candies. I recall thinking that this man was the most thoughtful human in the world. The next letter said we needed to canoe back to shore and go to the forest, to the "magic rock." As we walked through the woods with Sophia swinging between us, we spotted another treasure chest covered in some moss and leaves. Sophia lunged at it and opened it, revealing two smaller treasure chests inside. I turned to look at Ted and he was on his knee.

"I've crossed deserts, swam rivers, climbed mountains looking for treasure, but it was only when I met you that I knew I'd finally found it," he said. Tears filled his eyes.

Sophia and I opened the little boxes. They held two matching rings, platinum bands with a diamond and two sapphires on either side.

"Will you marry me?" he asked, voice quivering.

Sophia and I both said yes. She put her ring on herself, but I gave mine to Ted. He slipped it on my finger and held my hands. It was heavy and sparkly and perfect. My heart exploded in my chest. I felt like the luckiest person in the world, to have lost love and found it again.

But this is the mystery of love. It's never really lost. It just keeps showing itself if we stay open to it. It keeps revealing itself where and when we least expect it to. Sometimes, love tears us into pieces and we think we have met the opposite of love. I propose that love has no opposite. It's all love in this messy, sad, heartbreaking world.

Ted, with his business partner, Jessica Robertson, founded a company called Moksha Yoga (now Modo Yoga). When I came into the picture, there were six studios. Ted was part owner in three of them and was teaching full-time as well as running yoga teacher training programs. What I admired about them was their dedication to creating a company with the same deep integrity that mirrored their ethics. They were both activists and brilliant teachers. They grounded their teachings in yoga therapy and science, and were constantly learning and studying with different teachers. Modo studios have raised over seven million dollars for social justice and environmental issues. Both Ted and Jess embodied a profound humility and brought a lot of peace and healing to the world. Jess blew me away with her huge heart, humour and incredible musical ability.

Soon, they were opening more yoga studios all over the place, and they were booming. We began making plans to travel around the world so they could run training programs in retreat settings with the best faculty available, to create immersive experiences somewhere warm in February—almost every Canadian's least-favourite month. However, I was very pregnant.

With my return to Toronto, Kim and Damhnait welcomed me back into Shaye. EMI was wide-open to making another record after the huge success of the first one. I checked in with Terry and he just shrugged. I knew I was losing momentum in my solo career, but I just wanted to be in love, have babies and have a low-pressure music situation. The three of us laughed all the time and had created a sound that deserved more excavation and refining.

When I was five months pregnant, Ted and I decided to go on a babymoon, a romantic trip before the birth. We flew into San

Francisco and drove to the Green Gulch Farm Zen Center. As we drove up the long driveway, lined with eucalyptus trees, I felt something fall away and something peaceful wrap around me.

On the bedside table of our room sat a book: *Zen Mind, Beginner's Mind* by Shunryu Suzuki Roshi. It was a small book with a smiling monk on the cover. That night, I picked it up and read it cover to cover. It planted a seed.

When we got home, we decided to have a yard sale to make some space in the house. I found my grandfather Smiley's sword among my things, which he'd gotten in Egypt during the war. It was the very one he'd scared my sister with. I don't remember how it had come into my possession, but it was magnificent. Its sheath was carved with ancient symbols, and though the sword was now quite dull, it still shone as I held it up. I saw my reflection in the blade. I saw little Shaye. I saw him. I put it on the table outside.

Later, a man came around, picked it up and asked where it had come from. He was enamoured with it. I told him it had belonged to my grandfather, which upset him.

"You're selling it at a garage sale? Don't you think that's disrespectful?"

"Yes. Yes, I do," I replied. I told him he could have it for free, and he glared at me and stomped off with it in his hand.

Stella was born by candlelight at home in Toronto with midwives. It was a difficult birth, and at one point, I decided to get up and leave. I had changed my mind and wanted to go to the hospital to get drugs. Any drugs. All the drugs. By the time I got to the bottom of the stairs, Ted and the midwives running after me with their equipment, Stella began to crown. I fell to my hands and knees and realized that I wasn't going anywhere and there were no drugs coming my way. There was only one way through this, and I had a moment of absolute fear. *What if we die?*

Death sits beside the birthing woman. Thankfully, we were in a time and place where there was little chance of either of us crossing over. I looked him in the eye and knew him well. He'd already taken my sister, but he wasn't taking me or my baby that day. Birth can be a highly hallucinogenic experience when you're flooded with that cocktail of hormones.

Stella was born on the living room floor, caught by Tia, our beautiful midwife. Stella was perfect. She had the chubbiest cheeks and looked so much like Ted that it took my breath away. To see him holding his baby for the first time was one of the most beautiful moments of my life.

As with Sophia, I didn't tear at all. I was extremely pleased with my vagina.

A week later, Kim, Damhnait and I signed a deal with a film company, Breakthrough Entertainment, to do a series on our band, motherhood and how we made it as Canadian celebrities. Kim had baby Jack now. Damhnait was holding out. She was recently single and had her mind fully on music. The series was a great idea and we were all in.

Two weeks after that, Shaye had a performance booked to sing with a symphony in St. Catharines. Ted came to hold the baby while I was onstage. There would be two forty-five-minute sets with an intermission. No problem. I could do this.

I fed Stella before I went out for the first set, and she slept in Ted's arms. There we were, three East Coast girls in our full-length gowns in a beautiful theatre with a symphony behind us. At intermission, Stella woke and wanted to be fed again, but every time I handed her to Ted, she would cry. She wasn't finished. The audience was waiting, and the stage manager came to ask what was wrong. I grabbed my baby sling and put her in it. Ted undid the back of my gown again so I could expose my breast, and I managed to get her latched quickly. I used part of the sling to cover myself. We told the stage manager we were ready, and out we went onto the stage.

The audience thought it was wonderful, and Stella fell asleep for the rest of the set, lulled by the music, her little bare foot sticking out of the sling. It's no wonder she became a beautiful singer.

The very next day, I left Sophia with her dad, and Ted, Stella and I flew to Thailand for the yoga teacher training on Koh Phangan. We flew into Bangkok and then took a ferry to another island. Ted said we would take a water taxi to The Sanctuary, the resort where the training was being held. When I picture a water taxi, I envision the type you'd find going to Granville Island, in Vancouver, something sturdy and safe. I couldn't have been more wrong.

In Thailand, water taxis are more like big canoes with a smoky motor attached. As the wind picked up, the waves started splashing over us. Stella was in her sling attached to me, and I was livid. I couldn't believe I was in this situation with a three-week-old baby. I looked at Ted and tried yelling over the storm, "Are you fucking kidding me?"

Ted just laughed and said, "It's fine. We're close. This is fun."

This was to be the first of many experiences where I would find that Ted and I had exceptionally different opinions about what was safe and fun. He was a mountain climber, a whitewater rafter, a backcountry skier. This water-taxi ride was hysterical to him, and he thought I was overreacting. I think most people in their right minds would agree that having a tiny baby in a canoe in a storm in a foreign country isn't ideal, but Ted just saw it as an adventure.

I began to laugh. I laughed because I was so beyond mad that it was the only thing I could do. My best friend, Jenny, and sister Bryde were also at that training and on the boat with us that day, and they were equally horrified. As we approached the island, the waves calmed, and men waded out to our boat to get our luggage and to help us. I had to hand Stella to a complete stranger to portage over his head. I landed on the beach, drenched, exhausted and furious.

"See?" Ted said smiling. "Adventure."

I wanted to murder him, but that wouldn't have been very yogic of me.

We stayed at the resort for almost a month, living in a beautiful cottage at the top of a mountain. As the training went along, I began to notice something about Ted that I hadn't seen during the rush of the early dopamine days of love: he had a deep need for solitude. Being around all the students every day, teaching, and having a new baby and partner was a lot for him. He was an introvert. He grew distant. I took it personally. I asked him about his armour that had suddenly made an appearance. He didn't see what I saw. He didn't know that he needed to get away by himself. He just turned inward.

Something inside me panicked. This is what had happened with Bill, and I was so terrified that it was happening again. I'd been certain that I'd chosen someone who wouldn't abandon me, but now, a story began to form in my mind: *He will leave me. I will end up alone, now with two children. It must be me.* It felt like life or death, a biological imperative to hold on to my protector. This is the worst thing for a postpartum brain to spin out on. It's such a vulnerable time.

A dynamic began then, though almost imperceptibly, of him needing more space and me needing more love. Certainly, there was still a lot of joy and laughter and sweetness, but the seed had been planted, and it was watered by fear. I felt like I was starving for love and began contorting myself to fit what I thought he wanted.

Sophia had spent the month with Bill and was so excited to see us when we came home. She just wanted to hold Stella and kiss her face. It was hard to re-enter a winter environment, but filming was about to begin on the Shaye documentary, and we had an album to write.

The next months were a beautiful blur with the film crew around. I was juggling the girls and trying to get fit, while Ted was working twelve-hour days without an office of his own. At night, he would read the piles of projects from teachers, which sat beside the bed, until he fell asleep. It seemed like a way to avoid intimacy with me.

No matter what, we had yoga. I began to practise almost every day. I got strong and calm. In the beginning, when I would walk into class, where there were mirrors, I would see myself through the eyes of the culture I'd been raised in, through the eyes of my grandmother, the boys at school, the photographers and makeup artists, the magazines, the stylists, the music business. But as the class progressed, I saw what was really there: I was healthy, beautiful, mystical, a mother. Trillions of cells, galaxies of atoms, were all working together in concert. Perspective is everything.

I started going to belly dancing classes. I could move like a woman and figure-eight my hips like I was stirring a cauldron. I would leave feeling like a goddess again. Ted said he never saw me happier than when I came home from those classes.

Things felt all right with Ted. We were a great team, making our lives work, but when I'd bring up the subject of a wedding, he would ask that we not discuss it. The story got louder in my mind. It was as if, inside himself, he knew we weren't a perfect match, but he was trying to find a way to get to a place where it felt right.

We hired a part-time nanny to help with the girls, to get them out of the house so we could work a little, maybe have some time alone. This helped tremendously, and I began to feel connected to Ted like I had before. I was so relieved. We just needed space. He planted a little garden in the front yard and was proud of his heirloom tomatoes.

The music was flowing and the new Shaye album was soon finished. We were playing everywhere, constantly. The film crew was around most of the time, and between that process and the kids, I was starting to feel overexposed and exhausted. I lost the joy for it all and was irritable with my bandmates. I began to wonder, after a year of this, if motherhood and music could really be something I did at the same time. The film crew loved this angle, and it became well-known that I wanted out.

The funny thing about a reality TV show is that it has a writer. Doesn't that seem strange? They started to plant little scenarios to increase the drama between us, and that wasn't helping us connect. The timing couldn't have been worse. Our singles were being added to radio, and the next thing we knew, we were being asked to tour with—drum roll, please—Willie Nelson!

We couldn't say no, and our stage show was excellent at this point. Stella was still nursing at night, but Bryde said she'd come to help so I could focus. Off we went on an arena tour, and though our group dynamic wasn't optimal, we were knocking the shows out of the park. Kim and Damhnait would sing with Willie at the end of his show every night, but I usually had to get back to the hotel to feed Stella by then. I did stay to sing with them all at the end of one show, and it was a life highlight. But I paid for it when I got back to the hotel, because Stella was livid and was up a lot of the night.

These things snowball—an exhausted mother, an irritable baby, a band on the rocks.

One day on the tour, we were asked to come onto Willie's bus and sing him a song. I was nursing Stella in my sling while we sang him an a cappella version of a song we'd written called "Ocean of Sorrows." There he was, with his braids and bandana, his family around him, smiling at us as we sang. Talk about a surreal experience.

By the time we all got home, the girls and I weren't even speaking. I was done and they'd had it with me. They had to carry on together doing all the press for the singles. We tried to hide it from the press that we weren't a band, but they knew. I abandoned them when we should have worked it out like we always had before. They did a new photo shoot, just the two of them.

It took a long time for us to connect again and process what had happened, but luckily, we had built something beautiful underneath all the drama, and in the end, that is what survived. As with the aqueducts in Rome, there is evidence of how beautifully and perfectly we worked together. Even though it fell apart, the music remains and keeps flowing through the world. They are still two of my closest sisters.

I told Nettwerk that I was ready to proceed with getting back to my solo career, and Terry was overjoyed. He flew into Toronto to meet for dinner and make a plan. We decided that I would do some writing with other people—it was revolutionary for Terry to support that. I chose Ron Lopata and Simon Wilcox, two of Canada's best writer-producers, and off we went. Terry also shared that things had changed in the music business and the budgets would be smaller. He told me not to expect the red carpet.

Bill was back in Toronto for a while, and I asked him to set up a little studio in the basement of our house to make record-quality demos with me. Terry decided to release an EP called *Signs of Life* to put out an alert that I was making my way back. Ted took a photo of me in the front yard when the light was good, and the magic of John Rummen made it into an album cover. Gone were the days of the $25,000 photo shoot in a Moroccan mansion in the Hollywood Hills. I didn't care. I was just so desperate to make my music again.

Ted and I began to get passionate about raising money for the David Suzuki Foundation (DSF). As a child, I'd been such a fan of David Suzuki, the great Canadian environmentalist and broadcaster. To me, he was synonymous with protecting my safe place, my cabin, my forest, the sacred orchids. DSF was aligned in every way with our personal ethics, and it seemed like the perfect place to invest our money and time. David (we were on a first-name basis at this point) invited me to write a song for an album that they were making called *Playlist for the Planet*. I wrote "No Surrender" with Ron Lopata and Simon Wilcox, and was thrilled to be on that album with other amazing Canadian artists.

I was back on track. The album was almost finished, and mothering the girls felt manageable. The divide continued to grow between Ted and me, in terms of our connection, but we still worked great together in every other way. He was supportive of the record, I was supportive of his work, and he was a phenomenal father. I didn't have to worry about rent or groceries or gas. I had help with the girls. We travelled to exotic places like India, Hawaii, Brazil, Costa Rica and Thailand. During these trips, we had many magical experiences together, and there was a deep and profound love between us. No relationship is perfect. The push and pull of our dynamic had worn us down, and marriage was not on the table. Still, we found ways to be kind and sweet to each other, and those moments were enough to keep us together and occasionally reaching for each other in the night.

One morning, I woke feeling strange. Pretty soon, my suspicions were confirmed: I was pregnant. Ted and I sat there in shock. This was not what we'd planned. I called Terry to let him know that I needed to put the album on hold. Of course, he was happy for me personally, but he didn't know how long he could shelve an album while I had the baby, not with the music business being flushed down the toilet every day.

With this pregnancy, I went deep into my yoga practice. I had done doula training and thought I had adequate experience to be a strong advocate, but something was missing in my understanding. I wanted to be more courageous this time. I stumbled across a book called *When Survivors Give Birth* by Penny Simkin. In it, she shares stories about women who are survivors of sexual assault and their experiences of giving birth, which is a vulnerable time and can trigger old trauma. It can also heal it. This was the piece I needed.

I started painting and continued belly dancing. I got out of my head and into my body. I felt the most beautiful I'd ever felt in my life. Ted and I began to move toward each other again. Something was healing from the inside out. I wasn't afraid anymore.

Flora's birth was everything I could have dreamed of. I fearlessly leaned into the opening. Death didn't even bother to show for this one. It was about trusting, surrendering, following the river, reaching my arms to the light.

I danced to the mystical music of Dead Can Dance, *Toward the Within*, and the voice of Lisa Gerrard infused me with mythological power. This little girl burst into the world like the cork on a champagne bottle, with sounds of rejoicing. Bryde was there, cheering me on. I felt Shaye in the room, holding my hand. I felt all the birthing mothers in the world with me, all the mothers before me and all the birthing yet to come. This was the breakthrough. I wanted to guide mothers through this doorway, and this was the key I needed.

Flora was an easy baby who slept all the time. We started travelling to the Modo Yoga teacher trainings with all three girls. It was a lot, but the girls loved it. They experienced being loved by the entire community. I learned about motherhood from the other mamas who were around me, especially Jessica's mother, Janet Robertson, who often came to the trainings as the jubilant matriarch. She had raised three incredible girls and knew what I was going through in my hardest and most joyous mothering moments. I made close friendships at the trainings that will be with me for life.

We were making a good living, and thank goodness for that, because no one was buying music. I was never going to see a penny from my Capitol release, and I was still paying back Nettwerk slowly for the other records through album sales, but that would take eons. The Shaye records weren't selling either. I knew I had to approach Nettwerk and let them know I was ready to finally release and support the new record. Flora was a year and a half, and I couldn't put it off any longer.

I called Terry and he laid it out for me. He had been my manager for fifteen years, and though we'd had so many great opportunities and experiences, there was no way that I, with three children, could do what was required to break an album in the current climate. There was no money and I'd be starting from scratch, driving in a van from town to town to sing for no one until people started to care again. He told me that it was time for him to stop managing me, that there was nothing more he could do.

I hung up the phone in shock. I'd thought that he, of all people, would never give up on me. But he was right; I couldn't get in a van with my babies, stay in shitty hotels, pay for childcare while I was onstage or doing interviews.

It was done.

I was completely gutted. I had made my choices, and Nettwerk had stood by me for as long as they could—longer than they should have, really. I was incredibly lucky to have made three albums with them and to have had the chances I got. Nettwerk did release *Wake* digitally, but there was no way to support it or market it.

It took me three days to tell Ted, because I couldn't believe it myself.

I knew that I would never be satisfied with a completely domestic kind of life. I had details to distract me from how devastated I felt, and mercifully, they were enough to pull me through those first weeks. I was untethered, lost. I didn't even want to look at my name. Tara MacLean was someone with huge dreams of singing all over the world. But this incarnation of myself, she was different. She would find joy in the little victories—the first words and steps of my babies, my house, being Ted's partner. Something in me seemed to soften and Ted noticed. We began to talk about marriage again.

We flew to BC to be married in Tofino. We both felt so close to that land, having fought to save it. He'd been working for Greenpeace in 1993 while I was on the blockades. He'd been hanging off ships in an effort to stop the export of raw lumber, while I'd been sitting in front of the logging trucks. Though we hadn't met at the time, we were bonded by our love of this place. This land was very dear to us.

Ted and I were wed on Chesterman Beach at the Wick-aninnish Inn, a five-star, world-class resort with one of the most elegant and natural views of the rugged Pacific Ocean shoreline. We invited a small group of immediate family only. Bryde was my maid of honour. Dressed in my hemp silk dress and wearing tiny orchids in my hair, I nursed Flora that morning and looked out onto the beach from my hotel window. For a moment, I had a fear that Ted wouldn't show up. Minutes later, I saw him in a gorgeous tan suit, making a sacred circle of stones in the sand to surround us in our ceremony.

Our partnership made sense, and we created a beautiful container for the children to grow in. We loved each other, and though at times our differences were difficult to bridge, we stayed and fought hard for our family. Our relationship was grounded in building something sustainable. I even wrote a happy song about loving him called "Here and Now." That was a first!

I dropped MacLean from my name altogether and took Grand as my surname. I thought Tara MacLean was gone. I let her dreams go. But if we stop dreaming, we die. So I buried her as deep as I could.

But deep in the mycelium network and the roots of trees, she was wrapped in a shroud of spiderwebs and skeletonized leaves, held in stasis, all dreams intact.

20.

Sound of Water

The old pond
Frog jumps in
Sound of water
—BASHO

A ll bodies of water sound different. They all sing different songs. We are bodies of water, all connected, colliding, all moving toward something we can't even begin to fathom.

After a few more years in Toronto, our family decided (meaning that I begged Ted) to move to my beloved Salt Spring Island in the Salish Sea. It is known by the Cowichan First Nation as Klaathem, which means "salt." It is also known as Cuan by the Saanich, meaning "each end," referring to the mountains that bookend the island. In 1905, the Geographical Names Board of Canada named it Saltspring.

It felt important to raise the little ones in a place where they could be immersed in nature, like I had been. Whoever my mother had called upon to keep me safe that night in the river was certainly in the forest of the Pacific Northwest. I needed her to help me mother my girls. I needed her great arms around them. Maybe she is everywhere, but she felt closer in the trees. They serve as altars to the earth.

We found a gorgeous turn-of-the-century, French provincial farmhouse that backed onto hundreds of acres of protected forests and hiking trails along the Channel Ridge. We bought the land from the Pearsons, who'd bought it after the previous owners, the Chantelu sisters, died. The sisters had raised chickens on the farm and birthed baby lambs in the barn for over eighty years. At night, the owls called to each other across the valley, and the frogs sang us to sleep. The stars were so bright at night that it was hard to catch that first one to wish on before the others showed up. Trails cut through arbutus groves and giant fir and cedar trees.

Bill had asked us if he could take Sophia to live with him in LA, and I had reluctantly agreed, knowing that we were only a few hours away by plane. Bill wanted to live his dream of being in California and having Sophia with him. Stella and Flora, now five and three, were able to roam free, and we enrolled them in an alternative school.

On one of our first days on the island, we explored the little town. It had restaurants, a few clothing stores, a post office and a hardware store. You could even get sushi and authentic Italian pizza. The famous Saturday market was phenomenal.

My favourite restaurant, which had been there forever, was called the Tree House Cafe. Set in the heart of the island and built around a tree, the sweet little place was also a small music venue. Salt Spring was home to many artists who felt drawn to this peaceful place, including Valdy, Randy Bachman and Raffi. At the Tree House, you never knew who would show up and play. We went in and sat down. Around the corner, carrying menus, came someone who I recognized but couldn't quite place because it was so wildly out of context. It was Mark LeCorre, the master sound engineer who had rescued me on the road so many years ago.

"Mark!" I almost upended the table to hug him. He couldn't believe it either. When I told him I had moved there, he lit up. He had bought the Tree House and was running it through the summer as a full-time music venue with great sound and amazing food. He told me I had a gig in this little piece of paradise whenever I wanted. When I told him I wasn't really playing music anymore, he looked at me mischievously and said, "We'll see about that."

Ted fell in love with the lifestyle on Salt Spring and planted a magnificent garden. The girls flourished, and Sophia came to visit as often as possible. She once stayed with us for a year to try out the school. She didn't love it, so she went back with her dad in LA. It was just too small a town for her giant self.

I fell into a pattern of mothering, enjoying the harvests of pears and blackberries on the property, swimming naked in the lake at sunset and overseeing renovations on the house. I had begun writing a screenplay about the life of my sister Shaye, a long-term project that made me feel close to her. I played guitar and piano sometimes, but songs weren't coming through. Sony Music Publishing had told me that they would always be with me, and they were true to their word. They didn't push me to write, but they always let me know they were there.

I wondered if I would ever write a song again.

The world didn't present itself in poetry anymore. I would look at the white ringlets of Flora's hair, or the hazel-green of

Stella's eyes, or watch Sophia run like a wild colt in the fields and think that they were my poems now. Each one a little masterpiece. I had created them, and every day, between the ponytails and grilled cheese sandwiches, the laundry and the walks in nature, we wove a beautiful life for them.

Ted and I explored our marriage through varying expressions of affection and kindness, impatience and confusion, disappointment and deep love. It was the complex dance of two people who moved differently in the world to the extremes of introversion and extroversion. Some days, we met face to face in the middle of the floor; some days, we retreated to separate corners; but we kept dancing. Sometimes it was lovely, and sometimes it was lonely, but through it all, the children witnessed a climate of love and mutual support. Through those years, we created our own little house band, constantly playing the sounds of laughter, inside jokes, piano scales, lullabies and the songs of the land: the ravens, the frogs, the crickets, the owls, the neighbour's chickens, the rain on the metal roof.

My dad Danny would come from Victoria to visit, and he'd fix little things around the house and be a proper grandfather to the girls. His wife and stepson lived with him, and he loved escaping and coming over. His stepson dealt with hard-core addiction issues and was in and out of rehab. Our little home was an oasis of sweetness, little bouncy girls, and healthy living.

Sometimes, Mum would fly in from Ireland to spend a few weeks with us. After Shaye had died, she'd moved there to a house her husband had inherited in a magical little town called Newcastle, where heather grew on the mountains and she could wander the night in search of her daughter, a banshee of flesh and bone.

Even though she'd been drinking since Shaye's death, we were able to have a relationship, though I didn't feel that I could completely confide in her. I called her out once on her drinking, and she shot back that she didn't think Ted loved me. I didn't speak to her for a long time after that and had to keep a bit of an emotional distance. Sometimes, she'd call from Ireland, distraught and drunk, and make me wonder if these were her last days. Then she'd go for a cold swim in the Irish Sea and remember her wildness. She always sobered up and apologized. She'd lost a child, after all. How do you even go on?

Back on our little island, we had sweet rituals. We would wake up and drive the kids to school, have coffee dates at our favourite café and then go for a hike or run together in the forest most days. Salt Spring was good for us. Ted is incredibly intelligent and insightful, and our conversations were fascinating. I did like to talk much more than he did, especially when coffee was added to my already chirpy personality.

We had great friends and loved our home. The children were thriving.

Day after day, year after year, we lived this routine, but something was always missing for me. No matter how sweet our life was, I was restless. I wasn't used to being still for so long.

We had an old, wooden baby grand piano, and some days, I'd sit at it for hours, touching keys, hoping they'd open a portal to somewhere, but no combination seemed to work. One rainy West Coast day, I played and played until I burst into tears. *Who am I?* I turned around and saw that Stella and Flora had quietly set up a little audience of stuffed animals behind me. I worried they'd seen me crying, but soon that thought was erased by a new one: *They know me.* I stood up and bowed to the contingency of creatures. It wasn't a standing ovation, but it would do.

I needed people to sing to.

Our trips away for the Modo Yoga teacher trainings usually helped me feel less trapped, but one trip to Brazil had devastating consequences.

The year before, we'd had one of the best trips of our lives at a little place deep in the jungle on the coast of Brazil. We decided to return the following year. Ted travelled two weeks ahead of us and called the night before we were supposed to go, saying that he didn't think we should go, that people were getting sick. We were deep in winter in Canada, and I was desperate to get away and counting the minutes to our departure. We'd arranged to have people stay in the house while we were gone, and we'd had all our vaccinations and paperwork done. We were packed. How bad could it be? The training hadn't been cancelled, so I didn't imagine it was that awful. We'd been to India three times and people had gotten sick, but I was extra careful.

We flew down anyway, and I did the intense journey by car with the girls. What a relief it was to get to the coast after the hot, sticky ride. I loved Brazil and was excited to meet the new trainees. I was officially the prenatal consultant for the company, and if there were trainees that were pregnant, I got to take special care of them, which gave me a tremendous sense of purpose.

Within a few days, I got dysentery. The kids seemed fine, but I was the sickest I'd ever been. Ted told me I should take the kids, head to the nearby city and see a doctor. The night before I left, I was hallucinating under my mosquito net. I saw jaguars coming toward me out of the mesh. I heard little clicking sounds. I sat up, realizing I needed to get to the toilet. I turned on my flashlight, weakly climbed out of bed and got to the bathroom.

Something landed on my leg. It was a bat. I didn't have the energy to scream or even flick it off me. I just looked at it as its blue-black body shone in the light coming in from the moon and thought, *This is a new low.* I heard the clicking sound again. I lifted my flashlight and saw the biggest spider I'd ever seen in my life about four feet from me, between the bathroom and the bed. It was the size of my face. I couldn't identify the species in the moment, but tears began to run down my cheeks. Brazilian wandering spiders are the deadliest in the world. I could hear the kids breathing in the bed nearby. The spider quickly ran out of sight. I climbed back into bed under the net but stayed awake with my flashlight, guarding the children. Ted slept through all of it.

Stella, Flora and I took a small boat to a nearby town called Itacaré. It was an excruciating trip. At the hotel, I had the front desk call a doctor for me. She came to our room and put me on an IV while the kids played together peacefully on the floor. She said there were reports coming out of the jungle that the resort had become dangerous with staph infections and other serious risks due to issues with their water and sewage practices. When I asked if there was a board of health we could report them to, she laughed and said, "This isn't Canada." She told me to drink Coca-Cola to kill whatever was making me sick. What a funny prescription, but it turns out that a cold Coke when you have dysentery on a scorching hot day might be one of the best things ever.

I recovered enough in a few days to get on a plane headed for home. On the flight, Stella started itching her foot. I looked and saw a red line under her skin. What I didn't know at the time was that the tiny hitchhiker was a relatively benign parasite, if found in Brazil. The drug to kill it is an over-the-counter medication called thiabendazole. The hookworm, which causes an infection called cutaneous larva migrans, is commonly transmitted to children on the beach, as it lives in dog feces. Mothers carry the thiabendazole cream in their purses, and it's perfectly safe. In Canada, the doctors had no idea what the worm was, and it was growing. It was laying eggs in her feet. A local doctor who was a parent at the school Stella went to had done aid work in Africa and was able to identify it.

Stella was sent to a pediatric tropical disease specialist, who told me what medication she needed. I was so relieved, but it wasn't approved in Canada. The doctor said it shouldn't be a problem to get the government to release some for us, so she petitioned them. We were denied. Every night, Stella woke up screaming from nightmares and we'd ice her little foot.

I called the press. The film crew came to our house and interviewed Stella, who showed them her foot. The next day, someone sent us the medication.

Within days, the worm was dead. It had taken six weeks to kill it. We were exhausted, and Stella still wasn't thriving. We took her to a doctor who gave her antibiotics. She seemed to get better. As soon as the antibiotics were done, she would get worse.

One morning, on the drive to school, I looked in the back seat and saw that Stella had no colour in her face and wasn't breathing well. We ran to emergency. She was burning up.

We were rushed to a hospital off-island. I sat with my baby girl in the ambulance, holding her hand. She was on an IV and surrounded by cold packs for her fever, and her eyes were glossing over. When we arrived, the pediatrician said she was septic.

Over the next few excruciating days, they filled her with antibiotics, trying to kill whatever had invaded her system. A doctor walked in the room and asked me to sit down, which is never a good sign. She explained that the microbiology team at the hospital had discovered that Stella had a superbug called ESBL E. coli. All the antibiotics she'd been taking were making it worse because they couldn't kill it. It left all the strong ones to breed. She explained that if we had gotten there any later, Stella would not have made it. She said Stella had gotten this in Brazil, and possibly the hookworm was carrying it, but they couldn't be sure.

There were two options in terms of medicine: one could make her deaf, and the other one had unknown side effects, but it was one of the strongest antibiotics in the world. Stella was already proving to be a beautiful singer, so we chose door number two.

Through a plastic tube in her arm that went straight to her heart, the antibiotics began to take effect. I asked if we could take her home to heal. They gave me a course on how to administer them and flush the line with saline.

At home, I would flick the bubbles out of the lines before hooking her up to the drip. I thought of Nana, who'd been a nurse. I had to channel her. She'd given me her nurse's ring, and so I put it on, hoping it would give me the confidence to push salt water directly into my baby's heart.

We took her for walks outside between treatments. She would stand under the trees and close her eyes and listen to the wind. Sometimes, she'd walk to one spot and sit down and say she needed to be in that place, that it made her body feel good. We would follow her lead. Ted was amazing through this ordeal, but there was an unspoken accusation between us. If I had listened to him and not gone to Brazil, this wouldn't have happened. I knew him well enough to know that he was thinking what I was thinking, and I was silently blaming myself.

The side effects turned out to be cognitive. She had a hard time focusing at school and became easily overwhelmed. She also had severe pain in her body for over a year, but in time, her colour returned and her little light shone fully again. Her songs filled the house.

As much as time was gifting us with its healing, I'd been shaken. A friend invited me for a weekend retreat with the Zen teacher Peter Levitt, who lived on the island. I'd heard of him. He was a poet from New York, an old-school dharma bum teaching Soto Zen. He sounded fascinating, so I eagerly signed up.

The teacher was sitting facing us as we all entered. All I knew was that I was supposed to wear black. There may have been twenty of us in total. Peter looked right at me and smiled. "You know, you're already a Buddha. You just have to remember who you are."

The words went all the way through me. It was the same message that my wise friend Bruce had given me that day on the beach years before: "Who are you really?" That's how I knew in a flash that I had met my teacher.

Thus began a beautiful pilgrimage toward my centre. The centre of my centre. He taught me to sit in a way that had been done for thousands of years, to return to the silence, to find clarity, humility, compassion. I learned there was a reservoir of love that, though I had known it was there, I now had access to. I was hooked—hooked to getting unhooked. He was a genuine Beat poet from the Bronx. He'd hung out with Jack Kerouac and Allen Ginsberg in the 1960s. If anyone knew where my poems had gone, I figured it would be him.

He taught me to use the breath to follow the bread crumbs in the moonlight back to the source of the songs.

As I slowed down and became more tender with my life, more forgiving of myself, I noticed I was looking at my entire existence with the same lens, seeing clearly that the people who had hurt me, and who I had hurt, were simply part of the training. They were all my teachers. I was on my knees with gratitude and gave myself permission to drop the stories and find the space for love inside the pain. Surely this was a way to keep living. No matter where I was, I could find a cushion and sit. No matter where I was, I was home. It was revolutionary.

When it was time, I studied and took the Bodhisattva vows in an ordination ceremony called Zaike Tokudo. The ritual of taking these vows is ancient. To be on my knees, vowing to serve and free all beings, was incredibly humbling. I felt something rise within me that I had forgotten was there: a remembrance of our interconnectedness through space and time.

I was given my name: Koshin Suion. It means Ancient Faith, Sound of Water.

Here is the poem that Peter wrote for me that day:

In a place beyond seeing,
the sound of water. Listening
with the whole body and mind,
ancient faith rises
from the deepest source,
its song heard all the way through.
The wind of our ancestors
rustles the branches of autumn,
releases the rivers in spring.
A still voice gently singing
through the dark
brings all beings back to One.

Faith. There is that word again. Knowing that little bit of light can illuminate the darkest room, Mum had said. Could it be this simple? Could faith be a knowing? Inextricably linked to the will to live? To love? To evolve? Could it be the source of the songs? This little light of mine.

If this is so, then each one of us is the high protector of this sacred light within.

I began to organize Zen retreats with Peter, to be the reverend for funerals and weddings, and to support women in childbirth. I began to see my role as a gatekeeper, someone who stood at the thresholds of massive life events and helped people through. A hand in the darkness.

One day, while having lunch at the Tree House, I saw a sign for a Neil Young tribute night. Anyone could come and sing a song. I hadn't sung in front of anyone for ages, except my children and the stuffies. I went home and tuned my dusty guitar.

That night, I sat in my car outside the café, trying to find the courage to go inside. I'd get out of my car and then get back in. Out. In. I got out, took my guitar from the back seat and stood there in the parking lot for the longest time, leaning against my car, my heart in my throat. The Tree House kept getting farther away, like in a dream when you're walking down a hallway to open a door.

I had to move toward it.

Breathe. Remember who you are.

I thought of all the huge stages I'd played, all the incredible musicians I'd stood beside. I thought of who I'd been. What if I was still her? No one could take away my voice. Just because I didn't have a record deal, or a manager, or an agent didn't mean I wasn't a singer.

I slid a little note under my door. It read, *JFDI*—just fucking do it.

Glamour Spell activated. Shoulders back, chin up.

I walked into the Tree House and signed up to sing "Natural Beauty," one of my all-time favourite songs from the *Harvest Moon* album. As I sat on the stool, I looked at Mark, who was doing sound. He remembered who I was. He knew my voice so well. I started finger picking, and the sound was warm and carried out over the harbour, the boats, the purple starfish on the rocks, the mossy shoreline, the giant cedar.

As I began to sing, I felt the perfection of the lyrics move through me, words I felt deeply. It's such a simple melody. It's grounded, low, but then builds in the most unpretentious way. The song is a statement about the world being a mirror of ourselves. I sang it with all my heart. Though I was a little shaky in moments, there I was, the little girl on the plywood stage.

That was my reclamation.

I called Sony Publishing, and they were encouraged that I wanted to keep writing and singing. Ted was supportive and we decided that I would go to Nashville to write for other artists for now, and they hooked me up with Sony Music Nashville. I had loads of friends there, and Damhnait was going down to write all the time. She and I planned trips together and had the time of our lives. We didn't do dishes, drank red wine and wrote songs. We had breakthrough conversations deep into the night. She now had two little girls at home, and so we shattered our domestic selves for a moment to reclaim the other parts of us that we had no energy for otherwise. It was pure bliss.

Sony Music Nashville advised me that I would have more success as a songwriter there if I wrote songs from the male perspective. I didn't have a clue what men were thinking or wanting to sing about. It's a real skill for a female songwriter to do that, and it was one I didn't have. Also, *what the fuck?*

This was outside-in instruction again, and I just couldn't pull it off. I have women friends who are incredible writers, and they work with hard-core male rock bands and crush it. I couldn't. I wanted to write beneath all genders. But I would go into sessions with male artists and ask them what they were thinking, what mattered to them. I actually gained a lot of insight from that exercise, but I realized I was there at their service. No one asked me what I was thinking.

I started to spend time just going to shows when I was in Nashville. I'd dress up, walk downtown alone under the strings of lights in alleyways and find little blues bars, where I'd sit in a corner and listen. Seeing the great Colin Linden, a dear friend of mine, play with Whitey Johnson at the Bourbon Street Blues and Boogie Bar absolutely floored me. I felt so free, alone in the dark bar, soaking up the magic, with no one needing anything from me.

I needed a new plan. I began to wonder if I could create a live show that would be a ceremony, with many ceremonies inside it. Little breakthroughs to mimic life, and one giant push through to the other side at the end. Contractions and birth. Something transformational. Back home, I worked with my friend Naomi Jason, a brilliant dancer, as musical director on a show filled with local talent called *Imaginelle*. It was a play on *imaginal cells*. These are what allow for the process of metamorphosis to occur when a caterpillar turns into a butterfly. The caterpillar inside the chrysalis dissolves into a liquid, and then dormant imaginal cells come to life, creating something completely different than what was there before. It's the cell of dreams.

The show was a revelation. It wasn't a performance; it was a prayer. I was learning the difference.

I felt something stirring. My cocoon began to crack open. A few days after the show ended, I found myself sitting in my car outside my house. Something had shifted and I couldn't stop crying. My house was beautiful, my children were happy and healthy now, my marriage was fine, but where was I? I didn't recognize my life. Something inside me wasn't in alignment with my surroundings. Something in me felt bigger than my circumstances.

What was wrong with me? Was I depressed? Was I going crazy? Was I bored?

I picked up my phone, barely able to catch my breath, and called Bill.

"Are you okay, Little?" (This is one of his nicknames for me, referring to my diminutive stature.)

"No. I don't know what's wrong. I can't go in my house. I just feel so lost."

He was quiet for a moment, and then said, "This is not how you go down. You're Tara MacLean! Remember? You're supposed to be singing onstage. Ted loves you, but he doesn't understand that part of you. It's not his fault. He's never seen it. You have to find your way back to where you belong."

Where I belong? I looked at this beautiful life designed from choices I'd made, and thought, *Isn't this where I belong? Isn't this home?* I'd brought us here. Was it possible that I'd outgrown this somehow? What did I have that was really mine?

My voice.

My voice was screaming at me from the inside. I had to listen. Something had to change drastically.

Every now and then, all the randomness collides, and we glimpse something for a brief moment. A pattern emerges and then disappears before we can grasp it, and it tells us there is so much we can never understand about this miraculous existence. It tells us we are a part of something much grander than we can comprehend as we dance in orbit around this tiny star. It tells us to keep opening, to keep being brave, to keep letting go until we are gone. It hands us the key, presses it into our palms and closes our fingers around it. It whispers instructions on the wind. It sings us home.

I remembered that Sarah McLachlan had recommended reading a book called *Big Magic: Creative Living Beyond Fear* by Elizabeth Gilbert. One of the hardest things in life is discerning whether fear is controlling you, or if it is your intuition telling you something. I drove to the local bookshop and picked up the book. I read it cover to cover and then sat down at my desk, opened my computer and closed my eyes. *Deeper, under, lower. Breathe. What needs to come through? All the way through.*

I saw my life moving backward, from the moment I was now in, through the births of my babies, to meeting Ted, Bill leaving, Shaye's death, Sophia's birth, the songs and songs, finding my dad, the fire, the abuse, the cabin. I saw myself moving through the forest, a little wildling, singing to herself. I heard Marty singing to me, the nylon-string guitar, the wind in the trees, the birds, the lighting of the match for the kerosene lamp. I went further back, to my mother's birth, to my grandmother's birth, to my great-grandmother. I heard their songs and felt their love, and I understood that I was their dream and the dream of all my ancestors. I pushed back further, into fiddles and drums, the songwriters who came before me, the dancers, miners, loggers, sailors and farmers, the mothers. I saw them coming across the water on ships, bringing music. I saw the Indigenous Peoples and heard their songs, felt the rhythm. Further. Further. I landed on the shore by the Atlantic Ocean. I looked at the horizon line, where the water met the sky, and knew where I belonged. It was a primordial call home to the sound of water.

Come to the water, stand by my side.

I opened my eyes and began to write: *It's hard to know where anything begins, where life began, but it seems that it rises from the water.*

This was the first sentence of a show I began writing about the history of music in Atlantic Canada, the lineage that I was a part of. I needed them. I needed the voices of my ancestors to call me home.

I began to research the lives of the most legendary songwriters from the region, using what I knew of ceremony, of eulogy, of birthing, of celebrating and honouring the legacy of a life and the ripples it creates. They had dropped stones into ponds and I was simply following the circles outward. It turned out that these songwriters had left me clues, but I had to dive for them.

They were resilient, and nothing stopped them from sharing their music. Rita MacNeil was a singer and a mother. Gene MacLellan battled bipolar disorder and still found a way to create some of the most beautiful music in the world. Hank Snow had sold cod tongues in order to buy his first guitar and had experienced severe abuse as a child. Stan Rogers, gone too soon, gave us songs of the sea and love songs of exquisite longing. The Rankin Family rose again and again through unfathomable loss. On and on, I found evidence of unstoppable, fierce, powerful songwriters. These were my people. Surely, I was made of the same stuff.

My mother flew to PEI from Ireland to help take care of Nana, who was ill. In some ways, Nana was taking care of her as well—her drinking was getting worse. Nana had warned me that one day, I would be called back to the East Coast, that it was just something that happened to Islanders who lived "away," and I couldn't ignore it.

The call was clear.

I asked Ted if we could move east, and he took some time to seriously consider the possibility, but he just couldn't wrap his head around it and neither could the kids. They were happy where they were. We had a stunning home in one of the best climates in the country, surrounded by nature. He said he'd support me to create whatever I needed to make, but the family needed to stay there. I was gutted by this, but I had to honour their wishes.

Night after night, I researched and wrote the show that I called *Atlantic Blue*, after the Ron Hynes song. The house wasn't as clean, and I stopped cooking altogether. Ted picked up what I put down. Every word I wrote felt like a step closer to home. I contacted the families of the writers, or the writers themselves who were still alive. They gave me permission and insight and photos. It was coming together.

Finally, after months of writing, I called my dear friend Todd MacLean (no relation), a musician and writer on PEI, and asked him what he thought of the concept. It would be a multimedia presentation, with biographical films about the lives of the writers, live music and dancers. Todd loved it and signed on to help me. We got an incredible violinist,

Cynthia MacLeod, on board, as well as editor Jason Rogerson and director Jennifer Brock Abbott to help with the films. I booked two shows at the Harmony House theatre in PEI that summer to showcase the idea.

It was a hit.

The show sold out fast. I couldn't believe it. I realized that people remembered me and wanted to hear me sing. This was my home. This is where people really cared. Even the premier showed up. I was back, rowing my little boat.

After the showcase of *Atlantic Blue*, I signed a contract to play it for two summers at a theatre in downtown Charlotte-town called The Guild. People were coming back two and three times and bringing friends. We added more musicians to fill out the band, and all kinds of local companies were coming on board to sponsor it. Danny helped to produce it with me, and Marty flew in to perform on the show as a special guest. It was incredibly emotional for me to sing onstage with him, in a show that I had written, where I also told his story.

Mum and Nana came to the show often, and I was having the time of my life. The kids loved spending the summer on PEI. Even though I had to be away from them for stretches of time, I felt like the best mother in the world, watching them play in the waves by day and having them see me sing at night. Sophia got a job as an usher at the theatre.

Atlantic Blue evolved over time, and I was incredibly proud of it. It created the opening I wanted for people, allowing the audience to see themselves reflected in the creators of these great works. It showed their humanity, their vulnerability, their power. I wanted people to leave knowing they all had a key inside of them, one that opens the same mysterious door.

One warm night after a show, as I was walking home still high from performing, I got a call from the hospital. My mother was being held there after a breakdown. Suicidal, she'd called the police. She'd been drinking and had taken too much codeine for back pain and was sliding. When they found her, they told her that they wanted to bring her in to make sure she was okay. At the hospital, they put her on a psychiatric hold, which didn't go over well. She tried to fight security and was sedated. By the time I got there, she was calmer. When the psychiatrists came in, things got real. She couldn't run anymore.

I was scared to call out her drinking, afraid she would never speak to me again, but I knew that if we didn't do this now, we might not get another chance.

This was the moment when my mother knew there was no turning back. If she was to survive, she needed to dedicate herself to sobriety and to her deep spiritual practice. She needed to hand the wheel to her guardian.

I would wake early and drive her to the outpatient program at the addictions treatment facility in Mount Herbert. She worked harder than ever to face the broken parts of herself. Over time, she became my mother again in the way that I could trust her and rely on her, cry in her arms, let her be my nest, my safe place. She is now my closest confidante, a guide in my life and the wisest person I know. She has taught me that we are not victims of our lives or circumstances. Instead, we must always maintain a reverence for existence, for the world, for everything we must feel to experience the whole thing fully.

For all the things she's been and all the things she couldn't be, she's been the perfect mother for me, always. Her life is a triumph, and her legacy to me and my daughters is to rise, no matter what, even when your feathers are tattered, even when the winds are strong, even when there seems to be nowhere to land, to find the open sky.

So now, I had liftoff.

I got the dream offer of having *Atlantic Blue* play at the world-famous Charlottetown Festival, the very place where my parents had met and fallen in love in 1967. There was no higher honour for me personally. No Grammy award could have replaced what it meant to me to be starring in a show that I wrote at that festival. They brought in the brilliant Toronto director and playwright Mary Francis Moore, who took the show I had originally written and refined it into something more complete and powerful. She knew exactly where it needed to break through.

I was given a cast of world-class actors and singers to tell the stories. I had a string section, my band, a musical director, and it sold out every night. I even had someone to dress me. Prince Edward Island had called me home, and the community wrapped around me like a cozy knit blanket.

As well as being a beautiful show, it was funny and edgy, and at times, it pushed the envelope in terms of content. Somewhere along the line, I had lost the need to be anyone but myself and had cut the cords that bound me to the idea that being the good little girl, the sweetheart, was the way to be a woman in this world. I wanted to be evocative, and to challenge and provoke a response in people that was unexpected. I began to take joy in being a little shocking, mercilessly flirting with my audience, falling in love with them and having them fall in love with me back—not a version of me, but all of me, earthy, erotic, elegant and fierce.

I wrote and recorded new music with Island musicians. It turned out I didn't need to go anywhere else to find what I was looking for. There's no place like home.

Where I began was where I needed to be. My girls understood that I needed to sing to be complete, and I began to split my time between BC and PEI. I was West Coast Mary and

East Coast Aphrodite. There comes a time in the life of every mother when she has to decide whether or not to reclaim herself for all that she is. Ted was supportive, but we both knew this was the beginning of the end of our marriage. We wanted different things. Dreamed different dreams.

He needed roots. I needed to use my wings. He wanted to be still while I wanted to move. I could either follow the music or lose myself forever. I had no choice. Sink or sing.

We went down to the water for a ceremony and made new vows to each other, promising to let each other go, to put the children first, to remain a family, to support each other to live our best lives. The love remained as the container changed shape. It was painful, but it's what had to happen. I was terrified to start over without him, but I had a moment when I realized that I had no idea what life ahead of me looked like, and that was exhilarating. Anything was possible.

I bought a little house in Charlottetown, right around the corner from the one that burned down. Sophia came to live with me to finish school while Bill did some major renovating of his own life. Stella and Flora spend summers on the East Coast, and I spend as much time with them as I can out west. It's hard, but it works.

Both Bill and Ted are now my dearest friends and wisest counsel, and we are still on a most excellent adventure. They are amazing fathers. The success of a marriage isn't in the length of it, but the depth. We remain in the love.

Gene MacLellan posthumously bestowed his greatest gift on me: his daughter, Catherine. She and I wrote a song together in 2020 called "This Storm." It's the song I am most proud to have written. Our fathers had made music together with the intention of bringing faith where it was needed. Catherine and I had been training for this moment all our lives, immersed in hymns of beauty, praise and love since before we were born.

Together, we knew how to weave something strong enough to hold the human heart through turbulent times.

When the world is spinning round and round
Ashes ashes we all fall down
When we wake up in a scary dream
And all we want is to go back to sleep
I love you more than ever
Soon we'll be together
In each other's arms
I know that it will be all right
It's just gonna take some time
So hold on through this storm

At the age of eighty-seven, Nana died. I will never be able to thank her enough for a lifetime of support, and for showing me that music was my life raft, that it would carry me home, over and over again. She will be forever remembered for her giant laugh, her tremendous generosity and her sharp wit. Chin up, shoulders back.

My first dad, Marty, passed away as these last sentences were being written, but his songs live on in his children and grand-children. They are the safe place he created for us. His voice is the song of the sea. His other daughters, Donna and Kim, are still making music.

My father, Danny, decided to move to Prince Edward Island to be closer to me. His stepson had died of a fentanyl overdose, and soon his wife, Vanessa, distraught at the loss of her only child, took her own life. Bereft, he sold his home in Victoria and moved to the red shores of the Island, where he has found peace by the ocean.

My sweet brother, David, is the captain of a sailing yacht and has two children in Malta. Bryde is an incredible woman and knows my heart like no other. She's a brilliant film producer and yoga teacher, and is studying to be an osteopath.

She and I had the great honour of being with her father, Izzy, when he died. We anointed his head with oil and read his chosen prayers from the Bible. We dressed him in robes and flowers while singing songs to send him on his way through the gate. Wrapped only in a handmade shroud and quilt, he was lowered into the ground by his sons, just as he requested, so the earth would take him whole. I smiled to myself thinking of the chicken and the sheep in the car years ago, and when he taught me to drive, and how he brought me to the plywood stage and encouraged me to sing. He turned out to be one of the people in my life who saw me and loved me best.

My friend since childhood, Jenny is a passionate steward of the natural world. She and I still walk the forests and shorelines, looking for higher ground to launch from.

On PEI, I found that I could be useful in many ways, and I began to work on reconciliation projects with local First Nations. Dedication to social justice, to serving all beings, means that allyship is embedded in the vows I took. I misstep, but not trying isn't an option. Learning to decolonize is one of the most important gestures of love we can do in this world. Fighting for the equal rights of all human beings means not turning away from the history, the horror. It means not being afraid to take action, not being scared to check our privilege. We need to acknowledge the shadow side of our nature in order to transform it.

Within the stories and songs of the elders is woven the medicine that could very well save us all. If we don't listen, if we don't hear, we will all lose the most precious message from the ancestors: we are at home in the world, she will provide for us if we take care of her, and everything in this universe is our relation.

It is what the Vietnamese Buddhist monk Thich Nhat Hanh taught about "interbeing."

Now, the ancient songs echo again through the forests, taking their rightful place in the sonic landscape. Their language, the mother tongue of the land, has found its way home. Of course, it never really left. It was stored in the red clay, tucked deep into the minds of the survivors, and resurfaced as more truth and healing permeated the world, making safe passage for its return.

But whatever it is, wherever we feel the most love is needed, that is where we must go. We are all drawn to different wounds in the world to heal our own.

Find the key and harmonize.

Near the end of summer on Prince Edward Island is Old Home Week, when the Ferris wheel spins and the racehorses kick up red dust. It's the season of the Gold Cup and Saucer Parade. The local Tim Hortons was putting together a float. They invited me to be on it, in my blue, floor-length gown, singing with my musicians and step dancers. Off we went around town on the sparkling plywood stage, the sound system blasting as we sang "Sonny's Dream" over and over again. Joyful crowds lined the street, waving, dancing and beaming happiness.

As the parade came down the avenue, I realized we were passing one of the houses where I had lived as a child, where the monster used to take me into its lair. My eyes climbed the wall and rested on that window in the attic. I saw my little face staring back at me, my sad blue eyes watching the parade go by.

Time folded.

I looked up at her and smiled.

You're going to be okay, little one. You're going to fly out of there. Trust the wind. You won't always be lost in the world. Follow the river, the sound of the water. You'll find your way home.

Song of the Sparrow

I want to live my life
In constant prayer
Of gratitude
For the chance
To have placed my foot upon the earth
I want to waste no more moments
Begging for the love
That is my birthright
That is all around me
Within me
I want no magical thinking
Or superstition
To cloud my heart
I want to dance as the mystic
That understands it has been a dance all along
With every galaxy
In every cell
Spinning
Like a Sufi
In the desert
A spiral in the cosmos
Oh the wonder
Of everything
The awesomeness
The magnitude
The power
How could I have missed it
It's been here all along
Deceived by a story

Of separation
I did not see the web
The fabric
That wraps us all in her arms
That keeps us safe
That reminds us in our darkest times
That we are loved
Beyond our capacity
To understand
Because this is where we are going
It's the only thing I know
We are moving in circles
More deeply into love
Into reservoirs that have been
Excavated millennia before
Our flesh was sewn into this coat
Over our bones
We are the play of life
We are the music
We are the brutality
The beauty
We are the fools and the masters
We are woven into a mystery
That only love can guide us through
Keep looking
Keep moving toward the magnificent
But even if you hide
For your whole life
Even if you fall off the edge
Even if you don't find love this time around
It will find you
Because it always has you
Because it is you

And whenever you bravely open
And surrender
Even if it is at the moment of death
You will find you have never been abandoned
That you've never had to beg
That you were a child of life
Of grace
And that everything that has been
Uttered from your lips
Has been the prayer
Of the embodied
Has been the song of the sparrow
Has been the cry of the wind
As she kisses our forehead
And tousles our hair
And calls up the waves
And reminds us
We are held
I want to spend my life
Palms together
Tears streaming
Voice raised
In praise of existence
And then I want
All my wanting to dissolve
like ashes thrown into
The sea
And in my tiny boat
I will row toward the horizon
Held by an ocean of love

EPILOGUE

The Same Song

Thank you to life, which has given me so much.
It gave me laughter and it gave me longing.
With them I distinguish happiness and pain
The two materials from which my songs are formed,
And your song, as well, which is the same song.
And everyone's song, which is my very song.
—VIOLETA PARRA, "GRACIAS A LA VIDA"

I n the story of my story, I may have remembered some things out of order, but wherever possible, I've done what I can to confirm my recollections with those involved and to be as true to my life as possible.

Looking back, I am astonished at times by what I have done in search of love, and just to survive. I have learned to love this about myself. However, I am deeply sorry for any pain I have caused as my bulldozer of a heart tried to find its way.

Our emancipation begins with forgiveness, for ourselves and others, and when we dig down, we find that there is nothing to forgive. As my Zen teacher says, "We live mid-stagger with pure hearts."

A pure heart—that is what the witches gifted to me before I was born. Is it possible that we all have that gift? Original blessing, not sin. A reservoir of love. A shot at redemption. Even the monsters.

This is the bird's-eye view. What is seen from this vantage point is only gratitude for everything, only intimacy with life—and a deep bow to the mystery of it all. I will keep moving forward, one breath at a time, scars showing, belly-laughing, arms open, dancing and singing in my perfect, soft, aging body that has served me so well.

I still get lost sometimes, and that's when I remember to stop running, to be still, to breathe and get my bearings. I remember my vows and see where I've veered off course. I'm still just a little sparrow, after all, learning the directions, the constellations, the currents of the wind.

No matter what has happened or will happen, I know that in this lifetime, I have loved completely. I have given nothing less than my whole heart. I've had a kiss that resurrected me. I've let love wake me to the glory of what it means to be alive. I have cultivated love that has taken me to the outer limits of the human heart.

I've been devastated beyond recognition, drowned in despair, and I learned that grief can only go as deep as the love. The only choice was to lean into the pain and let it break me open. That breaking led me to songs that saved my life. I've learned what love is and what love is not. I've learned to ride the waves of heartache to shore, to be with the emptiness until life filled me up again, and it has, always.

This love is what I want to give to the world, to everyone.

This love is my true north.

This love is my wingspan.

What if all the love in the world is right here, has always been here, has never left because nothing can ever be lost? I knew it as a child in the forest. All I had to do was reach for it, and it would pick me up. This is grace. This is the tender mercy of life.

I am certain that it was my unaccompanied time in nature that gifted me with an inner compass, that taught me to make my own path, to follow my song as deep as I could go alone, a cappella.

But we are never really alone, are we? There is a witness, an accompanist, a symphony playing constantly, conducted by life, lifting us, moving us toward some crescendo, toward the light, communing, surviving, evolving.

Then we fall, scrape our skin, bleed, and we suddenly forget who we really are.

Pain can do two things: it can tear us into pieces, or it can tear us into oneness. Perhaps there is no difference. Perhaps we are all just pieces of the One, verses of the same song, making it up as we go along.

Acknowledgements

The lands this book was written upon are the traditional, unceded territories of the Mi'kmaq, Coast Salish, Saanich, Chemainus and the Cowichan First Nations.

I'd like to thank coffee, without which not one word of this would have been written.

I'd like to thank my Zen teacher, Eihei Peter Levitt, whose teaching and poems led me home. Deep gassho.

Thank you to my amazing mother, Sharlene, for sharing her secrets so fearlessly and entrusting them to me to tell. We took it to the limit. To Shaye, David, Donna and Kim—I love you. To my darling Bryde, who is my heart. To my daughters, Sophia, Stella and Flora, for understanding when Mama needs to fly. You are my world and my reason. To their fathers, Bill and Ted, for your unwavering support, love and wisdom. To my father Marty, for being my ship. To my dad Danny, for being my harbour. Thank you, Nana. I know you hear me still because I hear you. To the rest of my family who appear in these stories, named and unnamed, thank you for your love.

Thank you to my chosen family, who are the branches I leap from and where I find shelter through the storms: Damhnait Doyle, you know me by heart. This is for us, for our girls. Lisa Ray, your courage, honesty and fierce love paved the way for me to feel safe to open these stories. My Sam Taylor, you are mine and I am yours. You pulled me through this. Jenny Duquette, my heart, my conscience and my guide through the cosmos—from diapers to . . . diapers. Lauren Sherman, my sword and shield and sister for life. To Stasia Garraway—may we eternally be little girls together on the dance floor of life! You are a living poem.

Thank you to Catherine MacLellan, Harmony Wagner, Solange Rivard, Renee Layla and kids, Sarci Geddes, Jenn Abbott, Stasia Garraway, Pam Large-Moran and Alban, Starchild, Dido, Jann Arden, Sarah McLachlan, Bryan Adams, Cathy Barrett, Tonni Maruyama, Matt Rainnie, Steve Schnur, Rich Terfry, Chris Murphy, Avi Federgreen, Alicia Toner and family, Jordan Stratford, Channing Dungey, Amy Britt, Nathan Drake, Dalton Grant, Anya Coloff, Merrin Dungey, Joey and Christine Ponchetti, Michelle Lynch, Tressa DiFiglia and all my LA friends, Mary Francis Moore and family, Catherine Pacak, the Taylor family, Troy Greencorn, Neil Pearson, Jacob MacInnis, Beth Johnson, Sherry Sinclair, Cory Gray, Sarah MacNeill, C.C. Humphreys, Zandra Gutierrez, Heather Morrison and family, the Pearsons, Sheldon Elter, Kristi Hansen, Scott MacTaggart, Nadine Shelly, Kinley Dowling, Daryl Chonka, James Cowan, David Karr, Dan and Naomi Jason, Steve Bellamy, Kim Stockwood, Allan Reid, Kendel Carsan, Petra Hasenfratz and family, Julie MacKinnon, Clair Robertson, Serge Rousseau and Mélanie Rousseau, Renee LaPrise, Honor Griffith, David Cheverie (my angel), Asaya, Patricia Parkinson, Chad Willett, Nick Doneff, Oedipus and Amy, Natalie Williams-Calhoun, Michelle MacCallum, the Murphy family, Sheri Jones, Sarah Atkinson, Wayne O'Connor, Melanie and Carleton Stone, Jenene Woolridge, Patricia Bourque, Colin MacDonald, Lennie Gallant, Sharon Keller, Pam August, Colleen Sangye, Ric and Ken, Michael and Ayi, Ed May, Peter Bevan-Baker, Hannah Bell, Darcie Lanthier, Karen Bliss, Mark LeCorre, Pat Deighan and family, Craig Fair, Michael Dragland and family, Kindra Bernard and family, my darling cousins Naomi Costain, Shannon Carmichael and

Aaron Costain and the whole Costain family. Heidi Zinn, Dr. David Suzuki, WestJet, Jeff Reilley, Jeremie Saunders, Todd Wall, Brett Budgell and family, the Salt Spring Zen Circle and my dharma mama, Judy Daylen, Evan Solomon, Elan Mastai, Dr. Sobia Ali-Faisal, Tamara Steele, Alma MacDougall, Jamie Thomas, Lori St. Onge, Chief Darlene Bernard, Senator Brian Francis and family, for your love and wise counsel. Thank you to the Confederation Centre of the Arts, Trailside Music Hall and The Guild theatre and all my sponsors.

Thank you to my beloved Jess Robertson and family, and to the Modo Yoga community. Thank you to my *Atlantic Blue* family: Todd MacLean, Cynthia MacLeod, Daryl Gallant, Jon Matthews, Curtis MacNevin, Eric Fortune and Alanna Jankov.

Thank you to Daniel Lanois, Marsha Stevens-Pino and Peter Gabriel for allowing me to use your beautiful words in the book, and to all who helped with the licensing of lyrics. Thank you to Daniel Ledwell for producing the record, and to Jenn Grant and boys. To Karen Olender Kipnis, my steadfast therapist, who got me through the process. To Deanna Milligan for your beautiful cover photo, Zeena Baybayan for the cover design and Taiju Hasegawa and UA for the nest.

Thank you to Gary Furniss, Janet Baker, David Quilico and Mishelle Pack at Sony Music Publishing. Thank you to Terry McBride, Mark Jowett, Ric Arboit, Dan Fraser, Jon Rummen, Geoff Goddard, Crystal Heald, Dave Holmes, Catherine McLaren, Kim Hardy, Dave Holmes, Marc Alghini, George Maniatis, Catherine France, Shauna Gold, Aziyn Babayan, Andrea Lee-Aleoni, Christina Dunkley and everyone else who supported me at Nettwerk back in the day—I love you all. Thank you to everyone at Capitol Records US and Asia—including Bobby Gale, Sidney McCain and especially my dear Roy Lott. Thank you to Rob Oakie, Steve Love and everyone at Music PEI. Thank you to Sam Feldman and Richard Mills,

Marty Diamond and Larry Webman. Thanks to The Martels and Denise Donlon. I'd like to thank everyone who worked with me through the years, from the radio stations to the promoters, from the crews to the publicists, stylists, makeup artists, hair and glam squads, musicians, photographers, journalists, video directors, producers and co-writers.

Thank you to the shamans, the sacred medicines, the great sages throughout history, the activists who make this world better and to all Buddhas throughout space and time. Thank you to Mother Earth.

Thank you to Iris Tupholme, David Potter, Noelle Zitzer, Lisa Rundle, Lauren Morocco, Shayla Leung, Zanne Stachura and everyone at HarperCollins. And to my incredible editor, Jennifer Lambert; your steady encouragement and beautiful heart taught me how to do this thing. I love you! Thank you to my literary agent, Carolyn Forde at Transatlantic. You got me from the start. You made this happen and I am eternally grateful. Thank you to Stacey Cameron, copy editor. Wow! Your brain! You made this a real book. Thanks, too, to Catherine Dorton, for your expert proofread. Thanks to Sammy Volkov, for directing the audiobook.

Deepest bows to everyone I've ever loved and who has ever loved me.

Love never dies.

Photo Credits

p. 300   "Lady of the Lake," Tara MacLean (photo by Dave Brosha, 2021)

p. 327   Tara at Chantelu Farm, Salt Spring Island (photo by Billie Woods, 2016)

Permissions

Sparrow, the Soundtrack

Sparrow, the accompanying soundtrack to *Song of the Sparrow*, can be found at taramacleanmusic.com/song-of-the-sparrow.